OCMH MONOGRAPH 158M

OPERATION ARKANSAS

by

Robert W. Coakley

Histories Division
Office of the Chief of Military History
Department of the Army
Washington, D. C. 20315

1967

Published by Books Express Publishing
Copyright © Books Express, 2011
ISBN 978-1-78039-114-4

Books Express publications are available from all good retail and online booksellers. For publishing proposals and direct ordering please contact us at: info@books-express.com

Preface

This historical report on the Army's participation in the enforcement of an order of the Federal District Court at Little Rock Arkansas between 24 September 1957 and 20 May 1958, with regard to integration in the public schools of that city, was originally prepared almost contemporaneously with the events that it covers. It has not been extensively revised since that time. The circumstances under which it was prepared assured the preservation of the historical record for immediate use, but at the same time resulted in certain limitations in scope and breadth of coverage. The records used were primarily and almost exclusively those collected and maintained in Western Hemisphere Division, Office of the Deputy Chief of Staff for Operations, Department of the Army, (ODCSOPS) during the course of the operation. While these included periodic command reports and interim reports of various sorts, from field commands, and the records of daily exchanges with the commander and his staff in Little Rock, they did not include the actual records of the U. S. Military District, Arkansas, or of other field commands involved in the operation. This study is therefore primarily written from the vantage point of the command post in ODCSOPS.

The purpose of this history is, in terms of the many issues involved in the Little Rock affair in 1957-58, essentially narrow. It simply attempts to provide a record of the problems encountered by the Army in preparing for and carrying out a difficult and sensitive mission assigned it by the President and the Secretary of Defense. In order to do this, however, it has been necessary to show the essential background, just as it was essential to Army officers carrying out the mission to know about it. The essential background story has then been compiled in part from

Army records and in part from newspaper, magazine and other published material available in 1958.

In finally preparing this manuscript for circulation in its present form, the author surveyed most of the literature that has appeared in the last nine years on the Little Rock incident. There proved to be little in it that changed essentially what had initially been written in 1958 about the Army's role in the affair. However, some footnote references and a very small amount of text material have been revised in the light of these various accounts.

Some of the records on which the narrative is based have been since scattered and some of them destroyed. Once the troops had been finally withdrawn from Little Rock, it was no longer necessary to preserve a set of files for daily use in ODCSOPS. While the core of the records maintained there during the operation have been preserved, many documents used at the time can no longer be readily located and many probably no longer exist. This applies particularly to planning and working papers and to other materials that do not normally form part of the permanent files of a government agency, however valuable they may be to historians. In view of the great difficulty involved in rechecking every footnote to assure that the documents cited could be found, the author decided to let the footnotes stand in the form in which they were initially prepared and with the file references then pertinent. Readers will have to accept the fact, in some cases on faith, that the account accurately preserves the record as it then existed.

November 13, 1967   ROBERT W. COAKLEY

TABLE OF CONTENTS

	Page
Introduction	1
The Background of the Little Rock School Crisis	4
Preparation of Contingent Plans for the Use of Federal Troops	19
The President's Executive Order and Its Implementation, 24 September 1957	52
Enforcement of the Court Order at Little Rock, 25-29 September 1957	71
The Chain of Command and the Pentagon Organization	83
Preparation for Other Possible Contingencies	87
The Air National Guard and the Question of Command Channels	92
The Second Crisis, 30 September - 3 October 1957	99
Problems in the Arkansas National Guard	119
The First Reduction Plan, 4-15 October 1957	138
Release and Adjustments in the Arkansas National Guard, 15-23 October 1957	151
Reduction in Operations and the Second Reduction in Force, 23 October - 9 November 1957	175
Withdrawal of the Last Airborne Elements, 11-27 November 1957	189
The Third Reduction in the National Guard, 27 November - 18 December 1957	199
The Release of General Clinger	211
Phase Out Plans, School Incidents and Dynamite Scares, January 1958	216
Hesitant Reductions, 1 February - 4 April 1958	237
Final Withdrawal, 4 April - 29 May 1958	263

MAP AND CHART

The Central High School	opposite page 75
Chain of Command - Operation ARKANSAS	86

Introduction

During the course of this nation's history, the President has used federal troops in civil disturbances many times and under a variety of constitutional and statutory provisions either to uphold federal law, protect federal property, or assist the governments of the various states in dispersing violent mobs and restoring law and order. The first occasion under the Constitution was the Whiskey Rebellion of 1794 when President Washington placed himself at the head of a large militia army called into the federal service and marched them into Western Pennsylvania to put an end to resistance to the payment of federal excise taxes on distilled whiskey. Since that time instances have included such diverse situations as enforcement of the commercial embargo of 1808, repression of a slave rebellion in Virginia in 1831, enforcement of the Fugitive Slave Law in Massachusetts in 1854, maintenance of law and order on a host of occasions in the South during Reconstruction, similar actions in the great railroad riots of 1877, the Pullman Strike of 1894, and troubles in the mining areas of Idaho, Colorado, and West Virginia between 1892 and 1922, dispersion of the Bonus Marchers in Washington in 1932, numerous plant seizures during World War II, and preservation of order during a race riot in Detroit in 1944. For the most part the use of the Army in such civil disturbances since 1876 has been confined to industrial disputes of one sort or another. In almost all cases save the Pullman strike of 1894 and the plant seizures in World War II, action was undertaken at the request of state authorities. Between 1865 and 1957, no president exercised his power to call the state militia in such instances. In the twelve years between the end of World War II and the eruption of trouble at Little Rock in 1957, the Army was not called on for any duty within the Continental United States that involved the maintenance of law and order in civil disturbances, although it was used on several occasions in the same type of plant seizures that occurred during World War II.[1]

---

1. There is a considerable literature on this subject. The best single account covering presidential actions through 1941 is Bennett M. Rich, The President and Civil Disorders, (Washington, 1941). A more detailed account of earlier actions is to be found in Federal Aid in Domestic Disturbances, 1787-1903, Senate Doc. No 209, 57th Cong., 2d Sess. (Washington, 1903) and Senate Doc. No. 263, 67th Congress, 2d Session. There is no published work covering the period since 1941. However, John Ohly, History of Plant Seizures during World War II, MS located in the Office, Chief of Military History, covers most uses of the army for this type task during World War II.

Nevertheless, because troops had been so frequently employed in the past in civil disorders and because of the statutory provisions authorizing such employment, the Secretary of Defense and the Department of the Army had necessarily to recognize their continuing responsibility in this field. The basic guidance was Department of Defense Directive 3025.1, which outlined military policy for civil defense and other domestic emergencies. This directive prescribed that military assistance to civil authorities would be rendered only when requested or directed in accordance with Public Laws and Executive Orders except where "the overruling demands of humanity compel immediate action," and when "local resources available to State and municipal authorities are clearly inadequate to cope with the situation." It recognized that the Army had "primary responsibility for coordinating the planning and rendering of military assistance to civil authorities in domestic emergencies," while the Navy and Air Force would render necessary assistance.

Within the Department of the Army, Army Regulations (AR) 500-50, "Emergency Deployment of Army Resources, Domestic Disturbances," dated 22 March 1956 set forth briefly "the responsibilities, policy and guidance for the Army Establishment in operations involving military assistance during domestic disturbances." Two others, AR 500-60 and AR 500-70, provided the same type of guidance for disaster relief and civil defense. AR 500-50 prescribed that the Deputy Chief of Staff for Military Operations (DCSOPS) had staff responsibility for matters relating to intervention with Federal troops in domestic disturbances and that the Commanding General, Continental Army Command (USCONARC), had responsibility for carrying out such action.

For years training in handling civil disturbances had been included on Army schedules. The basic manual for such troop training in 1957 was Field Manual (FM) 19-15 entitled "Civil Disturbances", last revised on 24 April 1952. Army Subject Schedule 19-6, "Riot Control," provided information and guidance to commanders to insure maximum uniformity of training in this field. In the USCONARC training plans for the year 1957, this continuing responsibility for training under FM 19-15 was recognized, although its orientation was toward preparation for civil defense emergencies rather than the type of action that was to be required at Little Rock.[2] And at the time, it is evident, the subject was receiving little emphasis from commanders.

---

2. (1) See summary of these provisions in Incl 2, sub: DA Policy and Training Concerning Use of Troops in Domestic Emergencies, to Memo, Brig Gen T F Bogart, Dir O & T, ODCSOPS, for Asst DCSOPS (P & B), 17 Oct 57, sub: FY 59 Budget Hearings. DCSOPS Journal File, Opn ARKANSAS, item 891. (2) US CONARC Basic Plan, 28 Mar 57, Incl 4 (Training in Support of Civil Defense) to Tab C to App 2 to Annex D. See M/R by Lt Col H B Sewell, 19 Oct 57, summarizing these provisions, DCSOPS Journal File, item 567.

The Background of the Little Rock School Crisis[3]

---

3. Except where otherwise noted, this section mainly represents a digest of various contemporary newspaper and magazine accounts including particularly those in the Washington Post and Times Herald, Washington Evening Star, Newsweek, Time and U. S. News and World Report and the "Background Information and Summary of Situation" contained in the U. S. Army Military District, Arkansas, Command Report, 24 Sept – 30 Nov 57, App I to Annex B (Intell), pp. 1-7 (FOUO). Since 1957, a large number of first hand accounts have appeared covering these events. Most important among these are the following: Virgil T. Blossom, It Has Happened Here, (New York, Harper & Bros., 1959); Bishop Robert R. Brown, Bigger

than Little Rock, (Greenwich, Conn., 1958); Daisy Bates, The Long Shadow of Little Rock, A Memoir, (New York, David McKay Co., 1962); Sherman Adams, First Hand Report: The Story of the Eisenhower Administration, Chap. 16; Brooks Hays, A Southern Moderate Speaks, (Chapel Hill, Univ. of N. C. Press 1959); Dale Alford & L'Moore Alford, The Case of the Sleeping People (Little Rock, 1959); Harry Ashmore, "The Untold Story Behind Little Rock." Harpers, June 1958; Mayor Woodrow Wilson Mann's story appeared serially in the New York Herald Tribune. Corinne Silverman, The Little Rock Story, Inter-university Case Program, No. 41, Univ. of Alabama Press, 1959, is a good summary particularly of the legal questions involved. Wilson & Jane Cassels Record in Little Rock USA (San Francisco, Chandler Publishing Co., 1960) have assembled a good deal of the documentary record in the public domain. These various materials have been used occasionally to supplement that in contemporary periodicals originally consulted in preparing this account.

On 17 May 1954 the Supreme Court of the United States ruled that racial discrimination in public education was unconstitutional. On 31 May of the following year, the high court clarified this decision. It gave to the local authorities the task of eliminating racial discrimination in the schools and to the Federal district courts the task of seeing that they did so. Pursuant to its dictum in the original decision that integration should proceed "with all deliberate speed," the Supreme Court instructed the lower courts that they should require "a prompt and reasonable start" toward desegregation with the proviso that they might allow "additional time" for adjustments.[4] Shortly after the first decision of

---

4. *With All Deliberate Speed*, edited by Don Shoemaker, (New York, 1957), pp. 5-6. This volume is a good summary of progress and lack of it in carrying out the Supreme Court decision through the summer of 1957.

---

the Supreme Court, the Little Rock School Board announced its intention to comply, and over the course of the next year worked out a plan for this purpose. This plan was completed on 24 May 1955, and provided for gradual integration of the public schools in the city to commence at the opening of the 1957-58 school year provided a third general high school was completed by that time. Integration was to start with the Little Rock high schools rather than in the lower grades simply because it was found that less integration would be required at the high school level than any other. Following integration in the high schools in the session 1957-58, the plan called for integrating the elementary schools at approximately the rate of one grade per year.

The plan for integration of the high schools was carefully worked out. The new high school, Hall High School, was added to the Little Rock school system prior to the opening of the 1957-58 session as planned, making a total of three high schools and hence three school districts in the city. In District No. 1 was the Horace Mann High School, under the existing city and state laws an all-Negro school. In District No. 2 was Central High School, previously the all-white high school for the entire city. Hall High School was in District No. 3. The district boundaries were drawn so that very few Negro students were included in District No. 3 and none were deemed eligible to attend this new school. But in Districts Nos 1 and 2 there was a mixed school population, 328 eligible white students and 607 Negro students in District No. 1 (Horace Mann High School) and 1,712 white students and 200 Negroes in District No. 2 (Central High School). Under the integration plan, the white students in District No. 1 were given the option of attending either Mann High School or Central High School but the Negroes in the district were required to go to the previously all Negro school. Under this dispensation, the Mann school remained all Negro for the white students all chose Central. White students in District No. 2 were all required to go to Central High School, but the 200 Negroes were given the option of attending the Mann High School or of applying for entrance to Central. Those who applied were carefully screened by the school authorities and only seventeen were found eligible. Of these in the end only nine chose to assert their rights.[5] These nine Negro students,

---

5. (1) Information gathered by Hqs, USARMD, Ark. DCSOPS Journal File, Opn ARKANSAS, items 79 and 520. (2) Msg AKMAR 9-40, CHUSARMD, ARK, to TJAG, 28 Sep 57, DA-IN-865910. (3) Blossom, It Has Happened Here, pp. 9-24. The numbers given by Blossom, p. 17, for school population in the various districts differs markedly from that contained in the information available to the Army cited above.

---

who were from 14 to 16 years of age, became the chosen instruments for beginning racial integration in Little Rock and were to become the pivot around which a national crisis was to revolve.[6]

6. For a very sympathetic sketch of the nine Negro students, see Daisy Bates, *The Long Shadow of Little Rock*, pp. 113-51.

For two years the Superintendent of the Little Rock Schools, Mr. Virgil T. Blossom, carried on an educational campaign through the Parent-Teachers Association, citizens' meetings, and other channels to prepare the ground for acceptance of the integration plan. Although it is abundantly clear that the great majority of white citizens of Little Rock did not want any integration at all, there seemed every reason to believe, at least until the late summer of 1957, that they had sufficient respect for the law to allow the plan to proceed. Indeed the earliest opposition came from the National Association for the Advancement of Colored People (NAACP). On 24 January 1956, twenty-seven Negroes attempted to register at Little Rock schools and were refused. On 8 February 1956 the NAACP filed suit in the U.S. District Court for the Eastern District of Arkansas, charging that admittance had been denied to these students solely on the basis of race. On 28 August 1956, the District Court ruled against the NAACP, upholding the Little Rock School Board's gradual plan, and on 27 April 1957 the Eighth Circuit Court of Appeals upheld this decision. The district Court retained jurisdiction to see that the School Board carried out its plan, thus giving it the backing of a court mandate. In North Little Rock, a separate municipality across the Arkansas River, where a similar integration plan was also developed, no case was brought to court and no order issued obligating the school authorities to proceed with their plan.

The Little Rock and North Little Rock integration plans were generally similar to those carried out in other localities in Arkansas. By 1957 some form of integration had been started in the public schools at Fayetteville, Fort Smith, Van Buren, Charleston, Hot Springs, Hoxie, and Bentonville. The state university at Fayetteville had been integrated at the graduate level since 1950 and other state colleges had followed in its wake. The police force in Little Rock included Negroes and there was no segregated seating on Little Rock busses. Most of the school integration had come, however, in the western part of the state where the Negro population was sparse and the problem not acute. The old plantation area in eastern Arkansas remained solidly segregated. Little Rock, located almost exactly in the center of the state, partook of some of the characteristics of both sections.

The Governor of Arkansas, Orval Faubus, was until September 1957 regarded as one of the more liberal governors in the southern states and by some as almost an integrationist himself. He had been elected to a second two-year term in 1956, defeating a strong pro-segregationist candidate in the Democratic primary. While in that election campaign he had expressed strong opposition to enforced integration, prior to September 1957 he took no steps to halt the integration process in the various localities in Arkansas in which it was proceeding. The State Legislature, however, was strongly segregationist in sentiment and at the 1957 session passed a series of laws aimed at halting integration in the schools. Governor Faubus signed these laws.

Late in the summer of 1957, a highly vocal opposition to the School

Board's plan appeared in Little Rock itself, centering around the Capitol Citizens' Council and an organization called the Mothers' League of Little Rock Central High School. In an effort to halt integration at Central High School legally, a representative of the Mothers' League entered a petition in the Arkansas Chancery Court for Pulaski County asking that the School Board be prevented from proceeding with its plan. On 29 August 1957 Chancellor Murray O. Reed granted the injunction requested, basing it at least in part on testimony of Governor Faubus that "violence, bloodshed, and riots" would result if the integration plan were carried out.[7]

---

7. As quoted in U. S. News and World Report, 4 Oct 57, p. 55.

The following day, on petition of the Little Rock School Board, Judge Ronald N. Davies of the U.S. District Court for the Eastern District of Arkansas set aside the Pulaski County Chancery Court's order and specifically enjoined any action that sought to use the order to punish the School Board or in any other way "directly or indirectly" to hinder the execution of the School Board's plan. This injunction was also extended to "any and all persons" and thus constituted a broad court order against interference with the integration plan at Central High School.

Despite this development, Governor Faubus on 2 September, the day before the scheduled opening of Little Rock schools, ordered to active duty certain personnel of the Arkansas National Guard, citing information he had been furnished that violence was imminent in the city should integration be carried out. At the time the Governor did not reveal what orders had been issued to the Guard beyond stating that it was to preserve order at the school. The School Board then held up the enrollment of the Negro students at Central High School on the morning of 3 September and asked the federal court for clarification. At a special hearing on the afternoon of that day, Judge Davies said he would take the Governor at his word that the troops were present to preserve order, and again ordered that integration at Central High School proceed forthwith.

On 4 September the nine Negro students made an effort to enter Central High School only to be turned back by National Guardsmen and state troopers. The order issued by Governor Faubus shortly before the scheduled opening of the school was unofficially reported by a national news magazine as to "place off limits to white students those schools for colored students and to place off limits to colored students those schools heretofore operated and recently set up for the white students."[8]

---

8. As quoted in Ibid. For an interpretation of Faubus' actions and the decision to call the Guard, see Fletcher Knebel, "The Real Little Rock Story," Look, 12 Nov 57, pp. 31-33. Superintendent Blossom recounts his contacts with Governor Faubus, in which he found the latter non-committal up to the last moment, in It Has Happened Here, pp. 49-56, 58-59, 62-66, 70-72.

As a result, Judge Davies ordered U.S. District Attorney Osro Cobb to begin a complete investigation to determine responsibility for interference with the court order and to report his findings as soon as possible. United States Attorney General Herbert Brownell instructed the U.S. District Attorney, the U.S. Marshal, and the Federal Bureau of Investigation to take part in the investigation ordered by Judge Davies. The Mayor of Little Rock, Woodrow Wilson Mann, also took issue with the Governor, stating that "the only effect of his action is to create tensions where none existed," and claiming that but for the Governor's intervention the city police could have handled the situation with ease.[9]

---

9. As quoted in *Time*, 16 Sep 57, p. 24.

Meanwhile the city School Board, alarmed by the course of events, petitioned the District Court for a postponement of enforcement of its decision until the situation cooled off. Judge Davies again reiterated his previous decision that integration should proceed forthwith asserting that "In an organized society there can be nothing but ultimate confusion and chaos if court decrees are flouted whatever the pretext."[10] On 9

---

10. *Ibid*.

September he requested that the U.S. Attorney General and the U.S. District Attorney enter the case as "friends of the court," and start action immediately against Governor Faubus, Maj. Gen. Sherman T. Clinger, State Adjutant General, and Lt. Col. Marion E. Johnson, commander of the

National Guard troops at the school, "seeking such injunctive and other relief as may be appropriate to prevent the existing interferences with and obstruction to the carrying out of the orders" of the district court.[11]

---

11. As quoted in U. S. News and World Report, 4 Oct 57, p. 56.

Pursuant to this request, on 9 September the U.S. District Attorney reported to Judge Davies on the investigation ordered and declared that Faubus, Clinger, and Johnson were in fact obstructing and interfering with the execution of court orders. He then formally requested that they be enjoined from doing so. Judge Davies set 20 September as the date for these three officials to appear in court for a hearing on the petition for issuance of a preliminary injunction. Faubus and the other officials accepted the summons to this hearing served on them by the U.S. Marshal.

While these legal maneuvers were underway the fire that had begun in Little Rock spread across the river to North Little Rock. There on 9 September six Negro students who had been selected to begin integration in the high school were turned back on seeking to enter by a disorderly group mostly composed of teen-age students and adult railroad workers. The School Board, not being under any court order to integrate, simply decided to postpone any action and returned the students to the all-Negro high school in the city. In other sections of Arkansas and even in other parts of the nation, a certain restiveness began to assert itself where racial integration was involved. Little Rock had become, in the eyes of both domestic and foreign observers, a test case in the enforcement of a federal court's decision against the opposition of the Governor of a state.

In an effort to settle the crisis, President Eisenhower agreed to a meeting with Governor Faubus at Newport, Rhode Island, on 14 September. While the President afterward characterized it as a constructive discussion and Governor Faubus stated rather generally that he accepted the Supreme Court decision of 1954 as the law of the land, it soon became apparent that no firm agreement had been reached.[12] After his return from

---

12. The fullest account of the conference is in Brooks Hays, *A Southern Moderate Speaks*, pp.   . Hays arranged the meeting. Sherman Adams, *First-Hand Account*, pp. 346-53 also contains a summary. Adams concludes: "It is difficult to see anything of value that came from the meeting, but I felt that under the circumstances the President had to let Faubus come and talk with him." - p. 353.

Newport the Governor continued the same policy as before, retaining the National Guard at the school to prevent the Negro students from entering.

At the hearing held on 20 September before the Federal District Court, Judge Davies held that the integration plan had "been thwarted by the Governor of Arkansas by the use of National Guard troops" and ordered the Governor, General Clinger, and Colonel Johnson to cease "obstructing or preventing . . . the attendance of Negro students at Little Rock high school."[13] This was the fourth time within the course of less than a

13. See excerpt from decision in Record, Little Rock USA, pp. 53-56.

---

month that the Federal District Court had reiterated its order. This time Governor Faubus obeyed the Court's injunction and removed the National Guard from the school leaving the maintenance of law and order in Little Rock with the city and the state police. In so doing, the Governor again predicted that violence would result should the Negro children attempt to enter the school.

On Monday, 23 September, when the nine Negro students were scheduled to enter Central High School in accordance with the court's order, a crowd began forming early and continued to increase as the morning wore on. When the crowd was diverted to an attack on four Negro newsmen, the students were slipped into the high school by a side door. On learning of this, the mob became increasingly menacing, threatening to storm the school and do physical violence to the Negro students. By 1100 CST it had grown to approximately 1,000 persons and the police on duty had been increased from 50 to 100. Even this number was unable to cope with the situation, and City Chief of Police Marvin Potts decided it would be the better part of wisdom to escort the Negro children from Central High School by a side door. Mayor Mann charged that the violence was the result of a plan and that it "bore all the marks of professional agitators".[14] Governor Faubus, on the other hand, absent from

---

14. As quoted in U.S. News and World Report, 4 Oct 57, p. 57. For

a variant version of the events of 23 September which minimizes the serious character of the mob action, see Hqs, Arkansas National Guard, Cmd Rpt, Opn ARKANSAS, Pt I, 24 Sep - 23 Oct 57, App 2 to Annex B, p. 3 (FOUO).

Arkansas to attend the Southern Governors' Conference at Sea Island, Georgia, pointed to the development as a vindication of his earlier prophecies. Whichever view may have been true, it was clear that the oft-reiterated order of the Federal Court had been flouted and that only by drastic action of the federal government could that order be carried out.

A few hours after the mob action, the President, referring to "the disgraceful occurrences of today at Central High School," asserted that "The federal law and orders of a United States District Court, implementing that law, cannot be flouted with impunity by any individual, or any mob of extremists." He then promised that he would "use the full power of the United States, including whatever force may be necessary, to prevent any obstruction of the law and to carry out the orders of the federal court."[15] A few hours later, at about 1800 EDT, the President

---

15. U. S. News and World Report, 4 Oct 57, p. 57.

---

issued a proclamation commanding "all persons engaged in such obstruction to justice to cease and desist therefrom and to disperse forthwith."[16] This proclamation, authorized by the statutes of the United States, had been regarded since the time of President Washington as a preliminary step to the use of federal troops in domestic disturbances.[17] When this "cease and desist" order was not obeyed on the following day, the stage was set for the employment of federal troops to insure enforcement of the order of the federal court at Little Rock.

During the time that Governor Faubus employed the Arkansas National Guard at Little Rock under state control, the maximum force used at any one time was 280 men and at most times it was considerably less. These men were drawn from fourteen different units and included both Air and Army National Guard personnel. The Guard was supplemented by a few State Policemen, the maximum being 18 on 10 September. The Guard was apparently not called up by units but as individuals who were then formed into a provisional battalion under Colonel Johnson's command. Many of those called to duty were employees of the state government as well as members of the Arkansas National Guard. The National Guard Headquarters Command Report for the period of federal service states that under state control the men were "under orders not to load weapons under any circum-

---

16. Proclamation No. 3204, 23 Sep 57.

17. On the historic use of the proclamation, see Rich, *The Presidents and Civil Disorders*, pp. 201-06.

stances unless ordered to do so by Lt. Col. Johnson, bayonets to remain sheathed, and not to discuss anything concerning the situation with anyone . . . . There were no incidents in which a State Guardsman was involved that resulted in bodily or property damage."[18]

---

18. (1) Hqs, Ark NG, Cmd Rpt, 24 Sep - 23 Oct 57, Pt I, App 2 to Annex B, p. 3. (2) Information available at time in WHD, ODCSOPS.

The force employed by Governor Faubus was a very small one in contrast to that later to be used by the federal government in Little Rock. In making this comparison, it must be kept in mind that the task entrusted the Guard when employed under state control was one of keeping the Negro students out of the school, a goal with which any crowds that gathered at Central High School in the period 3-20 September were basically in sympathy. Under these circumstances, the preservation of order was no difficult matter and it was not surprising that a small National Guard force was able to accomplish it with no great difficulty. The task later assumed by the federal troops of preserving order while insuring that the nine Negro students were allowed to enroll peaceably in the school and attend classes there was of a different dimension.

Preparation of Contingent Plans for the Use of Federal Troops

The Department of the Army necessarily had to take cognizance of the developing situation in Little Rock, since it seemed possible any time from 3 September onward that the President might call on the Army for assistance in enforcing the District Court order. Newspapers and magazines openly speculated that he might either call the National Guard into federal service or use regular troops in Little Rock.[19] Prudence

---

19. See for instance U. S. News and World Report, 13 Sep 57, p. 30.

---

dictated that the Army prepare some contingency plans for either eventuality.

Little Rock fell within the area of responsibility of Fourth U.S. Army whose headquarters were at Fort Sam Houston, San Antonio, Texas. Fourth Army's area included the states of Texas, Louisiana, Arkansas, Oklahoma, and New Mexico. Under Fourth Army, located in Little Rock itself, was the headquarters of U.S. Army Military District, State of Arkansas /USARMD/, Maj. Gen. Edwin A. Walker commanding, charged mainly with administration of reserve and National Guard affairs in the state. General Walker had only recently assumed command. The only military installation in the city was a reserve armory. Immediately north of the city was Camp Joseph T. Robinson but it was no longer in use by the active army and part of it had been turned over to the State of Arkansas for use by the National Guard. The part remaining under federal control was used for reserve training activities. Some twenty miles north of the city was a Strategic Air Command (SAC) installation, Little Rock Air Force Base. The nearest active army base of any size was Fort Chaffee, an artillery training center near the city of Fort Smith, about 200 miles from Little Rock.

Under normal Army doctrine, any military action to be undertaken in support of the court order at Little Rock would be directed by the Secretary of the Army (pursuant to Presidential order) and carried out by CONARC order to Fourth Army. In view of its general responsibility, Fourth Army necessarily had to follow the developing situation closely. Region VI, 112th Counter Intelligence Corps (CIC) Group, covering the State of Arkansas began a complete coverage on 3 September within the jurisdictional scope of its mission, that is by close observation and following of news media. Based on information obtained in this manner, Fourth Army between 2 and 5 September sent several messages to CONARC and the Department of the Army officially informing both of developments in Little Rock, particularly as they related to the use of the National Guard by the Governor.[20] On 5 September the Chief of Staff, General

---

20. (1) Msg 9-001, CGUSARFOUR to ACSI, 2 Sep 57, DA-IN-850893. (2) Msg 9-0002 to ACSI, CGUSCONARC, CG Ft CHAFFEE, 3 Sep 58, DA-IN-851058. (3) Msg 9-0053, to ACSI, CG FT CHAFFEE, CGUSCONARC, 3 Sep 57, DA-IN-851269. (4) Msg 9-0175 to CGUSCONARC, TAG, 4 Sep 57, DA-IN-851956. (5) Msg CGUSARFOUR to DEPTAR & USCONARC, 5 Sep 57, DA-IN-852150. (6) Ltr, Maj Thomas J Mann, Region Cmdr, Region VI, 112th CIC

Gp, to CG, USAMD, Ark, 2 Oct 57, sub: Summary of Activities, Region VI, 112th CIC Gp fm 28 Aug 57 to 2 Oct 57.

Maxwell D. Taylor, became concerned and, after discussions with members of his staff and with the Deputy Commanding General of CONARC, then in Washington, telephoned the Commanding General of Fourth Army. On the same day, Col. William G. Easton, Chief of Military Affairs Division, Office of The Judge Advocate General, was sent to Little Rock on a temporary tour as special advisor to General Walker "in reference to the integration situation at Central High School."[21]

---

21. (1) Memo, Lt Col Robert B. Crayton, WHD, ODCSOPS, for Asst DCSOPS, 13 Sep 57, sub: Briefing for CGUSCONARC. (SECRET). (2) Hqs USARMD, Ark, Cmd Rpt, 24 Sep – 30 Nov 57, p. 1. (FOUO) (3) 4th US Army, Cmd Rpt, 1 Sep – 30 Nov 57, pp. 3, 13. (FOUO)

In accordance with the call from the Chief of Staff, Headquarters Fourth Army prepared preliminary draft plans for calling the Arkansas National Guard into federal service, and on 10 September Col. Lee L. Alfred, the Acting Deputy Chief of Staff for Operations, Fourth Army, was called to the Pentagon to discuss these plans. Mainly the plans provided for the personnel actions required in calling the National Guard to federal service and for assembly of the Guard at Fort Chaffee. In discussions with the Chief of Staff, Vice Chief of Staff, DCSOPS and Director of Operations, DCSOPS, the basis of Fourth Army planning was changed considerably. The Chief of Staff's decisions were reported to Fourth Army as follows:

1. The number of National Guard units will be held to a minimum and will be called to remain at home station. C/S stated that if individuals were not used they should be allowed to return home but not be released from the call. This system General Taylor feels will prevent the Guardsmen from local participation and will not have the effect of making them feel they are confined.

2. One battle group of the 101st Airborne will be employed should it become necessary to use active Army troops. DCSOPS was instructed to initiate riot training in the 101st.

3. General Taylor was satisfied with the Fourth Army plan but disapproved the command structure. The General stated that this is a DA problem and that except for basic information CONARC was not in the act. The C/S directed that General Walker be designated as commander of troops but that his command channel by-pass CG Sector D and CG Fourth Army, and go direct to Army C/S. General Taylor further directed that should the Guard be called or the active army used, a Major General from DA would be placed on the ground at Little Rock as his personal representative. The staff was directed to prepare the necessary directives for command structure as indicated above and to direct CG, Fourth Army to provide administrative and logistical support.[22]

---

22. (1) This quote was taken from an unofficial penned memorandum written by Col Alfred while in the Pentagon. Some rough notes of Lt Col Crayton of WHD made at the meeting generally confirmed Col Alfred's interpretation of the Chief of Staff's decisions. (SECRET) (2) Cmd Rpt, 4th US Army, 1 Sep - 30 Nov 57, pp. 3, 13. (FOUO).

These decisions became the basis for contingency planning in the two weeks that remained before federal troops would, in fact, be ordered to intervene at Little Rock. This contingency planning was carried on in the Department of the Army by the Office of the Deputy Chief of Staff for

Military Operations (DCSOPS) and in the field by Headquarters, Fourth Army in close coordination with Headquarters U.S. Army Military District, Arkansas, and the Commanding General, Fort Chaffee. Within DCSOPS, it was entrusted to the Operations Directorate (Brig. Gen. Francis T. Pachler) and within Operations Directorate mainly to Western Hemisphere Division (Col. Robert C. Williams, Jr.). Because of the extremely sensitive nature of the problem participation in and knowledge of this planning were limited to as few individuals as possible.

In all of this contingency planning, the presumption was that the Arkansas National Guard would be the primary force used should the President decide to act and that the use of regular troops was ~~described as~~ a "remote possibility."[23] With regard to this "remote possibility," in

---

23. Memo cited in 21 (1). (SECRET)

---

the conferences on 10 September, the availability and suitability of units from Fort Hood, Fort Polk, and Fort Chaffee, as well as a battle group from the 101st Airborne Division at Fort Campbell, Kentucky, were discussed. The choice fell on the battle group of the 101st because it was already on an alert status and could be moved to the scene more quickly than any other unit. The units of the 101st were in an advanced state of training and the battle group seemed a suitable organization from which to tailor a force for the task. The flying time from Fort Campbell to Little Rock was little more than two hours and there was an airfield on the military reservation where the troops could be loaded. This combination of advantages did not exist for any of the other units considered. The units at Fort Chaffee were mainly artillery training units, hardly suitable for the role under consideration. The units of the First Armored Division at Fort Polk and Fort Hood were scheduled for "gyroscope" rotation to Europe early in the following year, and were not particularly adaptable to air transport. Following the conferences on 10 September, Colonel Alfred called the Chief of Staff, Fourth Army and advised him that the Department of the Army desired a plan be prepared for the utilization of Airborne forces from Fort Campbell, initially, reinforced if required by ground forces from Fort Polk. DCSOPS plans after 10 September were all shaped around the use of the battle group of the 101st. At no time during the planning was any consideration given to the use of military police in anything more than a supporting role.[24]

---

24. (1) *Ibid*. (SECRET). (2) Verbal information from Lt. Col. R. B. Crayton, WHD.

On the basis of the decisions made by the Chief of Staff on 10 September, Department of the Army immediately sent a directive to the 101st Airborne Division at Fort Campbell instructing prompt initiation of training of one designated battle group in FM 19-15, an as a precautionary measure, to be carried out as a normal training procedure and in such a manner as to avoid speculation. Western Hemisphere Division drafted instructions for an alert to be dispatched to the 101st at the appropriate time either by letter of instructions or by TWX. The staff also prepared an operational plan providing for air movement of approximately 1,000 men in two increments to begin six hours after the alert was received from Washington (A plus 6) and to be completed by A plus 16, with the land tail of approximately 250 men to follow overland leaving at A plus 6 and arriving at their destination by A plus 54.[25] Initial

---

25. (1) (S) Msg DA 929321, DCSOPS to CG 101st ABN DIV, Ft Campbell, Ky., 10 Sep 57. (2) (TS) Memo, Col R C Williams, Chf, WHD for Director of Opns, ODCSOPS, 12 Sep 57, Sub: Implementing Instructions for Use of Army Troops in Arkansas (TS).

---

contacts were also made with the Air Force and tentative arrangements for coordination of the lift developed. In fact, Air Force Headquarters immediately sent out a tentative alert to the Military Air Transportation Service (MATS) outlining possible standby airlift requirements but promptly cancelled it on 12 September when it provoked too many queries from various headquarters involved.[26]

---

26. (U) Msg AFOOP-OS-T, Hqs, USAF to COMMATS, ANDREWS AFB, 12 Sep 57, DA-IN-857445.

On 14 September General Taylor approved a command structure, proposed by DCSOPS along the lines he had earlier indicated providing the Chief of Staff with "direct operational control from Washington through a commander on the ground over any units of the National Guard of the United States ordered or called to active duty from the State of Arkansas, as well as any Regular Army units employed in the Arkansas area." At the appropriate time the Chief, U.S. Army Military District, Arkansas, was to be designated field commander and CONARC, Third and Fourth Armies, XVIII Airborne Corps, and 101st Airborne Division notified. Fourth Army was also to be notified of its responsibility to provide necessary support. At the same time the Chief of Staff would dispatch a general officer, senior to the field commander and "thoroughly familiar with the views and prior actions of the Chief of Staff concerning this problem" from Washington as his personal representative on the scene, to guide General Walker but not to be in the chain of command. This direct chain of operational control would, it was argued, facilitate the transmission of instructions from Washington, enable the Chief of Staff to maintain close supervision and control over forces employed, enable him to take immediate action as directed by the Secretary of the Army and as the situation dictated, and speed up the ordering to active military service of units of the State National Guard, as well as early return to their status as National Guard. The presence of the Chief of Staff's personal representative at Little Rock would "greatly insure against any possible misinterpretation" of the Chief's directives. The authority of the Chief of Staff to exercise such command, DCSOPS pointed out, could not be questioned if the Secretary of the Army approved the plan since General Taylor would be acting as the agent of the Secretary in carrying it out.[27]

27. (TS) Memo, DCSOPS for CofS, USA, 14 Sep 57, sub: Command Structure in the Event of Civil Disturbance in Arkansas (TS). It was based on a WHD staff study.

In any event, this command structure outlined on 14 September was precisely the one placed in effect when the Army moved into Little Rock ten days later. In the ten-day interval, nevertheless, no formal instructions were sent out to inform the various headquarters involved and all plans remained in a very tentative stage. Questions inevitably arose in the field. The 101st Airborne Division responded to its training directive with a series of queries as to the exact size and destination of the force it was supposed to train in FM 19-15. On 12 September Fourth Army inquired as to the approximate strength of the proposed task force and the additional items of equipment that might be required at its destination, saying this information was needed for logistical planning purposes. USCONARC, Third Army and XVIII Airborne Corps unofficially indicated their concern. Department of the Army parried the cabled queries from Fourth Army and the 101st Airborne Division by stating that the required information would be made available at the appropriate time, but a staff representative was sent to USCONARC on 14 September to explain to general officers there the proposed command set-up and the reasons for by-passing that headquarters.[28]

28. (1) (S) Msg 205 AKADC-E, CGUSARFOUR to DCSOPS 12 Sep 57, DA-IN-53686. (2) (S) DA 929581, DCSOPS to CGUSARFOUR, 14 Sep 57.

(3) (TS) DA 929745, DCSOPS to CG, 101st ABN DIV, 18 Sep 57. (4) Memo cited n 21 (1). (5) Verbal info from Col. R. C. Williams, Chf WHD, ODCSOPS.

The 101st Airborne got additional clarification by telephone and sent its Chief of Staff, Col. D. P. Quandt, on a personal visit to the Pentagon. The First Airborne Battle Group of the 327th Infantry was designated as the unit to be used and the requisite riot training was initiated "under a cover plan which would not disclose its real purpose." On 12 September, Col. William A. Kuhn, Commander of the 327th, was sent to make a reconnaissance of the Little Rock area.[29]

---

29. (1) (FOUO) Cmd Rpt, 101st Abn Div, Opn ARKANSAS, 10 Sep - 27 Nov 57, p. 1. (2) Verbal info frm Col Williams.

The other matter requiring attention was a contingency plan for calling the Arkansas National Guard. The laws and the pertinent Army Regulations covering such a Call were reasonably clear but there was no real precedents involving actual use of the National Guard by the President in a domestic disturbance since the Civil War. The pertinent Army Regulations on bringing the National Guard into the federal service[30] provided

---

30. (U) AR 130-10, 27 Dec 50, National Guard: Induction of Army National Guard into Service of the United States.

for two distinct procedures, one a Call and the other an Order. The Call procedure was to be employed when the President wished to use all or part of the National Guard, as part of the militia of the United States, to repel invasion, suppress rebellion, or to execute the laws of the union when he was unable to do so with regular forces at his command. The Order procedure was to be employed when Congress declared a national emergency or authorized the use of armed land forces in excess of those of the regular army. When National Guard units were inducted under the Call procedure, they became part of the Army of the United States, but their units and members retained their state status as federally recognized units and members of the National Guard in a state of temporary suspension. Under the Order procedure those units and members merged with units and members of other components into one active Army of the United States without unnecessary distinction between individuals and units based on their component of origin. Under a Call, National Guard troops might be used on foreign territory only for limited purposes; under an Order there was no territorial limitation on their use. When called to federal service, neither officers nor enlisted men could be held to service beyond the terms of their existing commissions or enlistments, whereas guardsmen ordered to federal duty might be held until six months after termination of the war or emergency. "Department of Army plans," the regulation read, "contemplate induction of the National Guard by Presidential CALL in all circumstances in which Congress has not declared a national emergency but in which the President deems it necessary to use troops in excess of the Regular Army."[31]

31. *Ibid.*

Requirements for executing a Call for all or part of the National Guard were relatively simple. The laws of the nation required no other official act than issuance of such a call in prescribed form by the President. Department of the Army Regulations required that this Presidential Call be transmitted by the Secretary of the Army to the commander in whose area the units to be called were located. In accordance with these prescribed procedures, the Western Hemisphere Division, DCSOPS, prepared drafts of messages to be sent to Governor Faubus and to Fourth Army transmitting a Presidential Call to the Arkansas National Guard. These Call directives were prepared to cover two contingencies, the first that the entire National Guard of the state would be summoned to duty and the second that only units in Little Rock would be called.

The entire Army National Guard of the State of Arkansas was composed of 114 units with home stations scattered throughout the state. Only seventeen of these were located in Little Rock, and these were mainly service units. In addition there were eleven Air National Guard units. The total enrolled Army National Guard personnel was estimated at 8,870, with an additional 1,300 or so enrolled in the Air Guard units, making a total of something over 10,000 men. General Taylor's instructions on 10 September had stated that the number of Guard units to be called should be held to a minimum. There was no further guidance as to just what this minimum should consist of, and therefore the alternate plans for calling either the whole Guard or the units in Little Rock represented simply estimates of what might have to be done.[32]

---

32. (U) Estimates of National Guard numbers taken from working papers used in WHD, ODCSOPS at the time.

There were other problems and uncertainties, some revolving around the question of whether the Arkansas National Guard would actually respond to a Call if the avowed purpose was to create a force to enforce the court order at Little Rock. At the conference on 10 September, General Taylor suggested that Fourth Army make a survey of Guard opinion. The result of this survey was a general estimate, forwarded to the Department of the Army on 16 September, that 80 percent of Guard personnel would respond if called into service but not required to enforce the court order, 75 percent would respond if called to enforce that order, and 65 percent if the Guard were actually required to oppose other State forces such as state and local police, state militia, volunteers, etc. This uncertainty about the Guard's response to a Call was also reflected in DCSOPS planning. In the initial study prepared on the command problem on 12 September, officers of the Western Hemisphere Division outlined the various conditions under which federal forces might have to be used in Little Rock, among them the possibilities that the National Guard, under control of the State Governor, might disregard a Presidential proclamation to disperse or fail to respond to a Call to active military service by the President. Uncertainty about how the Arkansas National Guard might respond clearly affected all the contingency planning and was a primary factor making necessary consideration of the use of regular army units.[33]

---

33. (1) (S) Msg 208, CGUSARFOUR to DEPTAR, 16 Sep 57, DA-IN-54610
(2) (S) Msg 207, CGUSARFOUR to DEPTAR, 13 Sep 57, DA-IN-53993. (s) See memos cited n 22 and n 27.

Details of the contingent plans for bringing the Arkansas National Guard into the federal service and for supporting any regular army forces that might have to be moved to the Little Rock area were left to Fourth Army and Arkansas Military District. If the requirements for executing the Call at the Washington level were relatively simple, those for implementing the Call in the field were highly complicated, and the fact that the administrative agencies in the Department of the Army normally responsible for regulations governing this implementation were not brought into the planning eventually had serious consequences. The Fourth Army plan brought to the Pentagon on 10 September was revised, refined, and extended between 11 and 18 September. Headquarters, Arkansas Military District between 11 and 16 September prepared operation plans based on guidance in the proposed Fourth Army plan. On 18 September a meeting was held at Fourth Army Headquarters at which all plans were coordinated.[34] On

---

34. (1) (C) Cmd Rpt, 4th US Army, Opn ARKANSAS, 1 Sep - 30 Nov 57, pp. 3-4. (2) Cmd Rpt, Hqs USARMD, Ark, pp. 1-2. (FOUO).

20 September, the day that the order was issued in the U.S. District Court for the Eastern District of Arkansas enjoining Governor Faubus and National Guard officials from further interference with the integration plan in Little Rock, Colonel Alfred of Fourth Army and General Walker arrived in the Pentagon for a further round of conferences to put the contingency plans into relatively final form.

Five contingencies visualized in the revised Fourth Army plan were as follows: (1) Call to active duty of the Army and Air National Guard of the State of Arkansas and assumption of command of these Guard troops by the active army; (2) use of the 101st Airborne units in the State of Arkansas by air and surface movement; (3) use of 101st Airborne units in the State of Arkansas by surface movement; (4) air and surface movement of 1st Armored Division units to the State of Arkansas; and (5) surface movement of 1st Armored Division units to State of Arkansas. In each of the last four contingencies, it was assumed that the first, the call to active service of the National Guard would also be in effect. The movement of the troops from Fort Polk was predicated on the possibility that the original increments from Fort Campbell might need reinforcement.[35]

---

35. (FOUO) Copy of Fourth Army Plan in WHD, ODCSOPS Files.

The gist of the Fourth Army plan for calling the Arkansas National Guard was as follows: Commanding General, Fourth Army, was to issue general orders calling units to duty at home stations when directed by the Department of the Army, and issue movement orders for selected units to go mobilization station at Fort Chaffee. Commanding General, Arkansas Military District, was to assume command of the Guard units called to active service and operational control of the U.S. Army Advisory Group (NGUS), Arkansas, and issue orders for movement of units from home station to Fort Chaffee on receipt of movement directives from Fourth Army. Subsequent to the initial call, any Guard unit "which already has been or in future may be directed to move on State of Arkansas order to Little Rock and vicinity" would be immediately called to active military service at home station. Eventually it was anticipated it might be necessary to call the whole Arkansas Army National Guard and some of the Air National Guard. Air units, if called to duty, would be placed under the operational control of the Chief of Staff, U.S. Army, who would then issue further orders concerning their employment through the Chief of the Arkansas Military District. Commanding General, Fort Chaffee, was to receive the National Guard units and provide necessary administrative and logistical support. A detachment of the 53d Signal Battalion from Fort Hood would move to the Little Rock area to provide necessary signal communications with Fort Chaffee and Headquarters, Fourth Army.

The plan for air and surface movement of the 101st Airborne Division task force was roughly similar to that prepared in DCSOPS. One battle group of the 101st in two air echelons and one ground echelon was to move to Little Rock Air Force Base on order of the Chief of Staff and to pass to the control of Chief, U.S. Military District on arrival. Fourth Army would provide troops for security and transportation of the battle group air echelons by moving a provisional support company from Fort Chaffee,

and continue administrative and logistical support for both the regular
army and National Guard troops under control of General Walker as
required. A transportation truck company would move from Fort Sill to
Fort Chaffee to replace the one sent from Chaffee to Little Rock. The
Third contingency plan varied simply in that it provided for surface
rather than air movement of the task force from Fort Campbell, and the
last two provided for reinforcement of the airborne by an armored rifle
battalion from Fort Polk should it be required. A common annex to all
plans provided for the details of logistical and administrative support.
Supplies were to be transported forward from Fort Chaffee to forward
distribution points as required. Ammunition was to accompany troops from
home station, the National Guard to furnish its own initial issue to the
extent that it was available from its own stocks. Hospitalization,
laundry, salvage, and other miscellaneous services were to be provided by
Fort Chaffee for all troops under control of Arkansas Military District.
One L-20 aircraft was to be provided by Chaffee for emergency evacuation.
Similarly, a common intelligence annex provided that Fourth Army CIC
personnel (112th CIC Group) would support the local commander as directed
by Fourth Army, though remaining under control of Fourth Army G-2.

General Walker's "Operation Plan Nr. 1" was supplementary to and
generally based on the Fourth Army plan.[36] It assumed that a minimum

---

36. (S) Copy of General Walker's Plan in WHD, ODCSOPS Files.

---

number of units of the Arkansas army and Air National Guard would be called to active duty, that regular army units might be ordered into the Little Rock area about the same time, and that all units would be placed under Walker's control "for such purposes and to carry out such orders as may be directed." It postulated three possible phases in the calling of the National Guard: (1) a call to all units in the Little Rock area and their movement to Fort Chaffee; (2) a call to duty at home stations of any units which might subsequently be ordered to move on State of Arkansas order to Little Rock or vicinity; (3) a call for all units of the Arkansas National Guard at home stations "when and if necessary." The plan then went on to lay down in detail the functions to be performed by the Senior Army National Guard Officer, the Senior Army Advisors for the National Guard and Reserve, Arkansas, the Commanding Officer of the 101st Airborne Battle Group, the provisional support company from Fort Chaffee, and the detachment from the 53d Signal Battalion from Fort Hood in case the plan was placed in effect. A Logistics Annex and an Administrative Order No. 1 provided details of support to be rendered by Fort Chaffee and the steps to be taken in processing the incoming National Guard personnel, supplementing the Fourth Army plan in these areas. Distribution points for rations and petroleum products (POL) were to be established at the U.S. Army Reserve facilities at Camp Robinson; Class II and IV supply and ammunition were to be delivered from Fort Chaffee on call. Both regular army and National Guard forces were to subsist on C rations until such time as facilities for feeding A or B rations could be established. Regular Army troops would bring these operational rations with them; Guard units would draw a three-day supply of C rations upon being called into federal service. Processing of Guard personnel was to be accomplished by unit commanders of the Arkansas National Guard and was to follow generally the provisions of SR 130-10-1, a regulation used during the Korean War. However, this processing was to be considerably abbreviated and the complications that later were to develop in this regard were apparently not anticipated.

These plans filled in most of the details of the organizational framework for military intervention in the Little Rock school crisis. DCSOPS officers reviewed the Fourth Army plan on the morning of 20 September and accepted it as a tentative stand-by plan. They accepted General Walker's plan with some recommended revisions in detail in somewhat the same terms on Sunday morning, 22 September.[37]

---

37. Based on rough pencilled notes taken by Col Williams and Col. Crayton on a meeting on the morning of 20 Sep 57 and on verbal information from Col. Williams.

In filling in details of the organizational and logistical framework, these plans nevertheless left many questions unanswered. Neither plan contained any real concept for the employment of troops in Little Rock itself. Both were particularly vague in regard to the purpose for which the National Guard was to be called, implying rather strongly that it would be solely to keep it from being used by Governor Faubus to oppose carrying out the court order rather than for positive action to enforce it. In neither plan was the mission of the National Guard stated nor was there more than the vaguest of indications as to the number or types of units to be called. The Fourth Army plan did, however, state the mission of the regular troops should they be employed: "As directed by higher authority, to enforce the orders of the Federal Courts in the State of Arkansas, and to maintain order in the execution thereof only; to take such action as may be directed." It was assumed too that there would be a "Federal Proclamation" defining "the specific area involved, and provide other guidance."[38] Both plans also assumed martial law would not be

---

38. (FOUO) Fourth Army Plan, cited n 35.

---

declared and that any persons obstructing the action of troops would be turned over to the civil authorities for disposition. Beyond these very general assumptions they did not go.

The reasons for this vagueness are apparent. There had been no indications, at least at the staff working levels in DCSOPS or in the field, as to what action the President might in fact be contemplating. The most that could be done was to prepare generally for whatever specific action might be ordered. In this light the completion of plans for the organizational framework and preparations for movement of regular troops and for call to active service of all or part of the Arkansas National Guard were considerable accomplishments.

The plans for movement of the airborne task force from Fort Campbell were much better defined than those for calling the National Guard. It was reasonable clear that if the regular troops were to be used it would be for the positive purpose of enforcing the court order, while the Guard might simply be called to keep it from being used for a contrary purpose. Out of the round of conferences on 20-22 September emerged a much more positive plan for the movement of the airborne battle group. The necessary coordination with the Air Force, started and then stopped earlier, was carried through to completion. On 21 September, the Air Force issued a standby alert, this time not to MATS but through the Tactical Air Command at Langley Air Force Base and the Ninth Air Force to the commander of the 314th Troop Carrier Wing at Sewart Air Base near Nashville, Tennessee. This message instructed the commander at Sewart to place on standby alert effective 0800 CST on 23 September 1957 sufficient aircraft and crews to airlift 500 troops "in conjunction with probable surprise exercise involving airborne Western Hemisphere Reserve Forces." The troops were to be picked up at Fort Campbell AFB, would carry personal equipment and weapons, and their destination was approximately 350 miles away. The alert was to remain in effect until specifically cancelled by AF Headquarters.[39] On

---

39. (TS) Msg AFOOP-OS-T TS 7815, Hqs USAF to COMTAC, Langley AFB, COMNINTH AF, SHAW AFB, & COM 314th TROOP CARRIER WING, Sewart AFB, 21 Sep 57, DA-IN-56217.

Monday, 23 September, at the request of DCSOPS, a second requirement was placed on Sewart AFB to maintain sufficient additional aircraft on alert to transport the light vehicles of the task force (36 jeeps, 15 ¼-ton trailers, 2 ¾-ton command radio vehicles), and Sewart was informed that if the exercise were implemented a second increment of 500 airborne personnel and equipment with the same number of vehicles would be airlifted, using the same planes for a second trip.[40] The new plans

---

40. (1) (TS) Msg AFOOP-OS-T TS 7825, HQS USAF to COMATC, LANGLEY AFB, 23 Sep 57, DA-IN-56613. (2) Notes on events of 23 Sep 57 taken by Lt Col R. B. Crayton.

---

developed with the Air Force also speeded up the timing of the movement. Instead of departing Fort Campbell at A plus 6 hours as originally proposed, the planes were to depart at A plus 2 hours and the movement of both increments was to be completed by A plus 11 rather than A plus 15. Brig. Gen. Joseph J. Preston, commander at Little Rock AFB, was to assist in moving the troops from the air base to Little Rock, and direct contact between General Preston and General Walker was authorized so that coordinated arrangements might be made for landing and movement. In addition to these arrangements for possible air movement of troops, there was also some preliminary exploration with Air Force officials on preparation of parallel federalization orders to the Army and Air National Guard of Arkansas and on the use of the Air National Guard should it be called to service.[41]

---

41. (1) Pencilled M/R by Col Williams, WHD. (2) (S) Memo for Gen Sherburne, CG 101st Abn Div, prepared by Gens Walker and Eddleman, see below n 43.

40

During his visit on 20 September to Washington, General Walker showed some concern about public information policy and legal assistance for his command, since any federal intervention at Little Rock would inevitably become a <u>cause célébre</u> and involve complicated legal questions. To meet these needs, the Department of the Army arranged to place Col. William G. Easton of the Office of the Judge Advocate General, who had previously been assigned as legal adviser to Walker on the Little Rock integration problem, on TDY to his headquarters, and to form a public information team to handle public relations. A PIO plan was then prepared though it was not ready until the day after General Walker's departure. This plan provided for a very close Pentagon supervision over the release of information. An information section was to be created at Headquarters, Arkansas Military District, composed of four officers and three enlisted men drawn from the Chief of Information's office (CINFO) and from the information sections of Third and Fourth Armies. This information section was to handle the troop information program and contacts with the press and public in Little Rock. In the event a situation arose it did not feel qualified to handle it was to ask for guidance from the military commander, who would, if he felt it necessary, contact DCSOPS. DCSOPS would then coordinate with a projects officer in CINFO in furnishing the required guidance. In matters involving purely technical public information matters, direct communication was to be authorized between the Little Rock information staff and CINFO. The task force commander was to make no policy announcements to the press without prior clearance from DCSOPS. He was to be kept informed, however, of pertinent press releases made in Washington prior to their release, in order that he would not "hear of DA policy announcement from the press before receiving it through the chain of command."[42]

---

42. (1) (S) "Information Plan for Exercise" dated 23 Sep 57.
(2) (S) Sheet marked "Questions to be asked DA" filed with Walker's Plan.

On the morning of Sunday, 22 September, a conference took place in the office of Gen. Clyde D. Eddleman, DCSOPS, at which Maj. Gen. Earle G. Wheeler, Assistant DCSOPS, General Walker, General Pachler, Colonel Alfred, Colonel Easton, and officers from the Western Hemisphere Division were present. At this meeting General Eddleman made final the decisions that had been reached during the previous two days. It was agreed that General Walker should return to Little Rock via Fort Campbell and brief Maj. Gen. Thomas L. Sherburne, Jr., Commanding General of the 101st Airborne Division. The briefing paper, as finally revised by General Eddleman, read in part as follows:

The Chief of Staff had directed that I pass to you general information on what has been decided in DA to bring you up to date.

Specifically, it is necessary that your troops be able to become airborne on first sortie at A plus 2 hours which would land 500 troops at Little Rock Air Force Base at A plus 5, the second sortie landing at A plus 11. . . .

I have authority for direct contact with CG, Little Rock Air Force Base for planning purposes. You should not send anyone to that Air Force Base at this time. You should continue planning with my headquarters; send liaison officer there as I deem necessary. It is important that our plans be ready and that there be no delay in arrival of troops in accordance with plans.

. . . you should make direct contact with the commander 314th Troop Carrier Wing at Sewart Air Force Base without delay.

You should use utmost discretion in making some decrease in the colored strength of your task force, . . . Those arriving at destination should not be used operationally in the city where they have direct contact with the populace.

Your troops in the objective area will be under my direct command with logistic support furnished by CG, Fourth U.S. Army. Colonel Alfred is your point of contact if the need arises.

The operation, if necessary will be triggered by DA direct to you.[43]

---

43. (S) Memo for Gen Sherburne, unsigned. The final product was typed from a draft which General Eddleman had carefully gone over and rephrased. Col. Williams furnished verbal information on the meeting.

General Eddleman also went over a brief summary of guide lines for the operation which General Walker had prepared, and approved the following version, predicated as his own paper had been on the assumed existence of a Presidential Proclamation:

1. Observe use of the City Police and permit them normal authority.

2. Plan for the use of most desirable National Guard units.

3. Do not employ Active Army troops unless absolutely necessary and only if the Guard cannot do the job.

4. It is believed that there are no National Guard units in the state of Arkansas who have not received Federal recognition. This is being verified by Headquarters, Fourth U.S. Army.

5. Determine status of the white Citizens Council.

6. Integrated troops will be employed in Active Army if called, but colored troops will not be used operationally in direct contact with the populace.

7. The Battle Group of the 101st Airborne Division will be prepared to have first 500 man group airborne in two hours after alert.

8. General Walker is authorized direct communication with CG, Little Rock Air Force Base for planning purposes.

9. CG, Fourth U.S. Army is authorized to make necessary disposition of transportation to fulfill the requirement for the movement and supply of the 101st Airborne Battle Group.

10. DA will provide a PIO team consisting of 4 people to develop plans and programs. This work is to be done at DA except that one officer will be sent to General Walker's headquarters Monday, 23 September.

11. JA assistance is being provided by DA.

12. General Walker will be referred to as Chief, U.S. Army Military District of Arkansas, and his headquarters will retain present designation.

13. The Air Force plans to move the Air National Guard out of the Little Rock area.[44]

---

44. (S) Attachment to the memo for Gen. Sherburne cited above.

The second point of this summary of decisions is of particular note. While there are no records of these conferences, it does appear that General Walker discussed with Generals Wheeler and Eddleman the question of what units of the National Guard should be called if they were to be used operationally to enforce the court order. And these discussions apparently centered around the use of all or part of the 153d Infantry Regiment, Arkansas National Guard, an outfit whose home stations were outside Little Rock for the most part but within reasonable distance of the city. Though it lacked one infantry battalion, the 153d Infantry appeared to be the only suitable complete unit that could be used. In his original draft, General Walker had stated, "It is planned to move 1 battalion of the 153d Infantry Regiment, . . . to Little Rock should they be required for operational use." But he had also stated, "Do not use the National Guard unless absolutely necessary." General Eddleman marked out both these clauses and substituted: "Use National Guard units as directed in D/A. Plan for use of most desirable guard units."[45] Only the last sentence

---

45. (S) Working draft of above paper with revisions in General Eddleman's handwriting.

---

remained in the final draft.

It is clear therefore that when General Walker left Washington on 22 September a plan for operational use of selected National Guard units was at least in the formative stage. However, this remained the weakest link in the planning, since the guidance which General Walker took with him clearly stated that the Arkansas National Guard was to be the primary reliance and that the regular troops, for whom the plans were more meticulously worked out, were not to be employed "unless absolutely necessary." There remained some very serious questions about whether a suitable task force from the National Guard could be brought to the scene rapidly enough in case the need for action was an urgent and immediate one. It was fairly obvious too that in such case Fort Chaffee was entirely too far away to serve as a mobilization base and the finger pointed at the facilities, inadequate though they were, at Camp Robinson. In the plans submitted by Fourth Army and Arkansas Military District, Camp Robinson was mentioned only as a supply point.

In the afternoon of 22 September, General Walker and Colonel Alfred arrived at Fort Campbell, and briefed the Commanding General, 101st Airborne Division, and selected staff officers as instructed by General Eddleman. At the conclusion of this conference, Colonel Kuhn was ordered to execute Alert Phase ALFA of the Division Alert SOP, for the 327th Infantry, plans were put in final form for movement to an undisclosed destination, and personnel of the 327th were restricted to the battle group area. The previous prohibition on direct liaison with the 314th Troop Carrier Wing at Sewart AFB having been removed, the Wing Operation Officer came down from Sewart AFB to Fort Campbell to coordinate the air movement plan.

Over the weekend of 20-22 September, Fourth Army also began more advanced preparations for furnishing logistical and administrative support. On 20 September, warning orders went out to the Commanding General, Fort Hood, to prepare a light truck company for movement to any installation within the army area. On 21 September a Signal officer from Fourth Army was temporarily assigned to Headquarters, Arkansas Military District, further to coordinate signal planning and make preparations for installation of communications. Additional signal personnel and cryptographic equipment were sent in the next day and the Military District Headquarters was authorized to order such leased communication facilities as might be necessary, subject to confirmation by Fourth Army.[46]

---

46. (1) (FOUO) Cmd Rpt, 101st Abn Div, Opn ARKANSAS, 10 Sep - 27 Nov 57, p. 2. (2) (C) Cmd Rpt, 4th US Army, Opn ARKANSAS, 1 Sep - 30 Nov 57, pp. 4-5.

(3) (S) Memo, Lt Gen C D Eddleman, DCSOPS, for Sec Army, 25 Sep 57, sub: AF Support of the 101st Abn Div. DCSOPS Journal, Opn ARKANSAS, item 56.

On Monday, 23 September, the mob action of the school took place and at approximately 1800 EDT the President issued his "cease and desist" proclamation. The proclamation made it almost certain that some military action would be required, but what that action would be remained undefined until the next day. In the Pentagon last minute preparations were made for either contingency, the use of the Guard or of regular troops. DCSOPS began work on the final version of messages to be dispatched to various commands and to Governor Faubus. Definite arrangements for the air lift and for notification of the Air Force that the movement of the battle group of the 101st would begin were worked out. Under these arrangements the Department of the Air Force in Washington was to be notified simultaneously with the alert to the 101st Airborne Division and was then to send out an alert through its own channels. It was also the understanding of DCSOPS that Sewart AFB would immediately honor a request placed by the 101st Airborne Division. At 0700 CST, 24 September, the 327th Infantry was ordered to execute Alert Phase BRAVO, placing the battle group in "a posture of complete readiness to execute imminent movement orders."[47]

---

47. (FOUO) *Ibid.* (1) & (3).

On 23 September also, the PIO plan was submitted and Lt. Col. William A. Drake of CINFO was sent off to join General Walker's headquarters.

DCSOPS took steps to establish an operations room or command post in its
Operations Directorate as a channel of communication with Arkansas Military
District. A direct or "hot" line running from the command post to General
Walker's headquarters in Little Rock was installed. Arrangements were made
for a very rapid secure message system for direct handling of outgoing and
incoming messages on the Little Rock situation with the Staff Communications
Center, and for delivery of both news releases and up to date intelligence
reports from the Office of the Assistant Chief of Staff for Intelligence
(ACSI). ACSI assigned a representative to work with the DCSOPS Command
Post.[48]

---

48. (1) (FOUO) DCSOPS Rpt, Situation as of 0800 24 Sep, DCSOPS Sit
Rep Bk, Opn ARKANSAS. (2) The timing of the steps in setting up the
command post on 23 September are not completely clear. The first entry
in the command post journal was at 1740 EDT on that day.

Late in the afternoon of the 23d, the command post began operating.
By night it began to take on the sort of hectic atmosphere that was to
prevail there for the next two weeks. At 1740 EDT, and again at 1830,
General Pachler called General Walker for information on the situation
and discussed the problem of possible military action with him. Walker
reported that the situation at the school was currently quiet but would
not hazard a prediction as to what would happen the following day. This
information was immediately relayed to General Eddleman, but he apparently
was not satisfied either with it or with intelligence arrangements. At

1950 he came to General Pachler's office and called General Walker himself, querying him at some length on the sources of trouble and the size of force that would probably be needed. The Assistant DCSOPS, General Wheeler, joined him shortly afterward and Maj. Gen. Robert H. Wienecke, Deputy to the Assistant Chief of Staff for Intelligence and Brig. Gen. Royal Reynolds, Jr., Chief of Plans, Programs, and Security Division of ACSI were called in for consultation on the matter of gathering more accurate and timely intelligence. While the meeting went on, General Pachler and Colonel Crayton went to meet the Secretary of the Army at the airport. The Secretary of the Army was scheduled to talk to the Secretary of Defense shortly after arrival. Whether any guidance was received from either at this time is not apparent from the records. In any case, certain definite decisions did result from the conferences. General Wheeler, it was agreed, should depart for Little Rock the following morning by air. And at 2130 EDT General Wheeler telephoned instructions to General Walker directing him that if the Presidential Proclamation were issued to use the National Guard initially and to phone in a plan not later than 0800 EDT the following day to include the units and number of personnel to be used, how they were to be used, and a recommendation as to whether all the Arkansas National Guard should be federalized or only part of it. Wheeler also asked Walker to supply better and more timely information to DCSOPS. And following the call General Reynolds got in touch with G—2, Fourth Army, and obtained information that eleven of the twenty CIC agents in the Arkansas area had been instructed to report to General Walker and that his headquarters would be augmented with additional G—2 personnel from Fourth Army the following day.[49]

49. (1) (S) DCSOPS Journal, Opn ARKANSAS, items 1-11. These early entries are brief and not backed by items in the Journal File. (2) Sherman Adams in First Hand Report, p. 354, states that on 24 September, President Eisenhower "talked with Army Chief of Staff, General Maxwell D. Taylor, and later with Secretary of Defense Wilson as soon as he returned from Louisiana that evening." He does not elaborate on this statement.

In informing General Walker of the requirement for a plan for using the Guard, General Wheeler reminded him of the "complete unit we discussed" (evidently 153d Infantry), but suggested he might have to use the "1,000 odds and ends at the outset" (evidently units in Little Rock and immediate vicinity). Walker was advised with regard to calling the entire Guard that he should "federalize only that number needed, unless you deem it necessary to freeze people in place."[50]

50. (S) Ibid. (1), item 11.

Walker dispatched his plan from Little Rock at 0330 EDT on 24 September. He recommended calling up a task force composed of the 1st and 3d Battalions of the 153d Infantry Regiment plus the Military Police Company of the 39th Infantry Division and Company D of the 212th Signal Battalion (Corps), a total force estimated at 1,774 officers and men. He estimated that 70 to 80 percent of this strength would report for duty and that with deductions for "administrative loss" and "undetermined loyalty" some 1,240 men would be available for use in Little Rock. However, some of these units had home stations well over 100 miles away and while General Walker estimated he could have 140 men in two hours, it would take 16 hours to round up the entire force. The plan called for using National Guard transportation and for assembly of the Guard units at Camp Robinson. In choosing the 153d Infantry, General Walker noted that the troops in Little Rock would not form a suitable force because they were mainly service troops "not adaptable to situation," while the 153d was an infantry unit with capability of prolonged operations.[51]

---

51. (C) Msg, CHUSARMILDIST, Ark, to DCSOPS, 240740Z Sept 57.

Walker's plan did not include any recommendation as to how he would use the Guard units nor whether he thought it advisable to call all the Arkansas National Guard in order to freeze it in place. In reviewing the plan, Colonel Crayton carefully noted this ommission as well as the length of time that would be required to assemble the entire force. he recommended to Colonel Williams that the units furthest away be dropped and suggested that Walker be given a "preliminary reading" prior to noon on the 24th.[52] This

---

52. Pencilled memo from Lt Col R B Crayton for Col R C Williams attached to above message in WHD file.

---

in effect ended the preliminary planning. Very shortly after noon on the 24th the President and Secretary of Defense were to issue orders which finally removed all uncertainty and laid down a definite course of action. It was the existence of the contingency plans, nevertheless, imperfect though they were in some respects, that enabled the Army to take action so swiftly when direction from higher authority came.

The President's Executive Order and Its Implementation

24 September 1957

During the night of 23-24 September, CIC reports on the developing situation at Little Rock were regularly phoned in to DCSOPS. They revealed a high state of tension in the city, though there were no genuine race riots or extensive destruction of property. At 0720 CST (0920 EDT) General Walker reported that incidents had continued up to two o'clock in the night but then had died down, that the police were erecting two barricades near the school, but that no crowd had yet gathered. By the time school opened less than two hours later, however, a crowd estimated at 350 persons had gathered and it may be assumed that a repetition of the previous day's disorders would have taken place had the Negro students made any effort to enter the school. But they did not, and as the morning wore on the crowd gradually dispersed. At 0945 CST USARMD reported that the crowd had dwindled to 150 persons and by 1130 EST to 25. In anticipation of action by the President, nevertheless, General Wheeler departed Washington for Little Rock at 1040 EDT, planning to stop at Campbell en route to talk with General Sherburne. But events moved more rapidly than the Army anticipated.[53]

---

53. (FOUO) DCSOPS Journal File, Opn ARKANSAS, items 15, 17, 19, 25, 26, 27, 29, 30, 31, 33.

The reports that reached the President from Mayor Woodrow Wilson Mann portrayed a far more dangerous situation than the Army reports indicated.

Mann informed the President:

> The immediate need for federal troops is urgent. The mob is in much larger numbers at 8 A. M. than at any time yesterday. People are converging on the scene from all directions and engaging in fisticuffs and other acts of violence. Situation is out of control and police cannot disperse the mob. . . ."54

---

54. Dwight D. Eisenhower, Waging Peace 1956-1961, (New York: Doubleday & Co., 1965), p. 170.

In his memoirs President Eisenhower has indicated that even before the arrival of the Mayor's telegram he had decided to act and the question had become not whether to use force but what type of force to use. He discussed this matter with Attorney General Brownell and both of them rejected use of either the United States Marshall or the FBI. "General Maxwell D. Taylor, Army Chief of Staff," he says, "wanted to try the Arkansas National Guard before ordering out federal troops," but he (Eisenhower) rejected this suggestion. "After reflecting on the kind of troops to use, I decided to dispatch regular federal troops. Shortly after twelve noon, I telephoned the Attorney General that I was about to sign an Executive Order . . . which would federalize the Arkansas National Guard and send regular federal troops to Little Rock. At 12:15 I called General Taylor and gave him the decision."[54a] At 1222 EDT, the President issued Executive Order No. 10730

54a. Ibid.

---

from the temporary White House at the U.S. Naval Base at Newport, Rhode

Island, resolving any remaining doubts about the question of federal intervention at Little Rock.

Since this Presidential Executive Order became the basis for all actions taken by the Army in the crisis, it requires examination in some detail. To begin with the President cited his proclamation of the preceding day and stated that the fact that it had not been obeyed indicated that "willful obstruction to enforcement of said court order still exists and threatens to continue." He then authorized the Secretary of Defense "to take all appropriate steps to enforce any order of the United States District Court for the Eastern District of Arkansas for the removal of obstruction of justice in the state of Arkansas with respect to matters relating to enrollment and attendance at public schools in the Little Rock school district, Little Rock Arkansas." Specifically, the Secretary of Defense was authorized and directed to order into the active military service of the United States "any or all of the units" of the Arkansas National Guard to serve "for an indefinite period and until relieved by appropriate orders." He was further authorized to use any of these Guard units and "such of the armed forces of the United States as he may deem necessary" to enforce the court order. Finally, the Secretary of Defense was authorized to delegate to the Secretary of the Army or the Secretary of the Air Force, or both, any of the authority conferred upon him.[55]

---

55. (U) Executive Order No. 10730, PROVIDING ASSISTANCE FOR THE REMOVAL OF AN OBSTRUCTION TO JUSTICE WITHIN THE STATE OF ARKANSAS, 24 Sep 57.

As legal basis for this action, the President cited particularly Title 10, Sections 332, 333, and 334 of the Revised United States Code. Section 332 provides that the President may use the armed forces of the United States or call into federal service the militia of any state to enforce the laws or suppress rebellion whenever he considers "that unlawful obstructions, combinations or assemblages, or rebellion" against federal authority make it impossible to enforce federal laws by "the ordinary course of judicial proceedings." Section 333 provides more specifically that the President may use the militia or armed forces when necessary to suppress, in a state, insurrection, domestic violence, unlawful combination, or conspiracy that "so hinders the execution of the laws of that State, and of the United States within the State, that any part or class of its people is deprived of a right, privilege, immunity, or protection named in the Constitution and secured by law, and the constituted authorities of that State are unable, fail, or refuse to protect that right, privilege, or immunity, or to give that protection; or opposes or obstructs the execution of the laws of the United States or impedes the course of justice under those laws." Section 334 provides for the issuance of a proclamation as a preliminary to action under either of these other sections. The other law cited by the President, Section 301 of Title 3 of the U.S. Code, establishes his right to make the delegations of authority to the Secretary of Defense.[56]

---

56. (U) Laws governing the entire military establishment, Army, Navy and Air Force were recodified and combined in a new Title 10 to the

U. S. Code by the 84th Congress, 2nd Session. Approved 10 Aug 56. See Special Pamphlet No. 17, United States Code: Congressional and Administrative News, (St. Paul, Minn. and Brooklyn, N. Y., 1956).

Pursuant to the President's Executive Order, at 1425 on 24 September the Secretary of Defense, Charles E. Wilson, issued his implementing order. While the President had said "any or all" of the units of the Arkansas National Guard, Wilson's order called "all of the units and the members thereof of the Army National Guard and the Air National Guard of the state of Arkansas" into federal service. The members of these National Guard units were to "hold themselves in readiness for further orders as to the time and date of reporting to active duty by the Secretary of the Army acting for me." Copies of this Call by the Secretary of Defense were to be "furnished forthwith to the Governor of Arkansas and to the commanding officers of the Army National Guard and the Air National Guard in the state of Arkansas." Finally Wilson sub-delegated the authority given to him by the President to the Secretary of the Army:

> I further direct that the Secretary of the Army take such actions as he deems necessary to implement such executive order and this order, and I hereby vest in the Secretary of the Army the right to exercise any and all of the authority conferred on me by sections 2 and 3 of the above mentioned order, as of 24 September 1957.[57]

---

57. (U) Copy from New York Times, 25 Sep 57.

This sub-delegation of powers covered everything the President had ordered done except the actual issuance of the initial Call to the Arkansas National

Guard.

As of 1425 EDT on 24 September, then the affair was in the Army's hands. But the nature of the action the Army was to take had been largely determined by the directives from higher authority. The whole import of the President's and Secretary of Defense's orders was that not only should the task force from the 101st Airborne Division be used but that the entire Arkansas National Guard, Army and Air, should be called to federal service. DCSOPS planning up to that time on the 24th had been proceeding along the line of using a selected force from the Army National Guard. The decision to use both the entire Guard and the airborne battle group therefore came as a surprise.[58] It meant, in effect, that all phases of the contingency

---

58. Verbal info frm Col R. C. Williams, Chf, WHD.

---

plans would be in effect rather than any single one of them. The concept that rapidly took shape was one that contemplated using the task force from the 101st Airborne, the most dependable resource and the one that could be moved most quickly to the scene of action, initally, and then replacing it by the units of the Arkansas National Guard that General Walker had recommended. The rest of the Arkansas National Guard would be mobilized at home stations as a possible reserve.

The implementation of the Executive Order actually began immediately after the President's call to General Taylor at 1215 EDT. At 1230 EDT (1030 CST) General Eddleman called General Sherburne telling him that his battle group was alerted "to move immediately to designated area," and that

57

he should "Get Sewart to get Air Force." At the end of the conversation, General Taylor passed the message to the 101st Commander that "The President of the United States is watching your move personally. Make it expeditious and a good airborne move."[59] Simultaneously the Air Force was

---

59. (FOUO) M/R by Maj Charles D. Daniel, Aide to CofS, of tel call, Lt Gen Eddleman to Maj Gen Sherburne, CG 101st Abn Div, Ft Campbell, Ky, 1230 hrs, 24 Sep 57. DCSOPS Journal File, item 27A.

---

notified of the movement requirement. General Eddleman then called General Walker informing him of the President's decisions and of the order to the 101st, saying that the first increments of the battle group should be at Little Rock Air Base by 1530 CST (A plus 5). He told Walker briefly that he was to take command of the battle group on arrival and of the National Guard called to federal service, that he was to use the regular army units initially, replacing them with the Guard as he deemed feasible. The units of the Guard were to be mobilized at home stations except for the 153d Infantry (-), which was to be moved into Camp Robinson. He was not to interfere with the city administration in other parts of Little Rock but was to take over "the critical area around the school" and carry out the President's directive to enforce the court order.[60]

---

60. (FOUO) Ibid., item 32. The original entry is timed at 1240 EDT, but another version at 1230 EDT.

Formal messages soon followed these telephonic instructions. The drafts prepared in DCSOPS were quickly revised to fit the situation. At 1310 EDT a message went out to the 101st Airborne Division confirming verbal orders for movement of the Battle group.[61] At 1439 EDT a second

---

61. (S) Msg, DA 930027, to CG 101st ABN DIV, FT CAMPBELL, KY, 24 Sep 57, Excl for Maj Gen Sherburne from Lt Gen Eddleman.

---

message carried formal instructions to General Walker. It confirmed his command over the National Guard called to active duty and "any U.S. Regular Army units that might be employed in the Little Rock area to enforce Federal authority." He was to report directly to the Chief of Staff but was informed that General Wheeler was designated as the personal representative of General Taylor in Little Rock to effect liaison, not to be in the chain of command but still "authorized to issue orders for the Chief of Staff, U.S. Army." Detailed instructions to Walker consisted simply of the following:

You will carry out the orders of the Presidential Executive Order, 24 Sept. You will employ the minimum force necessary in carrying out this assignment. Initially you will use units of the Regular Army placed under your command replacing them with units of the Arkansas National Guard as you deem advisable and feasible. For this purpose you will order into the Little Rock area such units of the Arkansas National Guard as you may require; you will direct the remaining units to remain in their home areas, subject to your order.[62]

---

62. (U) Msg DA 930038 to CHUSARMD ARK, 24 Sep 57.

A third message at 1440 EDT to General Wheeler informed him of the Chief of Staff's action in designating him as his personal representative at Little Rock.[63] A fourth dispatched at 1505 EDT informed CONARC and Fourth

---

63. (U) Msg DA 930039 to CHUSARMD ARK, 24 Sep 57, Lt Gen Eddleman to Maj Gen Wheeler.

Army of the actions taken, confirmed the direct command channel, and charged Fourth Army with providing necessary logistical and administrative support to the forces involved.[64]

---

64. (TS) Msg DA 930046 to CGUSCONARC and CGUSARFOUR, 24 Sep 57, Excl for Gen Wyman fm DCSOPS.

There remained the formal Call to the Arkansas National Guard. In the event, this was not carried out as the DCSOPS planners had anticipated, apparently because the Call did not come directly from the President but from the Secretary of Defense. The draft messages to the Governor of Arkansas and to Fourth Army with their detailed lists of units appended were therefore not used. At 1450 EDT Secretary of the Army Wilber M. Brucker telephoned Lieutenant Governor Nathan Gordon of Arkansas (Governor Faubus was en route to Little Rock from the Southern Governor's Conference at Sea Island, Georgia) communicating the Call.[65] This was followed by a

---

65. (U) See Time-Table in Washington Post and Times Herald, 25 Sep 57.

message to Faubus and Gordon at 1517 EDT that simply cited the Presidential Executive Order and transmitted the substance of the Secretary of Defense Call.[66] To carry out the Secretary of Defense's instructions that copies of

---

66. (U) Msg DA 571834, Secretary of the Army Wilbur M. Brucker to Hon Gov Orval E Faubus, Gov of Ark, & Hon Nathan Gordon, Little Rock, Ark, 24 Sep 57. Info copies to CGCONARC, CGUSARFOUR, AG of State of Arkansas.

---

the Call be delivered to the Governor and the commanders of the Air and Army National Guard, a second message was dispatched to General Walker at 1539 EDT transmitting the Secretary of Defense Call in full and instructing that he ensure that copies of it were delivered to these parties in person.[67] An

---

67. (U) DA 571836 to CHUSARMD, ARK, 24 Sep 57.

---

information copy of this message to Faubus and Gordon went to Fourth Army, but no copy of the Call was sent directly to that headquarters as had been planned. Fourth Army was asked directly, however, to notify The Adjutant General of the State of Arkansas that General Walker was designated commander of all Army units of the National Guard to be inducted under the Call.[68] The list of units to be called was not appended to any of the

---

68. (U) Msg DA 930052 to CGUSARFOUR, 24 Sep 57.

---

messages; instead it was incorporated in a TAG information letter almost a week later.[69] Under these arrangements the whole burden of calling the

---

69. (U) TAG ltr to CGs, USCONARC & Fourth US Army, Chf, NGB, 30 Sep 57, sub: Ordering to Active Duty NG Units of State of Ark, AGAO-O (M) 322 (27 Sep 57) DCSOPS. Copy in DCSOPS Opn ARKANSAS Out-Cable Book.

Arkansas National Guard to federal service and issuing initial movement orders fell on Headquarters, Arkansas Military District and the National Guard Headquarters itself, not on Fourth Army as had been stipulated in the Fourth Army Plan.[70]

---

70. (FOUO) See Fourth Army Plan cited n 35.

These were, in essence, the principal orders sent out by the Department of the Army on 24 September 1957 to implement the President's Executive Order. Their rapid execution made possible the carrying out the purpose of that order at Little Rock on the morning of the 25th.

The force chosen from the 101st Airborne Division to execute the mission was an especially tailored one, consisting of most of the elements of the First Airborne Battle Group, 327th Infantry, reinforced by certain division support personnel. It consisted of five rifle companies, a mortar battery and part of the Headquarters and Headquarters Company to which the division support personnel had been added. The battle group was preparing to move within ten minutes after the receipt of the alert at 1030 CST. The plan for movement, as worked out with Sewart AFB, called for the separation of the battle group into two air serials each consisting of approximately 500 personnel plus necessary command and communications vehicles. Each of the two serials was to be deployed by 26 medium (C-123) type aircraft operating a shuttle. Owing to some last minute confusion, the plan was not executed in this manner. The 101st contacted the 314th Troop Carrier Wing at Sewart AFB at 1040 CST but the latter did not understand that it was to dispatch planes until it received its own alert through Air Force channels. The USAF did not contact Sewart directly but sent the alert through normal Air Force channels via TAC and Ninth AF and this alert was not received at Sewart until 1145 CST. The first of the twenty-six C-123's arrived at Campbell AFB at 1237 CST with the others following at two minute intervals. Loading began immediately, but there was a further delay while the Air commander talked to the USAF Headquarters in Washington. The first aircraft did not depart Campbell until 1329 CST, just one minute short of three hours after the alert, and one hour after the time (A plus 2) stipulated in the plan. Nevertheless, the last of the 26 planes carrying the first serial arrived at Little Rock AFB at 1547 CST, only minutes after the scheduled five hours from the initial alert. The delay apparently produced a change in plan and the scheduled shuttle was cancelled "by telephonic order from the Department of the Army."[71]

---

71. (FOUO) Cmd Rpt, 101st Abn Div, Opn ARKANSAS, 10 Sep – 27 Nov 57, p. 7 & Incl 6.

All aircraft on station at Fort Campbell (2 C-130's, 11 C-123's) were ordered loaded and dispatched to Little Rock and six additional C-130's sent from Sewart. There was again a short delay because the on-base planes had to be de-rigged and loads adjusted to allowable weight limits that were substantially lower than normal. Moreover, for a time the Air Force commander insisted that he had no authority to use the on-base planes though General Eddleman later stated that they had been placed at Fort Campbell "ostensibly for training of the 101st Airborne Division, but actually on alert status for the Little Rock operation."[72] All these

---

72. (FOUO) Memo, Lt Gen C D Eddleman for Sec Army, 25 Sep 57, sub: AF Support of the 101st Abn Div. DCSOPS Journal File, item 56.

---

problems were straightened out and the last plane carrying the second increment departed Fort Campbell at 1809 CST, 24 September, and arrived at Little Rock at 2019 CST. Eleven C-123's and seven C-130's were used in the second serial. Despite all delays, the movement was completed nine hours and 49 minutes after the first alert, a slight improvement over the eleven hours stipulated in the plan. Total personnel moved by air in the two echelons consisted of 42 officers and 814 enlisted men. An overland echelon (land tail) consisting of nine officers, 90 enlisted men, and 24 vehicles departed Fort Campbell at 1430 CST, 24 September and closed at Camp Robinson at 1300 CST the following day. Not until they were en route were the airborne troops officially briefed on their mission.

From Little Rock AFB, most of the airborne troops were moved directly to the vicinity of Central High School, the rest to Camp Robinson. The first group, consisting of selected headquarters and communication personnel, the reconnaissance platoon, and one rifle company, departed Little Rock AFB at 1740 CST and arrived at the school at 1843 CST. The other units followed. Organic transportation brought by air movement was limited and had to be supplemented by vehicles furnished by the Air Force Base. General Preston, the base commander, cooperated to the fullest in expediting the movement.[73]

---

73. (1) (FOUO) This account is based mainly on 101st Abn Div Command Report, pp. 3-5 & Incls. 2 & 8 with some additional material drawn from Memo, Col D P Quandt, CofS, 101st Abn Div, for DCSOPS, Attn Col Reaves, 25 Sep 57, DCSOPS Journal, item 49 and memo cited n 72. (2) (FOUO) See also items 38B, 41B, 42, 42C for interim information received in DCSOPS during movement. There are no records in the Journal of contacts with the Air Force during the movement.

Fourth Army, acting quickly on instructions received, dispatched a provisional support company from Fort Chaffee consisting of five officers, 153 enlisted men, and 53 vehicles that arrived at Camp Robinson at 2130 CST to assume the task of administrative and logistical support. At the request of General Walker, two H-13 helicopters were also brought up from Fort Polk, and one L-23 aircraft furnished from Fourth Army Flight Detachment. Four motor messenger teams were ordered to Little Rock from Fort

Hood on 24 September, and two refrigerator vans with operating personnel were sent from the same installation on the following day. Region VI, 112th CIC Group, was augmented by ten additional personnel from other Fourth Army regions and directed to keep the Chief, U.S. Army Military District, Arkansas, informed of local situations that might affect the accomplishment of his mission. Headquarters, U.S. Army Military District, Arkansas was also rapidly augmented on the 24th and 25th by 29 officers, six warrant officers, and 53 enlisted men, all from Fourth Army installations except three officers and one enlisted man from the Department of the Army and one officer from Headquarters, Third Army. This more than doubled the size of a staff that prior to 20 September had consisted of only 13 officers, 1 warrant officer, 17 enlisted men, and 35 civilians.[74]

---

74. (1) (C) 213 AKADC-E, Msg CGUSARFOUR to CG FT CHAFFEE, 24 Sep 57, DA-IN-56913. (2) (S) Msg AKPCH-DC 9-265, CG ATC FT CHAFFEE to CGUSARFOUR, 25 Sep 57, DA-IN-57309. (3) (FOUO) Msg 251300Z, USARMD ARK to DCSOPS, 25 Sep 57, Sit Rep #1, DA-IN-863853. (4) (FOUO) 4th U.S. Army Cmd Rept., pp. 5 -8. (5) (FOUO) Hqs. USARMD, Ark., Cmd Rpt., p. 3, & app 1, pp. 1-2.

Department of the Army took one additional action to see that General Walker had an adequate force to accomplish his mission. On the night of the 24th it was arranged that four specialist personnel from Fort Myer, Virginia with an irritant gas dispenser, supplies of tear gas and vomiting gas, and gas grenades be flown to Little Rock the following day.[75]

75. (C) MR, Col Kelsie L Reaves, Dep Dir Opns, OCODCOPS, 24 Sep 57, sub: Rpt of Conf w/Reps of CG, MDW and Dir Opns, ODCOPS w/notes by Lt Gen Eddleman and Lt Col Crayton. DCSOPS Journal File, item 39e.

While the regular army force at Little Rock was taking shape in this manner, the Arkansas National Guard was also being mobilized. It is worth noting at this point that a force of 150 Guardsmen had been assembled at Camp Robinson by the Lieutenant Governor of Arkansas, acting in Governor Faubus' absence, on both 23 September and the morning of the 24th on alert for possible use at Central High School. But this force was never used and at 1500 CST 24 September after news of the Presidential Call was reported on local radio stations the men were dismissed.[76] The Call issued

76. (FOUO) Hqs, Ark NG, Cmd Rpt, Pt I, 24 Sep - 24 Oct, App 2 to Annex B, p. 3.

from Washington was for the entire National Guard of the state. There was some doubt for a time whether Faubus, Gordon, and General Clinger would accept this Call and issue the necessary orders, and General Walker was instructed that if they did not, necessary action must be taken to inform all individual Guardsmen of the Call. These doubts were soon resolved. At 2000 CST General Walker and General Wheeler met with General Clinger, State Adjutant General and Commander of both the Army and Air National Guard, and informed him of the list of units called to the federal service and those to be moved immediately to Camp Robinson. After this conference and with the concurrence of General Walker, the State Adjutant General conferred with the Governor of Arkansas. At 2100 CST General Clinger again met with General Walker and agreed to issue the necessary orders. At 2110 CST he instructed the Assistant State Adjutant General to take necessary steps to assemble the selected units at Camp Robinson. At 2113 the Arkansas National Guard Alert Plan was put into effect with notices on radio and television and telephone calls to all subordinate unit commanders. The general call to all units of the Arkansas National Guard was regularized the following day by issue of General Orders by the Adjutant General's Department of the State of Arkansas calling the Arkansas National Guard to federal service, and the orders to selected units for assembly at Camp Robinson were confirmed by messages from Headquarters, Arkansas Military District, to Headquarters, Arkansas National Guard on 5 and 8 October. On 24 September General Walker issued an operational order setting forth the mission of the Guard and the concept of its operations.[77]

---

77. (1) (FOUO) DCSOPS Journal, items 42, 42a, 42b. (2) (FOUO) Chronology of actions with copies of pertinent orders furnished by Ark Mil Dist in DCSOPS Journal File, item 409. (3) (U) GO 12, State of Ark, AG Dept, 25 Sep 57 and amendment dated 26 Sep 57. (4) (FOUO) DCSOPS Journal, items 43a, 44, 384 and unnumbered item 0015 EDT 25 Sep 57. (5) (FOUO) Hqs. Ark NG, Cmd Rpt., Pt. I, pp. 2-3.

During the night and the next day these orders were carried out. The units selected to report at Camp Robinson were the same ones General Walker had recommended for use in the early hours of the morning of 24 September. The force, later to be known as the Alert Force, consisted of two battalions of the 153rd Infantry, the regimental headquarters, tank, truck, service and signal companies, the 39th MP Company, and Company D of the 212th Signal Battalion. These units began assembling at 2300 CST on 24 September and the last unit was reported in at 1210 CST the following day. The total assigned strength of these units was 1,586 officers and men, of whom 1,240 were reported at Camp Robinson at 1335 CST 25 September. By 1 October this strength had increased to 1,455.[78]

---

78. (1) (U) Journal File, item 409. (2) (FOUO) Journal File, unnumbered item, 1535 EDT, 25 Sep 57. (3) (FOUO) Rpt USARMD ARK, Personnel Daily Summary for Ark NG as of 2400 hrs CST 1 Oct 57.

Thus within less than twenty-four hours after the President's Executive Order both a regular army and National Guard force had assembled in Little Rock and at Camp Robinson ready to carry out the President's wishes. There is considerable doubt, however, whether the Guard units would have been ready to act by themselves by the morning of the 25th of September. They had been called hastily from their homes, lacked training in the sort of task they would have to undertake, and though they had responded to the Call, individual members of the guard could hardly be expected to apply themselves to the task with any enthusiasm. The well disciplined and trained troops of the battle group therefore were undoubtedly required to take the initial action, if the initial show of force was to be sufficiently positive and commanding to establish firm military control of the situation. The President's feeling on the matter was communicated to DCSOPS late in the afternoon of the 24th by Brig. Gen. Andrew J. Goodpaster: "President wants to insure that troops are not employed until Army has preponderance of force on hand."[79] General Eddleman notified Generals Walker and Wheeler of this

---

79. (FOUO) DCSOPS Journal File, item 38a.

---

note, with his interpretation that it meant the first echelon of the airborne troops at Camp Robinson and the second echelon one hour away. The interpretation, however, was less important than the general concept that the President's instructions implied. This was, very plainly, that there should be no confusion or lack of firmness in the military action, and that the military force should be sufficient to halt immediately any mob action and assure peaceable entry of the Negro students in Central High School. This was the general concept that motivated the assembly of a force at Little Rock that included both the regulars and the selected units of National Guard, and dictated the mobilization of the rest of the Arkansas National Guard at home stations. Put in its simplest terms, the philosophy was that if the federal government acted, that action must be successful.

Enforcement of the Court Order at Little Rock, 25-29 September 1957

The mission assigned General Walker at Little Rock can best be stated in the words of the Executive Order of 24 September authorizing the Secretary of Defense "to take all appropriate steps to enforce any order of the United States District Court for the Eastern District of Arkansas with respect to matters relating to enrollment and attendance at public schools in the Little Rock school district, Little Rock, Arkansas."[80] It remained

---

80. (U) Executive Order No. 10730, 24 Sep 57, cited.

---

for General Walker, acting with the advice of General Wheeler and in close touch with authorities in the Pentagon, to work out on the ground the method by which the troops, once assembled, would be employed to carry out this mission. Instructions from Washington were at first confined to the very broad principles that he should use the battle group initially, replacing it with National Guard troops as he deemed feasible, and that he should seek the cooperation of local law enforcement agencies to the maximum extent possible. The President's conception was contained in another message from General Goodpaster that was relayed to General Wheeler at 1820 EST on 24 September: "Lines established some distance from the school to keep mob a block or two from school to allow police to deal inside. Only students and teachers permitted inside school and troop cordon."[81]

---

81. (FOUO) DCSOPS Journal File, unnumbered item, 1820 EDT 24 Sep 57.

This concept, that the troop action should be confined simply to controlling any mob and assuring the Negro students entry in the event proved impossible of fulfillment. In order to carry out the mission, it proved necessary not only to control crowds but to provide close protection to the nine Negro students on their trips to and from school and even within the school itself, and to secure the school building when classes were not in session. Indeed, after the first day genuine riot control measures were but a minor part of the task, and the other aspects of the operation assumed the greater importance.

The nature of the action required was very largely determined in conferences held by General Walker, General Wheeler, and members of the military district staff with the principal city, county, state, and federal law enforcement officials, and with the Mayor and school authorities on the night of 24 September. The Little Rock Police would not agree to operate within the troop cordon established around the school but would only consent to accept custody of offenders apprehended by the military and to place charges against them for trial in local courts. The Chief of Police in Little Rock, Marvin Potts, firmly told Army authorities that:

. . . he was sworn to maintain law and order and that he and his force would do so without regard to their personal feelings in this matter. However, he further stated that he had issued an order to his Department prohibiting his force from escorting the Negro students to or from school, providing personnel to man guard posts in a joint operation with the Army at the school, and from patrolling the school corridors. He explained that his order was predicated upon the Army having the responsibility to insure compliance with court orders and that the Little Rock School Board has the responsibility for control of the students inside the school. He also stated that upon notification from either the military authorities or school officials that an individual had committed an offense, he would take action either in or outside the school to place the persons under arrest.[82]

---

82. (1) (FOUO) Hqs, USARMD, Ark, Cmd Rpt, 24 Sep - 30 Nov 57, Annex F (PM), p. 6. (OUO) (2) (FOUO) M/R by Col Alan B Todd, JAGD, 25 Sep 57, unnumbered item in DCSOPS Journal, Opn ARKANSAS. (3) (FOUO) Journal File, items 37, 41A, 43b, 44a.

At the same time, Virgil T. Blossom, Superintendent of Schools, and Mayor Woodrow Wilson Mann were anxious that the Army undertake as broad functions as possible in carrying out the President's Executive Order. General Wheeler later stated that:

> They had many proposals, many of which were infeasible. Mr. Blossom wanted us to take over the security of all high schools to prevent them from being sabotaged. We could not do it because it was not our mission. We didn't have the people, even if we had the will and mission. However, he made several proposals that were sound and were adopted. He feared for the personal safety of the Negro students in proceeding to the school and he requested that they be escorted to and from school by the military. . . . Mr. Blossom also requested that General Walker speak to the students at a school assembly at the opening of school the next day and explain to them why the troops were there and the fact that individuals who did not obstruct a Court order had nothing to fear.[83]

---

83. (FOUO) Talk by Maj Gen E. G. Wheeler at Army Commanders Conf. 2 Dec 57, Incl 1 to TAG Ltr, 7 Feb 58, Sub: Transcript of Army Cmdrs Conf, pp. 29-30.

General Walker's disposition and use of troops the following day conformed to these decisions. Oral orders issued to Colonel Kuhn, the battle group commander, on the night of 24 September and confirmed in writing on 25 September were as follows:

1st ABG, 327th Inf will, in the area of Little Rock Central High School, restore and maintain order, protect lives and property, and enforce the orders of the federal courts with respect to attendance at the public schools of Little Rock of all those properly enrolled. In carrying out this order the following minimum tasks will be executed:

(1) Deny access to Little Rock Central High School to all unauthorized persons.

(2) Provide security escort to individuals or groups as desired by this headquarters.

(3) Disperse assemblages which are, or may become, inimical to the maintenance of order.

(4) Arrest and turn over to proper authorities all persons who create a disturbance or fail to obey lawful orders.

(5) Prevent vandalism.[84]

---

84. (FOUO) Cmd Rpt, Hqs USARMD, Ark, 24 Sep - 30 Nov 57, Tab D to App 4 to Annex C.

The Central High School property occupies an area approximately 220 yards in width and 440 yards in depth. The main entrance was on the east facing Park Avenue which ran north-south past the school. Fourteenth Street ran east-west past the school on the north, and 16th street past it on the south. Immediately in the rear of the school proper was an eight-foot cyclone fence with two gates. Back of the fence lay an athletic practice field and back of the practice field a school stadium. Jones street ran north-south at the rear of the stadium wall. In addition to the main entrance there were sixteen other entrances along the sides of the school and in the rear. There were two gates to the stadium, one on 14th Street and the other on 16th, each located just past the cyclone fence separating

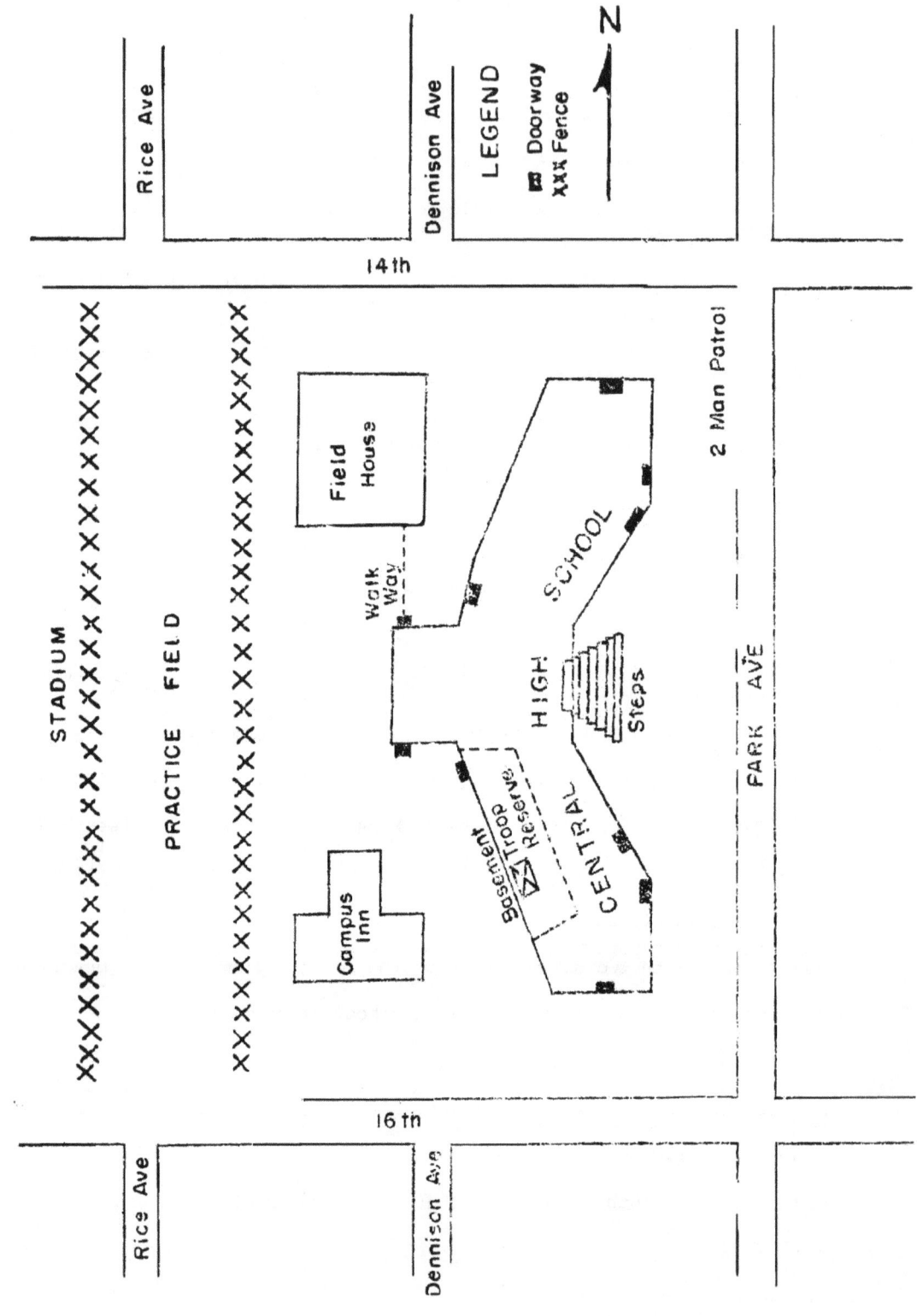

the practice field from the school proper. During the night of 24-25 September, the airborne troops moved in and employing three rifle companies threw a cordon around the school starting at the stadium gate on 14th Street and extending to the gate on 16th Street. A comand post and bivouac and reserve areas were established on the practice field and in convenient portions of the stadium. The two other rifle companies were held as a group reserve, one at the school and the other on 30-minute alert status at the Army Reserve Armory in the city about three miles away. The troop cordon employed 319 men. The reserve force consisted of 60 men on the school grounds in front of the school and 283 in the stadium behind the school. The mortar battery was assigned responsibility for the entrances and interior of the school. At least two guards were posted at each of the entrances (a total of 36 men were used) and a detail of 4 officers and 31 enlisted men was assigned to patrol the hallways and maintain order inside. The military police detachment from the Fort Chaffee support force established road blocks a city block from the perimeter at most points to prevent congregation of dissident groups. Sixteenth Street was closed to traffic from Park to Jones Street and Park Street was closed to traffic from 14th to 16th Streets. Students were prohibited from using the student parking lot. At the request of the City Police, Fourteenth Street remained open for through traffic past the school, and military police were directed to keep the traffic on this street moving.[85]

---

85. (1) (FOUO) Ibid., App 1 to Annex C, p. 1. (2) (FOUO) Cmd Rpt, 101st Abn Div, p. 5. (3) (U) Msg AKMAR 9-19, CHUSARMD, ARK, to DSCOPS,

25 Sep 57, DA-IN-863979. (4) (FOUO) Msg 251300Z, USARMD, ARK to DCSOPS, 25 Sep 57, DA-IN-863853, Sit Rep # 1. (5) (S) Msg 262245Z, CHUSARMD, ARK to DCSOPS, for Eddleman fm Wheeler, 26 Sep 57, DA-IN-57627. (6) DCSOPS Journal, item 41.

All troops were in position by 0500 CST 25 September. They took up their outside posts wearing steel helmets and gas masks and carrying individual arms with bayonets fixed. The troops inside carried night sticks and wore bayonets on their belts. Both small arms and chemical ammunition were held at a central point in the reserve area under control of the Commanding Officer, 1st ABG. A communications system connecting all elements was established with organic tactical equipment, and a commercial line was established between the command post in the stadium and Headquarters, Arkansas Military District. An FM radio, borrowed from the city police, was netted with their system. A central collection point was established at the stadium where any civilian offenders apprehended were to be brought immediately, and a liaison officer from the city police was stationed at this point.[86]

---

86. (1) (FOUO) Cmd Rpt, Hqs USARMD, Ark, 24 Sep - 30 Nov 57, App 1 to Annex C, p. 2; App 5 to Annex C, p. 1-3. (2) DCSOPS Journal, items 44a, 65, 254, 285, and unnumbered item 0015 25 Sep 57.

The 101st Airborne Division was an integrated unit and the battle group contained on its arrival at Little Rock 114 Negro enlisted men. In accordance with the guide lines agreed in Washington on 22 September, none of these Negro soldiers was employed in the operational force where he would come into contact with the civilian population. Three were employed in the command post under the stadium at the school and five in communications work at the reserve center. The rest were used for guard duty at Camp Robinson.[87]

---

87. (U) Info fm USARMD, Ark, 28 Sep 57, DCSOPS Journal File item 128.

On the morning of 25 September, an Army station wagon picked up the nine Negro students at a central assembly point at the home of Mrs. L. C. Bates, President of the Arkansas NAACP, and transported them to the school with an escort of one jeep with a soldier guard in front and another following in the rear. At 0900 CST, prior to their arrival at the school, General Walker addressed the student body as requested by Mr. Blossom, explaining the purpose of the presence of the troops.[88] The nine Negro children arrived

---

88. (U) Msg, PIO USARMD, ARK to CINFO, 25 Sep 57, DA-IN-863951, contains text of General Walker's remarks. They were prepared by the JAG representative, Col. Easton.

---

at 0930 CST. When they dismounted from the station wagon a platoon of soldiers immediately surrounded them and escorted them into the school building where they were met by the hall guards. When they departed for their class rooms, a soldier guard followed each student and this guard remained outside the door of the classroom. Between classes he kept his assigned student under general surveillance.

Meanwhile, starting at about 0800 CST a crowd had gathered along Park Avenue, 14th and 16th Streets in front of the school, and milled around just beyond the troop perimeter, many on the porches and lawns of private houses. A reserve force had to be used to rectify a slight buckle in the troop line caused by the converging crowd when the Negro students entered the school. After their entry, the crowd increased and certain elements began to show open hostility in both words and action. It was believed that if the perimeter were extended to deny observation of the school grounds and building by the crowd, there would be considerably less incentive for individuals to remain, and a part of the reserve was again employed to disperse the groups crowding around the road blocks and on private property. During the course of this maneuver, two incidents occurred. One involved Mr. Clifton R. Blake, who refused to move away and attempted to wrest a soldier's rifle from him. The soldier retaliated with a butt stroke and Blake suffered a cut on his head. The other involved Mr. Paul C. Downs who moved away too slowly and swung his arm back onto the bayonet of a soldier who was trying to persuade him to move faster. Investigations of both cases established that the soldiers had acted in accordance with their duty.[89]

---

89. (FOUO) (1) Cmd Rpt, Hqs, USARMD, Ark, 24 Sep - 30 Nov 57, App 1 to Annex C, pp. 2-3. (2) Cmd Rpt, 101st Abn Div, pp. 5-6. (3) Talk by Gen Wheeler, cited n 81. (4) Rpt of Inquiry, Hqs, USARMD, Ark, Re: Incidents in Which Mr. Clifton E. Blake and Mr. Paul C. Downs Received Injuries

in Connection with Operation ARKANSAS, 2 Oct 57. DCSOPS Investigations File, Opn ARKANSAS.

There were also numerous cases where high school boys were reluctant to move out; these students were isolated and turned over to the police, admonished, and released. In addition, some eight adults who failed to obey the order to move were taken into custody and turned over to the city police at the designated collection point in the stadium. However, the city police turned the offenders over to the County Sheriff and failed to charge them. The Judge Advocate, Colonel Easton, and the officer who had specific cognizance of the case went to the county jail, secured identification of four of the people, lodged loitering charges against them, and recommended that the other four be released. The four who were charged posted bail which they forfeited the next day. It was obvious, however, that the system in use whereby the police filed the charges was not an effective one and at a conference between the Judge Advocate, the city, county, and federal attorneys, the city police, and the judge of the Little Rock Municipal Court on 26 September, it was agreed that the soldier apprehending a civilian should make a sworn complaint before turning him over to the city police.[90]

---

90. (1) (FOUO) Cmd Rpt, Hqs USARMD, Ark, 24 Sep – 30 Nov 57, App 1 to Annex C, p. 3; Annex H (Judge Advocate), p. 1. (2) Msg AKMAR 09-22, CHUSARMD, ARK to DCSOPS, 26 Sep 57, DA-IN-864245. Sit Rep # 2. (3) Talk by Gen Wheeler, cited n 81.

The crowd around Central High School began to disperse about 1000 CST and by 1200 the area was relatively clear of spectators. There were no further significant incidents during the day. A formation of one officer and eight enlisted men escorted the Negro students from the school to the waiting station wagon and they were taken back to the assembly point at the home of Mrs. Bates in the same manner that they had been escorted to the school in the morning.[91] This day's action in fact proved to be the

---

91. (FOUO) (1) N 90 (1) and (2). (2) Msg AKMAR 09-24, CHUSARMD, ARK tp DCSOPS, 26 Sep 57, DA-IN-864502. Sit Rep # 3. (3) Cmd Rpt, 101st Abn Div, p. 6.

---

last one in which troops were required to disperse any sizable crowd. Thus the initial show of force had accomplished its purpose and could be called an unqualified success.

For the night mission of securing the building and school grounds, General Walker proposed to move in National Guard units as the first step toward their eventual employment to carry out the mission. Generals Taylor and Eddleman approved at an afternoon briefing for the Secretary of the Army on 25 September. Accordingly, at 2000 CST, the 3d Battalion of the 153d Infantry replaced the airborne battle group on active guard duty at Central High School, employing a force of 15 officers and 200 enlisted men with a reserve of 5 officers and 60 enlisted men. Two-man fixed posts were set up at each of the entrances, two-man walking patrols placed every 25 yards around the perimeter of the building areas, and six-man road blocks at three points near the front of the school. The Guard troops carried their individual arms, but bayonets were worn sheathed on belts. The rifle companies of the airborne battle group took up their bivouac in the stadium with one company on 30-minute alert prepared to assist the National Guard if necessary.[92]

---

92. (FOUO) (1) DCSOPS Journal, items 59, 63, 83. (2) Hqs Ark NG Cmd Rpt, 24 Sep - 30 Nov 57, Pt 1, App 1 to Annex C, p. 1. (3) Hqs USARMD Ark Cmd Rpt, 24 Sep - 30 Nov 57, App 1 to Annex C, p. 4. (4) Msg CHUSARMD, ARK to DCSOPS, 26 Sep 57, DA-IN-864987, Sit Rep #4.

On Thursday, 26 September, the airborne troops relieved the 153d Infantry at 0600 CST and carried out their operations in the same manner and with the same dispositions as the previous day, except that the number of enlisted hall guards was reduced from 31 to 20. At night they were relieved by the 1st Battalion, 153d Infantry. On Friday, 27 September, the last day of the school week, the same pattern of operations was repeated but a beginning was made on a program of "reduction in visible effort." The number of troops in the cordon was reduced from 319 to 270; the door guard was reduced from 36 men to 18; the escort of the Negro pupils into the school was "materially reduced in force"; in the evening 16th Street was opened to traffic past the school.[93]

---

93. (FOUO) (1) DCSOPS Journal, item 112. (2) Hqs USARMD, Ark, Cmd Rpt, App 1 to Annex C, p. 4; App 5 to Annex C. (3) USARMD, Ark, Sit Reps

5 & 6, DA-IN-865238, 27 Sep 57 and DA-IN-865729, 28 Sep 57.

With the situation relatively quiet and no incidents reported, the school authorities proposed to proceed with a football game and dance scheduled for the night of Friday, 27 September. There was some question at first whether the game should be transferred from the high school stadium to the Municipal stadium, but on receiving assurances from the city police that they would assume full responsibility for maintaining law and order at the game, General Wheeler recommended that the high school stadium be used. DCSOPS approved on 26 September. To make room for the game, General Walker removed two of the airborne rifle companies with their administrative support to the reserve center, and placed the other in front of the school as a local reserve. The football game and dance proceeded without incident. Over the weekend, guard at the school was continued by the airborne battle group, employing one company. Posts were established at each door, and seven walking patrols were employed on the exterior. Park Street continued barricaded at 14th and 16th.[94]

---

94. (S) (1) Msg, CHUSARMD, ARK to DCSOPS, 26 Sep 57, DA-IN-57627. (2) DCSOPS Journal, items 75, 81, 87. (3) USARMD, Ark, Sit Reps 7-10, DA-IN-865846, 28 Sep, DA-IN-865986, 28 Sep, DA-IN-866018, 29 Sep, & DA-IN-866044, 29 Sep 57. (3) (FOUO) Cmd Rpt, Hqs USARMD, Ark, 24 Sep - 30 Nov 57, App 1 to Annex C, p. 4.

The Chain of Command and the Pentagon Organization

The command structure established placed the actual burden of decision on all questions of importance on Headquarters, Department of the Army. Even the replacing of the airborne troops with the National Guard on the night of 25 September and the holding of the football game on the 27th required Pentagon approval. The Chief of Staff, the Secretary of the Army, and the Office of the President all kept in very close touch with the situation, and it was the Secretary who, on the Army side, made the major decisions. The chain of command as it actually operated ran from the Secretary and Chief of Staff through DCSOPS to the Commanding General, Arkansas Military District. Within DCSOPS, General Pachler, Director of Operations, was responsible for staff work and for keeping in constant touch with General Walker. Under General Pachler, Colonel Williams, Chief of the Western Hemisphere Division, was in charge of a special operations room or command post, as it was sometimes called, set up initially in General Pachler's office. This operations room was manned mainly by officers from the Western Hemisphere Division, but they were supplemented by personnel temporarily assigned from other sections of DCSOPS. And ACSI maintained one representative on duty at all times. Operating around the clock, the operations room became the center for the transmission of orders and instructions from the Chief of Staff and the Secretary of the Army to General Walker, for the flow of information from Arkansas and its dissemination in Washington, and for staff work on the Little Rock problem. Arrangements were made for contacts and coordination with specified officers in other general and special staff sections and with the Air Force. To provide a closer liaison direct with the staff of Arkansas Military District, Lt. Col. Robert B. Crayton of the Civil Activities - Ground Defense Branch of Western Hemisphere Division was dispatched to Little Rock on a tour of temporary duty. At the behest of General Walker a second direct line was installed between DCSOPS and Little Rock for the use of the staff, freeing the other line strictly for use as a command line, mainly by the general officers on both ends. The command line terminated in General Pachler's office but had one extension in General Eddleman's office and another in the operations room. Operations room personnel used the staff phone for conduct of their own business with Arkansas Military District and monitored the command line when conversations went on among the generals involved.

To provide up to date information to the Chief of Staff, the Secretary, and the White House, summary reports were submitted at 0800, 1200, and 1700 EDT daily, situation reports covering the previous day at 0800 EDT. Moreover, spot reports were distributed immediately on receipt of any information of importance from Little Rock. Situation and summary reports received a rather wide distribution to interested officers in DCSOPS and other staff agencies, but spot reports went only to the high level agencies. In addition to information forwarded by telephone, Headquarters, Arkansas Military District also forwarded formal situation reports every twelve hours during the early phases of the operation and every 24 hours after 1 October. These situation reports were also given a limited distribution to interested agencies.[95]

95. (1) Summary and situation reports of DCSOPS are contained in a separate notebook in WHD Operation ARKANSAS Files. Spot reports are filed in the Journal File. (2) CHUSARMD, Arkansas, situation reports are filed in In-Cables file.

Chain of Command – Operation ARKANSAS

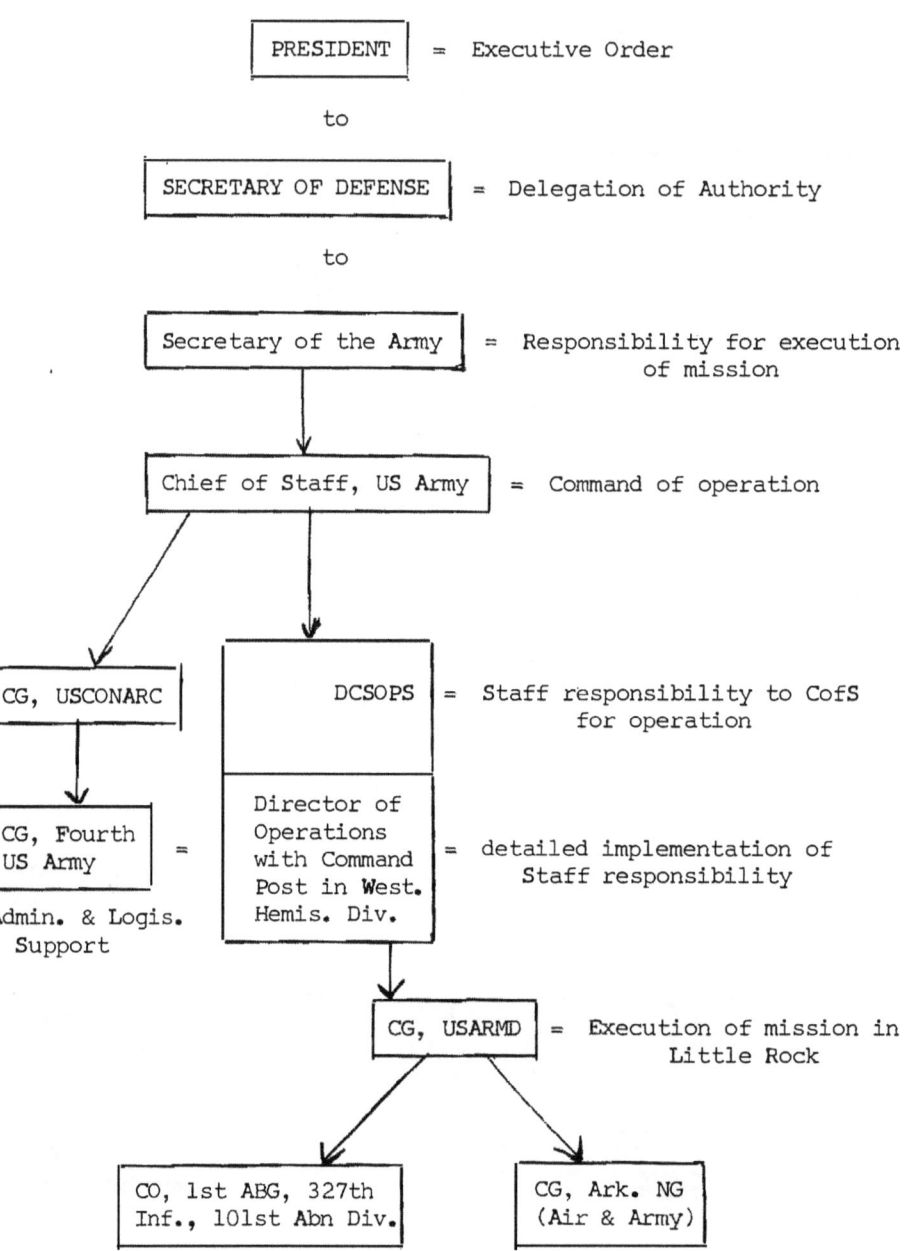

Preparation for Other Possible Contingencies

The possibility of more widespread riots in the vicinity of Little Rock or of the need to use troops elsewhere to quell disturbances arising out of the segregation problem weighed heavily on the minds of the Army staff during the first two days of Operation ARKANSAS. General Walker was concerned about the possibility that riots might arise in North Little Rock where there had been trouble earlier in September. His Judge Advocate expressed the opinion that since the District Court order only covered the Little Rock School District, no action could be taken in North Little Rock under the executive order. Walker referred the matter to Washington and the Chief of Staff suggested the possibility that the Federal judge might be asked to prepare but not issue an order covering North Little Rock for use in the event conditions there required it. In the end the Secretary of the Army referred the question to the United States Attorney General who rendered the following opinion:

> The authority of the Presidential Executive Order does not extend the authority to use federal troops to assist in the integration of Negro children into North Little Rock schools or any schools outside of the jurisdictional limitations as stipulated in the court order. . . .
>
> However, if in the considered judgment of the military commander of federal forces, a mob or a conspiratorial gathering forms close to but outside the Little Rock School District with the intent to obstruct the performance of the prescribed mission, the senior federal commander may use such force as is necessary to remove a threat prejudicial to his primary mission. The commander must insure that his estimate of the situation is most carefully analyzed and studied. If time permits, the Chief of Staff of the Army and the Secretary of the Army should be consulted prior to the commitment of federal forces to such purposes.[96]

---

96. (1) (S) Memo, Sec Army for CofS, 25 Sep 57, DCSOPS Journal File, item 73. (2) (S) Msg DA 930164 to CHUSARMD, ARK, 26 Sep 57. (3) (FOUO)

Tel Conv, Gen Wheeler - Gen Pachler, 0015, 25 Sep 57, Journal unnumbered item. (4) (FOUO) MR, Col Alan B. Todd, JAGC, 25 Sep 57, sub: Sit at LR, 0900 Hrs, 25 Sep 57, unnumbered Journal item. (5) (FOUO) Journal items 73, 80, 88.

In any event, no circumstances arose that required any intervention beyond the boundaries of the Little Rock School District.

Nevertheless, it was thought prudent to make the necessary preparations should additional force be required in the Little Rock Area. On 25 September, Department of the Army instructed the 101st Airborne Division to organize a reserve task force of approximately 500 men to be prepared for air movement by A plus 2 hours, and made arrangements with the Air Force to pre-position 6 C-130 and 15 C-123 aircraft at Fort Campbell for the purpose.[97]

---

97. (1) (S) Msg DA 930118 to CG 101st ABN DIV, 25 Sep 57. (2) (S) Msg AFOOP-OS-T 47327, HQ USAF to COMTAC, 25 Sep 57.

In this way a stand-by reserve was set up against any possible need at Little Rock. On the same day steps were taken toward preparing for any possible requirement imposed by the President for the use of troops in the same sort of situation elsewhere. Department of the Army instructed CONARC to organize task forces of 1,000-1,200 men in the 82d Airborne Division at Fort Bragg, North Carolina, the 3d Infantry Division at Fort Benning, Georgia, the 1st Armored Division at Fort Polk, Louisiana, and the 1st Infantry Division at Fort Riley, Kansas, to give them training under FM

19-15, and to prepare plans for air and motor movement "as a precautionary measure in event troops are required in situations similar to that now current in Little Rock."[98]

---

98. Msg DA 930103 to CGUSCONARC, 25 Sep 57, from Gen Eddleman to Gen Wyman.

CONARC was also to determine availability of Military Police units for this type of duty. As a final precaution, DCSOPS requested the Provost Marshal General to make a survey of the availability of riot control materials at supply depots in the United States.[99]

---

99. DF, Lt Col George C Williams, Chf, Opns Div, OPMG, for DCSOPS, 25 Sep 57, sub: List of Items Used in Riot Control w/Quantity Available and Depot Location, DCSOPS Journal, item 108.

These precautions were normal under the circumstances. The outbreak of further segregation riots certainly seemed possible in the wake of the Little Rock incident. The Army must always be prepared for any likely eventuality in which the President might call upon it for action. Although it was still carried on, riot duty training under FM 19-15 had a rather low priority in most units since the Army had not been called on for such duty in the Continental United States for a number of years. Nevertheless, the dispatch of the "riot training order" proved unfortunate. The gist of its content leaked to the press and to Congress almost immediately and Secretary

Brucker promptly revoked it the next day.[100] But the damage had already

---

100. Msg DA 572966 to CGUSCONARC, 25 Sep 57.

---

been done, for some members of Congress interpreted the version of the message which they had heard to mean that the Army was planning to use troops to enforce integration throughout the South. In this situation Secretary Brucker finally decided on 11 October to release the full text of the message to Senator Richard B. Russell of Georgia, Chairman of the Senate Armed Services Committee. In so doing he gave the following explanation:

> Field Manual 19-15 . . . prescribes the basis for training in "Civil Disturbances" to be given to Army troops. This training is incorporated into training schedules as a routine matter. However this type of training occurs at varying times in the annual training cycle. Consequently, following the sending of U.S. Army troops to Little Rock on 24 September 1957, it appeared prudent in the military judgment of the Chief of Staff to send a precautionary reminder to the Commanding General, Continental Army Command, to assure the status of readiness and training of elements of certain units under his command for possible duty covered by FM 19-15. This reminder took the form of the above directive which was prepared and issued by the Army Staff under the overall cognizance of the Chief of Staff. The units involved were designated primarily because of training considerations rather than because of their geographical location. They were not "alerted" in the military sense of the word, nor was consideration given to their employment in any specific area or for any particular unit.[101]

---

101. Msg DA 577432, SEC ARMY to HON RICHARD B RUSSELL, CHMAN SENATE ARMED SVCES CMTE, WINDER GA, 11 Oct 57.

It did not prove necessary to carry out any of the precautionary moves taken. On 26 September, the Air Force alert was modified to provide that the planes should be prepared to move within five hours after receipt of an implementing directive. Then because it was interfering with both Air Force and airborne troop training the alert was finally cancelled altogether on 10 October. And on the following day the reserve force of the 101st Airborne Division reverted to its normal status of being on six-hour alert under the Western Hemisphere Defense Plan.[102]

---

102. (1) (FOUO) Msg AFOOP-OS-T 47948, Hqs USAF to COMTAC, 26 Sep 57, DA-IN-864828. (2) Msg AFOOP-OS-T 31308, Hqs USAF to COMTAC, 10 Oct 57, DA-IN-872160. (3) DCSOPS Journal, items 90, 230, 414, 427. (4) Cmd Rpt, 101st Abn Div, p. 8 states that "approximately two weeks of training time were lost" by troops on this alert.

The Air National Guard and the Question of Command Channels

The fact that the Arkansas National Guard was included in the call issued by the Secretary of Defense created certain problems of Army-Air Force coordination. Others arose out of the fact that Maj. Gen. Sherman T. Clinger, State Adjutant General and Commander of the Arkansas National Guard, was an Air and not an Army National Guard officer. Since the Secretary of Defense delegated to the Secretary of the Army the execution of the Call for both Army and Air National Guard units, the Air Force did not initially enter into the channels by which the guard units were brought to federal service. Also on 25 September, the Department of the Army informed General Walker that his command included the Arkansas Air National Guard. But the question soon arose as to who would care administratively for these Air Guard units since the Department of the Army had no authority to do so. General Walker immediately raised the question of who was to exercise general court martial jurisdiction, pointing out that the Fourteenth Air Force had declined to accept responsibility since the Air Guard was under "command" of Walker's headquarters. Department of the Army then made arrangements with the Air Force that it should take care of administration, logistical support, and general court martial jurisdiction for the air units while General Walker would retain the right to use them in the operation as he deemed necessary.[103]

---

103. (1) Msg DA 930117 to CHUSARMD, ARK, 25 Sep 57. (2) Msg AKMAR-A 9=20, HQ USARMD, ARK, to DCSOPS, 25 Sep 57, DA-IN-864115. (3) Msg DA 573175 to CHUSARMD, ARK, 27 Sep 57.

On 27 September, Headquarters, U.S. Air Force, directed the Commander, Continental Air Command (COMCONAC) to issue general orders confirming the Call and furnished detailed instructions on steps to be taken in processing the individual members of the Arkansas Air National Guard into the federal service. It was stipulated that "all command responsibilities will be retained by Continental Air Command except for operational control which will be given to the Chief of Arkansas Military District."[104]

---

104. (1) Msg AFOOP-OC-R 47968, Hqs USAF to COMCONAC, Mitchell AFB, NY, 27 Sep 57, DA-IN-865467. (2) Msg AFPMP 48091, HQS USAF to COMCONAC & COMAMC, 27 Sep 57, AF-OUT-48091. (3) Msg AFPMP-R 48163, HQS USAF to COMCONAC & COMAMC, 27 Sep 57, AF-OUT-48163.

Under this arrangement, COMCONAC directed the Commanding General, Fourteenth Air Force to assume command of the Arkansas Air Guard and Headquarters, U.S. Air Force issued instructions to Little Rock Air Force Base to pay them.[105]

---

105. Msg AFAAF-5-48290, HQS USAF to COMCONAC, 27 Sep 57, DA-IN-865875.

On 28 September, the Commanding General of the Fourteenth Air Force, Maj. Gen. John W. Persons, informed General Walker that he was assuming command of the Arkansas Air National Guard units and placing them under Walker's operational control. He further stipulated that "As senior United States Air Force officer present, Maj. Gen. S. T. Clinger will assume command of Federalized Arkansas Air National Guard units under my command."[106]

---

106. Msg AKMAR 9-41, CHUSARMD, ARK to DCSOPS, 28 Sep 57, DA-IN-865976-C.

This message disturbed General Walker in that it seemed to put him in a peculiar position vis-a-vis General Clinger, who as Commander of both the Army and Air National Guard was in charge of the National Guard Headquarters established at Camp Robinson as a subordinate command to Arkansas Military District. General Walker immediately protested to DCSOPS that the Fourteenth Air Force message did not seem to be in consonance with the Department of the Army messages prescribing his command responsibilities. He wanted to know specifically whether General Clinger, as an Air Force officer, could continue to act as commander of Camp Robinson, an Army Camp, and of the Army National Guard, and whether he could issue orders to General Clinger in his status as Air Force Commander in regard to the training of Air Guard troops for missions he (Walker) might want them to perform. These questions were presented informally to the National Guard Bureau and to The Judge Advocate General and off the cuff opinions were rendered that Walker, in view of his operational control could tell Clinger to "go ahead and train" or stipulate "you know my mission, I expect the troops to be ready." But both had doubts that General Clinger could, as an Air Force officer, command Army troops.[107]

---

107. DCSOPS Journal, item 140.

General Eddleman, however, felt that the relationship could be adjusted informally as the situation demanded and on 29 September notified General Walker that "he visualized no problem in regard to the command relationship existing between Major General Walker and Major General Clinger." Walker, he said, "was in effect a task force commander exercising operational control over the National Guard units through Major General Clinger." The CG, USARMD, at this point agreed that he "could not foresee any problem in this regard."[108]

---

108. (FOUO) (1) Ibid., item 152. (2) Msg 14 COM 92, COMAFOURTEEN to MAJ GEN EDWIN A WALKER, CHUSARMD, ARK, 30 Sep 57, DA-IN-866768.

Then on 30 September Fourteenth Air Force addressed another message to General Walker requesting that he provide his concept of operations for all Arkansas Air National Guard units under his operational control, and information copies of all orders issued to them by Headquarters, Arkansas Military District. These were needed, General Persons said, to provide the necessary administrative support and particularly to determine fund requirements for flight training. General Walker again protested to DCSOPS, recommending that he not comply with the Fourteenth Air Force order since it would place him in an "untenable position" with respect to a subordinate commander, General Clinger, "currently commanding the Arkansas Army National Guard and . . . the federalized Arkansas Air National Guard units of which I would only have operational control."[109]

109. (1) (S) Msg AKMAR 9-54, CHUSARMD ARK to DEPTAR, 1 Oct 57, DA-IN-58601. (2) Msg 14 COM 92, COMAFOURTEEN to MAJ GEN EDWIN A WALKER, CHUSARMD, ARK 30 Sep 57, DA-IN-866768.

As a result of General Walker's second protest, Colonel Williams conferred with a representative of the Office of the Director of Operations, U.S. Air Force, and a clarification of the command channel was agreed upon. This was, in general, precisely as it had been understood at first. Logistical and administrative matters, including pay, processing, training, medical services, funding, court-martial, and so forth, were to be handled entirely through Air Force channels while General Walker exercised all operational control. Under this arrangement, the Air Force agreed that General Clinger was under General Walker's control for operational matters and under that of General Persons for logistical and administrative matters. General Clinger could thus issue operational orders to both Air and Army National Guard units under General Walker's command, while issuing administrative orders to Air Force units under Fourteenth Air Force command. It was agreed that General Clinger could answer the message from Fourteenth Air Force, speaking for General Walker. In effect, the Fourteenth Air Force was to be in the administrative and logistical channel on the Air Force side much as was Fourth Army was in it on the Army side.[110]

110. (FOUO) DCSOPS Journal, items 198, 199, 221, 495, 499.

With a clear understanding on the matter apparently reached between the Army and Air Force in Washington, DCSOPS on 1 October told Walker that the original orders on 24 September had given him the necessary authority over the Air National Guard to accomplish his mission, and that his authority had not been changed by the institution of procedures for administrative and logistical support through Fourteenth Air Force by the Department of the Air Force. However, his administrative channel on Air National Guard matters was to run through General Clinger to the Fourteenth Air Force, and Walker was to inject himself into this channel "only as necessary to accomplish your mission, so that the Department of the Air Force bears the administrative burden of federalization of their Air Force units." There was to be no change in the wording "of any messages so far dispatched," both the Department of the Army and the Department of the Air Force preferring to "handle any questions on a case-to-case basis."[111]

---

111. (C) Msg DA 930401 to CHUSARMD, ARK, 1 Oct 57.

Meanwhile, the Air Force had found its own solution for General Clinger's anomalous position. On 1 October Headquarters, U.S. Air Force instructed Fourteenth Air Force to issue appropriate orders calling Clinger to duty as an Air Force major general but in such a manner that he could not assume command of the Arkansas Air National Guard in federal service "since such action would place flying tactical units under the command of an officer who has not received the aeronautical rating of pilot."[112] General Clinger

112. Msg AFPDC-G 48 753, Hqs, USAF, to Cmdr 14th AF, 1 Oct 57. Typed copy in DCSOPS In-Cables, Opn ARKANSAS, # 60.

thus remained as an operational commander under General Walker in charge of both Army and Air National Guard at Little Rock, but the administrative channel for the Air National Guard troops was changed to run through a regular Air Force officer, Col. Timothy A. Shea. On 2 October General Walker informed the Fourteenth Air Force that he understood the terms of his operational control over the Air National Guard, that he did not contemplate using any of these units "except in dire emergency and then only the necessary Air Police units," and that he would inform Fourteenth Air Force of any requirements as far in advance as possible. This, in effect, closed the issue, for the only member of the Air National Guard who was to take part in the operation was General Clinger. The rest of the Air Guard personnel remained mobilized at home stations undergoing a part-time training program prescribed by COMCONAC.[113]

113. (FOUO) (1) Msg, AKMAR 10-16, CGUSARMD, ARK to COMAFFOURTEEN, 2 Oct 57, DA-IN-867771. (2) DCSOPS Journal, items 389, 391.

The Second Crisis, 30 September - 3 October 1957

The week end of 28-29 September was quiet in Little Rock. There were no incidents arising out of racial tension, and the city police reported a noticeable decrease even in the number of arrests for the usual run of offenses. During the next week the Arkansas Livestock Exhibition was scheduled to run from Monday, 30 September through the following Sunday, and was expected to attract crowds of 30,000 - 40,000 daily, but there seemed little reason to apprehend any race disturbances growing out of it. That despite the surface quiet there were undercurrents there could be little doubt. There was reliable information of a telephone campaign designed to dissuade students from attending the integrated school for the next few days. School attendance had risen from a low of 1,250 on Wednesday, 25 September to 1,415 on Friday, 27 September, but this was still considerably below normal for a total enrollment of around 2,000. Nevertheless, the time seemed propitious to start phasing back the military effort at the school.[114]

---

114. (FOUO) (1) DCSOPS Journal, items 149, 151, 154, 157, 162, 164, 165. (2) USARMD, Ark, Sit Rep 11, DA-IN-866191, 30 Sep 57. (3) School attendance figures from DCSOPS Sit Reps on designated days and USARMD, Ark, Sit Rep 13, DA-IN-867262, 2 Oct 57.

Another factor that entered into the situation was the prospect of a settlement at a higher level. A committee selected by the Southern Governors' Conference proposed to talk to Governor Faubus and then meet with President Eisenhower on 1 October. There were high hopes on all sides that the meeting would result in a settlement of the question of integration at Central High School. The Secretary of the Army on 26 September had made it "unequivocally clear" to General Walker and all others in the Army concerned with the Little Rock operation that there was to be no "speculation . . . as to the timing of the withdrawal of federal troops," that both the National Guard and the airborne contingent would remain on duty in Arkansas until relieved by proper authority.[115] However, this did not mean that the effort could

---

115. (FOUO) Msg DA 572549 to CHUSARMD, ARK, 26 Sep 57.

---

not be made to phase down the numbers of the Guard and progressively reduce operations, or that the National Guard could not be phased in to replace the airborne troops in accordance with General Walker's initial orders.

On Sunday, 29 September, General Walker presented to DCSOPS his concept to "progressively reduce show of force consistent with the situation returning activities at Central High School to complete normalcy at earliest practicable date." In carrying out this "concept of progressive reduction effects," he proposed five actions:

    1. Reduce troop density in the area; eventually no troops visible on school ground proper.

    2. As troop density decreases gradually increase employment of 153d Infantry to include daylight mission in lieu of the 1st ABG.

    3. Restore to normal activity, usage of Park St. and 16th St.

4. Wearing of bayonets on the belt.

5. Reduce as the situation permits troops escorting Negro children. Includes from pick up point to school and from front of school into building. Work toward Negro children coming to school with their own transport under minimum observation and protection of troops.

In communicating this plan, General Walker stated the concept of the specific tasks required at Central High School in somewhat more comprehensive terms than had been previously used in the order issued to the First Airborne Battle Group:

1. Permit entrance to the school by authorized persons such as students, teachers and staff, employees, utility repairmen, and delivery men.

2. Prohibit entrance to the school by unauthorized persons.

3. Provide safe conduct for Negro students to and from Central High School and within the school from classroom to classroom as required.

4. Maintain law and order as required to accomplish the mission.[116]

---

116. (S) Msg, CGUSARMILDIST, ARK to DCSOPS, 29 Sep 57, DA-IN-58342.

The first steps in reducing troop density had actually been taken on Friday, 27 September. On Monday, 30 September, General Walker started to move more rapidly to restore the situation to normal in accordance with his program. When school opened, the troops stood guard without gas masks and with bayonets on their belts (bayonets had actually been removed from rifles on Sunday, 29 September). The cordon was discontinued. Instead seven two-man walking patrols were employed along with four jeep patrols of four men each operating on the four sides of the school. A total of eighteen men remained on the various entrances, but the hall guard was reduced to four officers and eleven enlisted men. The escort to the school from the assembly point (changed from the home of Mrs. Bates to that of the father of one of the students) was maintained as before, but only one lieutenant accompanied the Negro pupils from the station wagon to the school door and this was done "so unobtrusively that some observers believed that the students were not escorted."[117] At noon Park Avenue was opened to traffic

---

117. (1) DCSOPS Journal, items 153, 161, 166, 171, 172, 179, 220, 415. Quote from item 179. (2) USARMD Sit Rep 11, DA-IN-866191, 30 Sep 57. (3) Hqs USARMD, Cmd Rpt, (FOUO) 24 Sep - 30 Nov 57, App. 1 to Annex C, p. 4.

---

past the school and restrictions removed on parking in the student parking lot restoring normal traffic conditions. At noon also the guards were removed from the doors. Concurrently with these latter steps, the number of jeep patrols was increased to seven operating to a depth of eight blocks in all directions from the school.[118]

---

118. (1) DCSOPS Journal, items 174, 179. (2) Hqs USARMD, Cmd Rept., Annex C, App 1, p. 4 & App 5, p. 3.

No repercussions resulted from any of these steps. The attendance at the school rose to 1,520, an increase of 105 over the previous Friday, despite the purported telephone campaign. In the afternoon, General Walker asked and received permission from the Department of the Army to use National Guard units for the full time security mission during daylight hours the following day. He was, however, instructed to hold one rifle company of the airborne troops on alert in the high school gymnasium as a reserve.[119]

---

119. (FOUO) (1) Msg DA 930355 to CHUSARMD, ARK, 30 Sep 57. (2) Msg AKMAR 9-50, CHUSARMILDIST ARK to DCSOPS, 30 Sep 57, DA-IN-866526. (3) DCSOPS Journal, items 195, 196. (4) USARMD, Ark, Sit Rep 13, DA-IN-867262, 2 Oct 57.

At 0600 CST, Tuesday 1 October, the National Guard took over the daylight duty at the school, employing 13 officers and 132 enlisted men in the active guard and 3 officers and 57 enlisted men in a reserve. The replacement of the airborne elements with the National Guard was accompanied by further steps in the program of reducing the visible effort. Inside, the hall guards were replaced by a detail of one officer and eight enlisted men stationed in the principal's office on call for duty wherever needed. Door guards were placed only on the main entrance and at the stadium gates. The motorized patrols were reduced from seven to three. The plan for escort of the Negro students into the school called for one National Guard officer to accompany them a few steps and point the way to the door, but then let the children proceed on their own.[120]

---

120. (FOUO) (1) Hqs, Ark NG, Cmd Rpt, Pt. 1, Annex C, App 1, p. 1, App 5, p. 6. (2) DCSOPS Journal, items 203, 209.

The orders under which the troops were acting inside the school should be noted at this point because of the importance they later assumed. Instructions issued by Headquarters, U.S. Army Military District, Arkansas, on 28 September were as follows:

    a. The primary responsibility for handling students who create disturbances rests with the school authorities. All teachers and others in a position of responsibility have been instructed that such students should be brought to the principal's office for disposition. All military personnel will conduct themselves in such a manner as not to interfere with the exercise of disciplinary control by the school authorities.

    b. Should military personnel on duty in the school observe an incident which takes place out of the presence of a teacher or other school official or should such an incident be reported to military personnel on duty, the soldier concerned will immediately report the incident to the nearest teacher. Ordinarily, no further action need be taken by the soldier.

    c. Only in the event that the incident is such that the teacher cannot handle it will the soldier actually intervene. In such a situation the soldier concerned will confine his activities to escorting the offender with the teacher to the principal's office. All military personnel are cautioned to use tact and common sense in dealing with students.[121]

---

121. (FOUO) Ltr, Hqs, USARMD, Ark, 28 Sep 57, sub: Handling Disturbances in CHS, Hqs USARMD Cmd Rpt, 24 Sep - 30 Nov 57, Annex H (JA), App 4. Copy in DCSOPS Journal, item 497.

The Arkansas National Guard Command Report described the entry of the Negro students on 1 October as follows:

    At 0108 22 October, nine (9) students reported to school, four (4) entered SE entrance, five main entrance. At top of steps, 30 to 35 white male students formed side by side. Colored students stopped. On call, escort troops dismounted from jeeps and started toward steps. When they had covered about half the distance, the white students broke up and the colored students entered. Some jeers, not too noisy.[122]

122. (FOUO) Hqs Ark NG Cmd Rpt, Tab C to App 2 to Annex C, p. 2.

This was the beginning of a day that General Walker described at its end as "the most disagreeable in school since the arrival of federal troops" for the Negro children. Minor harassing actions such as the throwing of spitballs and pencils were carried on against them all day.[123]

---

123. (FOUO) (1) USARMD, Ark, Sit Rep 13, DA-IN-867262, 2 October 57. (2) DCSOPS Journal, items 203, 204, 211, 217, 220.

In retrospect, it appears that there had been a shift in segregationist tactics. Instead of boycotting the school, habitual trouble makers began to return on 1 October and adopted the tactic of harassing the Negro children while promoting a mass student walk-out to be carried out later in the week. The day's school attendance shot up to 1,692. Nevertheless, the school authorities tended to regard the incidents that occurred as minor and apart from the statement quoted above, the military command in Little Rock seemed not to regard them as portents of future trouble. In Washington hopes were high that the President's Conference with the delegation of Southern Governors would produce a solution and the troops could be withdrawn. At midday, the Secretary of the General Staff asked DCSOPS to prepare a plan for relieving the Arkansas National Guard from the federal service.[124]

---

124. (FOUO) (1) DCSOPS Journal, items 203, 210, 217. (2) Statement by Elizabeth Huckaby, Teacher, CHS, Exhibit G, Hqs, Ark NG, Rpt of

Investigation Concerning Incidents Inside Little Rock CHS on 2 Oct 57. DCSOPS Rpts of Investigations File.

These hopes were doomed to disappointment. At the meeting the Governors informed the President that Governor Faubus had authorized them to state that he was prepared to assume full responsibility for maintaining law and order in Little Rock and that he would not obstruct the orders of the federal courts. The President responded that if the Governor of Arkansas would personally give such assurance he would direct the Secretary of Defense to return the command of the Arkansas National Guard to him and withdraw all federal troops as soon as practicable. The delegation of Governors then got in touch with Faubus who issued a statement concluding as follows:

> I now declare that, upon withdrawal of federal troops, I will again assume full responsibility, in co-operation with local authorities, for the maintenance of law and order, and that the orders of the federal courts will not be obstructed by me.[125]

---

125. (U) Quoted from U.S. News and World Report, 11 Oct 57, p. 103. Other documents on the meeting and its aftermath are in this issue, pp. 103-09.

In the President's view, the words "by me" made the statement unacceptable. It seemed to leave Governor Faubus free to take no action to prevent the removal of the Negro children from Central High School by mob action, as had occurred on 23 September, or by means of more subtle pressure. He consequently rejected the Governor's terms - ". . . the statement . . . issued by the Governor of Arkansas does not constitute in my opinion the assurance that he intends to use his full powers as Governor to prevent the obstruction of the orders of the United States District Court. Under the circumstances, the President of the United States has no recourse at the present time except to maintain federal surveillance of the situation." In a later press conference he said the troops would be withdrawn only if one of two conditions existed, the first being unequivocal assurances from Governor Faubus along the lines indicated, the second the actual development of peaceful conditions to the point where the city police could say that they foresaw no difficulty they could not control in carrying out the court order.[126] The

---

126. (U) Ibid., pp. 103, 108.

Army apparently was in for a long stay at Little Rock unless Governor Faubus changed his position or unless public opinion in Arkansas underwent a significant change.

The extent to which the Army had been committed to almost complete protection for the Negro students in Central High School became apparent the next day when the continued harassment of these students by white pupils produced a minor crisis which had wide repercussions, definitely setting back General Walker's program of progressive reduction. On 2 October, in accordance with the battalion rotation plan under which the National Guard was operating, the 3d Battalion, 153d Infantry, took over the duties at the school that the 1st Battalion had exercised the previous day. The reserve force was doubled and the active guard slightly increased, but there was basically no change in dispositions. The 3d Battalion was not familiar with the lay-out of the inside of the school and had not completely posted its interior guard when school opened. The Negro children were escorted to the school as usual but again allowed to proceed on their own from the station wagon to the entrance. Because a crowd of approximately 60-70 students had formed what appeared to be a blockade at the main entrance, the Negro students entered by a side door. A group of white students kicked the books from the hands of one of the Negro boys. He and another Negro boy were subjected to another attack inside the school, two white boys kicking them and throwing can openers at them in the locker room. During the rest of the morning Negro students were subjected to shoving, crowding, jostling, and jeering. The National Guard detail was unable to intervene in the first incidents and did not feel that its orders permitted intervention to prevent the sort of incidents that occurred later. However, at 1030 CST, two hours after the opening of school, the National Guard assigned 18 men from the reserve to provide two escorts for each of the Negro students. Around mid-day General Walker went to the school to meet with General Clinger with a view toward arranging for more positive action on the part of the National Guard to control school incidents.[127]

---

127. (FOUO) (1) Ark NG Investigation cited n 124 (2). (2) DCSOPS Journal, items 218, 226, 227, 231, 247, 251. (3) USARMD, Ark, Sit Rep 14, DA-IN-867925, 2 Oct 57. (4) Hqs Ark NG, Cmd Rpt, Annex C, App 1, p. 1, App 5, p. 7.

Nonetheless, the Negro students had already become dissatisfied with the protection they felt they were getting from the National Guard, and this dissatisfaction soon made itself felt not only at General Walker's Headquarters but at the highest levels in Washington. At 1440 EDT, General Goodpaster informed the Chief of Staff's office that he had had a call from the Protestant Episcopal Bishop of Arkansas, saying that Mr. Blossom, Little Rock School Superintendent, wanted to talk to the White House "concerning the security and order within the school." The bishop was advised by General Goodpaster that it would be more appropriate to talk to General Walker in Little Rock or to Secretary Brucker in Washington, and asked that these parties be alerted to the possibility they might receive a call.[128] In fact, General Walker received a call before

---

128. (FOUO) DCSOPS Journal, item 243.

---

he received any alert, not from Mr. Blossom but from the Field Secretary of the NAACP in the Southwest, Mr. Clarence A. Laws. The Chief of Staff of the Military District took the call for General Walker, who had gone to the school to confer with General Clinger. Laws said that the parents of the children were very much concerned "about the failure of the Guard to give adequate protection to their children." He urged that General Walker meet with these parents and with NAACP representatives to work out a positive program for protection of the Negro students. "They felt they were entitled to adequate protection," Mr. Laws said, "since the President had directed General Walker to see that they did receive adequate protection . . . and if we can't get the protection from the

Guard that we received from the 101st that the President sent here, then we will have to report that to our Washington office." After considering the implications of the message, General Walker declined the meeting and instructed his Chief of Staff to inform Mr. Laws that he was "well informed on the situation and is making appropriate adjustments."[129]

---

129. (1) (C) Msg AKMAR 10-18, CHUSARMD, ARK to DCSOPS, 2 Oct 57, DA-IN-59199. (2) (FOUO) DCSOPS Journal, item 235.

These adjustments at first were conceived to involve strengthening the protection given by the National Guardsmen. In the meeting at the school with General Clinger, the increase in the interior guard and the assignment of two escorts for each Negro student was agreed upon. Moreover, a stronger order was drafted on the handling of incidents in the school, replacing that issued on 28 September. The new order read:

    a. All military personnel will conduct themselves in such a manner as not to interfere with the exercise of disciplinary control by the school authorities.

    b. Should military personnel on duty in the school observe an incident which takes place or should an incident be reported to military personnel on duty, the soldiers concerned will immediately intervene, quell the incident, and escort the offender(s) to the principal's office.

    c. All military personnel are cautioned to use tact and common sense in dealing with students.[130]

---

130. (FOUO) (1) Ltr, Hqs, USARMD, Ark, 3 Oct 57, sub: Handling Disturbances at CHS, Hqs USARMD Cmd Rpt, 24 Sep - 30 Nov 57, Annex H (JA), App 4, p. 2. (2) The written order is dated the following day but the

gist of it was evidently communicated verbally to National Guard officers at the time. In the Report of Investigation (cited n 124 (2)) 1st Lt Malcolm E. Moore, in charge of the interior guard detail testified as follows: "Later in the day when it became apparent that our previous orders of staying in the background and handling the students with 'kid gloves' had been completely rescinded I notified my people that they were to take immediate action at the slightest disturbances."

The stronger order resulted in the Guard's intervention in a shoving incident in the cafeteria in the afternoon, but in the meantime sufficient news of these incidents had reached the Secretary of the Army and apparently the President to lead them to believe that even stronger action was required. At 1830 EDT, the Secretary called General Walker and talked to him for about thirty minutes. He apparently informed the General that more positive steps would have to be taken the next day to insure the safety and well-being of the Negro students inside the school. At 2135 EDT, an officer representative of the Secretary's office called DCSOPS and stated that "Mr. Brucker was quite concerned about the situation at Little Rock," and requested that the Secretary be informed immediately whenever there was any significant change.[131] The Secretary was evidently

---

131. (FOUO) (1) DCSOPS Journal, items 244, 245. (2) N 124 (2).

---

not entirely satisfied with the information distributed by the DCSOPS operations center on the incidents of the day. There is no question that all of the information received on these incidents had been reported but

111

it had not been evaluated to make the situation appear quite so serious as it did when reported to the Secretary through other channels.

Under existing circumstances, it appeared that the next day would be critical, both in Little Rock and in the Pentagon. What made it seem even more critical was the receipt of information indicating that the prosegregationist element among the students was planning a mass walk-out. Acting on instructions received from the Secretary, General Walker quickly readjusted his plans and reversed his previous policy of cutting down on the guard inside the school and replacing the airborne troops with the National Guard. The mortar battery of the 1st Airborne Battle Group, 327th Infantry, was again assigned full responsibility for the entire school building, to include steps and entrances. Two guards were again to be posted at each entrance and two guards assigned to escort each Negro pupil to and from classes and to remain available outside classrooms on call. A reserve force was to be located in the basement, available on five-minute call to move to any scene of disturbance within the building. A system of communication was established between hall and door guards and the reserve force. The original wording of an order to the airborne battle group commander instructing the troops to "maintain order" in the school was strengthened to read "prevent disorder."[132] The instructions on "handling

---

132. Msg AKMAR 10-22, CHUSARMILDIST, ARK, to CO, 1st ABG, 327th Inf, 3 Oct 57, DA-IN-868053 and corrected copy, DA-IN-868053-C.

---

disturbances in Central High School" were further revised on the night of 2 October by the addition of a paragraph prescribing that students also might, at the discretion of the High School Principal, be handled as adult civilian offenders.

The decision as to the disposition of the student(s) is the responsibility of the principal. Should he decide to handle it administratively, military personnel will take no further action. Should the principal decide that the matter cannot be handled administratively, the student(s) will be conducted by the apprehending soldier to the collection point established at the Command Post at Central High School for processing in accordance with letter, this Headquarters, subject: 'Disposition of Civil Offenders', 27 September 1957 as amended by letter, same subject, 28 Sep 57. If the soldier is not an eye-witness to the incident, an eye-witness must accompany him to make the necessary affidavit.[133]

---

133. (FOUO) Ltr, Hqs, USARMD, 3 Oct 57, sub: Handling Disturbances in CHS, Hqs USARMD, Ark, Cmd Rpt, Annex H (JA), App 4, p. 3.

The National Guard remained responsible for the exterior of the building and for motor patrols but with its strength increased to 16 officers and 166 men in the active guard and 11 officers and 156 men in the reserve. An escort of no less than 30 Guardsmen was to accompany the nine Negro students from their vehicle to the school steps where they would be turned over to the protection of the airborne mortar company. Park Street between 14th and 16th was again blocked to traffic during the morning.[134] It was a show of force again, not this time to quell a mob

---

134. (FOUO) (1) Msg AKMAR 10-23, CHUSARMDILDIST, ARK to CG, ARK NG, 3 Oct 57, DA-IN-868054. (2) DCSOPS Journal, items 245, 248, 249, 252, 253. (3) Cmd Rpt, Hqs Ark NG, Pt 1, Annex C, App 1, p. 1, App 5, p. 8.

---

but to assure protection for the Negro children against a more subtle form of pressure inside the school.

The show of force was accompanied by effective action by the school authorities to discipline students who had been involved in disorders. The three white boys who had kicked the Negro boys and thrown can-openers at them were suspended. The school authorities officially notified students that if they participated in the rumored walk-out on Thursday, 3 October, they would be suspended and not permitted to re-enter the school until their parents appeared to re-enroll them.

These twin actions by the Army and the school authorities were effective. On the morning of 3 October the Negro students were escorted to the school without incident although there was "some spasmodic, half-hearted jeering from the on-lookers," and "four or five boys stood in the passage in the school until the Negroes approached them, then fell back into line."[135]

---

135. (FOUO) DCSOPS Journal, items 241, 247, 257. Quote from item 257.

Under the protection of the paratroopers, the physical persecution inside the school practically ceased. The scheduled walk-out was a failure. A few minutes after the school opened a small group of students, estimated at between 40 and 60, straggled out of the high school and joined a similar small group who had not entered the school at all and about 25-35 adults who assembled across the street. A black dummy had been secreted in a tree and one of the boys set the dummy on fire. The National Guard troops handled the situation very well, quickly putting out the fire and dispersing the crowd. Its members moved off very quietly and orderly with the exception of one adult, Vernon Duncan, who had to be taken into custody and turned over to the city police, and one obstreperous girl student who hurled insulting remarks at the guardsmen and slapped one of them. She was turned over to the school authorities, suspended from school, and escorted from the school area by a soldier escort. The only other incident of the morning arose out of the fact that a soldier peremptorily ordered a newsman from the Washington Star out of the phone booth, dispersing him with the rest of the crowd.[136] The Duncan case, however, later became the basis

---

136. (FOUO) (1) Ibid., items 258-60, 269, 274-77, 284, 286, 345. (2) USARMD, ARK, Sit Rep 15, DA-IN-868672, 4 Oct 57.

---

for a test of the authority of the Military in Arkansas state courts.

The situation had been brought under control but at considerable cost. Any hopes that the airborne troops could be pulled out soon and the whole effort turned over to the National Guard were dashed. There were many fears that a wedge was being driven between the Guard and the airborne troops, since the Negro students, their parents, and the NAACP showed a definite preference for the airborne guard. General Walker on the night of 2 October sent a letter to General Clinger stating clearly his mission to enforce the court order and adding.

This includes providing necessary protection and assistance to the process of integration at Central High School and to prevent any interference with this process. It requires the maintenance of law and order, including the prevention or suppression of incidents which might affect the mission throughout the school district.

To this statement, General Walker requested that General Clinger reply by indorsement "indicating that you understand the above mission, and that you and the troops at your disposal are capable of carrying it out." General Clinger called his principal officers together and asked if any had any reservations. None being expressed, he replied to General Walker that: "It is my belief that I and my command understand the mission as stated, and that Arkansas National Guard troops in numbers as presently assigned to me are capable of carrying out the assignment." In forwarding this statement to General Eddleman, Walker indicated that he accepted it.[137] Both he and General Wheeler indicated in other instances that they

---

137. (FOUO) (1) Ltr, Gen Walker to Gen Clinger, 2 Oct 57, sub: Mission, w/1st Ind by Gen Clinger to Hqs, Ark Mil Dist, sub: Mission. Forwarded w/covering note by Gen Walker to Gen Eddleman, 3 Oct 57. DCSOPS Journal, item 393. (2) DCSOPS Journal, item 371.

---

believed the National Guard was capable of taking over and deplored the circumstances that had set back the plan for such an early turn-over. General Wheeler on 3 October expressed his belief that relationship with the Guard had been set back a "good two weeks," and that General Walker by being forced to take over responsibility for what happened inside the school was being placed in a "near untenable position."[138]

---

138. (FOUO) DCSOPS Journal, item 345. See also item 261.

If in retrospect it appears that the incidents inside the school on 2 October were blown up and in the end assumed greater proportions than they should have, the indications at the time were that the situation had grown so unpleasant for the Negro students that they were ready to withdraw. Withdrawal would have defeated the whole purpose of the operation the President had ordered. The only other solution was to persuade the city police to take over the task of preserving order inside the school, and the Secretary asked General Walker for another effort to achieve this end. But again it was fruitless, the police saying they did not have the authority "to physically restrain children," and maintaining their previous stand that they would not undertake any activity within the troop cordon except to receive and charge such violators as the troops turned over to them.[139]

---

139. (FOUO) (1) *Ibid.*, items 261, 270.

The students who walked out on 3 October were suspended by the Superintendent and not permitted to return until their parents accompanied them to the school and vouched for their future behavior. Secretary Brucker also ordered that action be taken against the National Guardsman who had refused to take action at the request of a Negro student on 2 October. A thorough investigation by the National Guard Headquarters, however, concluded that the Guardsman had been acting in accordance with orders and that a delay in getting the men to their assigned posts inside the school on 2 October prevented any interference in the kicking and can-opener throwing incident that had occurred that morning.[140]

---

140. (FOUO) (1) <u>Ibid</u>., items 255, 261, 290, 302, 318, 330, 339, 349, 353, 395, 426, 347, 366, 369, 372, 406, 407. (2) Msg AKMAR 10-27 CHUSARMD, ARK, to CG, ARK NG, 3 Oct 57, DA-IN-868397. (3) Ark NG Investigation cited n 124 (2).

Problems in the Arkansas National Guard

The hasty call issued to the Arkansas National Guard on 24 September left a myriad of problems in its wake, involving both the Alert Force at Camp Robinson and the rest of the Guard mobilized at home stations scattered throughout the state. The handling of these National Guard problems was one of the most complicated aspects of Operation ARKANSAS. This was almost necessarily so since the Call issued on 24 September was without precedent in the recent history of the United States and because the National Guard authorities could not, on account of the situation, be brought into the planning so that they would be at least partially prepared. Similarly, even the administrative agencies in the Pentagon responsible for defining procedures for handling the Call were practically in the dark until after the Call was issued. For the Guardsmen themselves the Call came as an abrupt and unexpected interruption of their daily lives.

The assigned strength of the Army National Guard of the State of Arkansas according to the last morning reports filed while under state control (23 September 1957) was 8,549. On 30 September, Arkansas Military District reported this total at 8,619, and later revised the figure to 8,611. But the official morning reports on the same date set total assigned strength at 8,504. Of this total assigned strength, Arkansas Military District reported that 7,577 had reported for duty on 24 September. The assigned strength of the units in the initial Alert Force at Camp Robinson was 1,586; by midnight 1 October, 1,455 were reported as present for duty with this force.[141] Many of the absences, both in the Alert Force and the

---

141. (FOUO) (1) APR 12-A, 30 Sep 57, National Guard. (2) Msg AKMAR 9-52, CHUSARMD, ARK to CGUSARFOUR, 30 Sep 57, DA-IN-866587-C. (3) Msg AKMAR 10-18, HQ USARMD, ARK, to DCSOPS, 2 Oct 57, DA-IN-867794. (4) DCSOPS Journal, items 84, 156, 917. (5) Morning report strength figures from OCA were used in computing cost of the operation.

---

units mobilized at home station, were accounted for by personnel already on active duty for training status. On 2 October it was reported that 36 were attending service schools and 385 were engaged in active duty training for periods varying from 11 weeks to four months. Officially these Guardsmen were transferred from their active duty for training status to an active duty status effective 24 September although they were not called back to their parent units until they completed their assigned tours. However, no new active duty for training tours were authorized for the period of the Call. Other absences were attributable to the fact that personnel were out of the state or unable to complete personal arrangements to enable them to report for duty on time. There were no reported cases of refusal to report. However, accurate accounting was largely confined to the Alert Force. Because of distance, delays in forwarding morning reports, and the lax control exercised over the Guard mobilized at home stations, the strength for duty reports received were almost meaningless.[142]

---

142. (FOUO) (1) DCSOPS Journal, item 240 (OUO). (2) Msg DA 577481 (TAG Book Msg), 11 Oct 57. (3) Msg, CGUSARFOUR to AG, STATE of ARK,

2 Oct 57, DA-IN-867566. (4) Hqs Ark NG Cmd Rpt, 24 Sep - 30 Nov 57, Pt 1, Annex A, p. 1. (5) Fourth U.S. Army comment on National Guard strength reports is worth noting: "Initial morning reports and corrected monthly personnel rosters from individual National Guard units revealed almost total unfamiliarity by administrative personnel with the Active Army regulations on preparation and correction of these vital records and resulted in duplication of assignment of personnel and in many cases no strength accountability." This situation must be taken into consideration in compiling any figures on the Arkansas National Guard during this period. Cmd Rpt, 1 Sep - 30 Nov, p. 20.

In practice the Army National Guard mobilized at home stations became a pool from which both units and personnel could be drawn for the Alert Force as needed. Other than this, National Guard personnel in this status were at least supposed to report to a point of assembly daily and engage in two hour drills four times weekly. Reporting and drill times were arranged to minimize interference with schooling and routine business. No training program was prescribed by the National Guard Bureau; General Clinger's headquarters drew up a general training program on its own initiative, leaving considerable discretion to unit commanders as to the actual schedules to be followed. Subjects prescribed for attention were basic combat training, maintenance of equipment, and domestic disturbances. In sum then, personnel of the Army National Guard mobilized at home stations simply went about their own business, and suffered only minor inconveniences but were subject to call for service at Little Rock. There is little question that it was a system calculated to cause resentment on the part of personnel assigned to the Alert Force. "This plan favored personnel remaining at home station," comments the Arkansas National Guard Command Report, "in that they were paid a ration allowance of ($2.57) per day and service pay in addition to pay received from civilian employment."[143]

---

143. (FOUO) (1) Hqs Ark NG Cmd Rpt, 24 Sep - 30 Nov 57, Pt 1, Annex A, p. 3; Annex C, App 3, Tab A. (2) DCSOPS Journal, Item 397.

The assembly of the Alert Force at Camp Robinson and the provision of logistical support for it were by no means inconsequential problems. The initial transportation to Camp Robinson was accomplished in National Guard vehicles. Because neither gasoline nor courtesy cards were available responsible Guard officers had to "borrow" gasoline from the U.S. Purchasing and Fiscal Officer. No meal tickets or other arrangements for meals or sleeping facilities en route had been made so that the Guard had to arrange for these services as best they could. General Clinger later stated that "delay in getting papers processed for money allocations for the payment of these meals was in excess of one month."[144]

---

144. (FOUO) (1) Hqs Ark NG Cmd Rpt, Pt 1, p. 4. (2) Ltr, Maj Gen Sherman T. Clinger to CG, USARMD, 18 Nov 57, sub: Ark NG in Opn "Arkansas," WHD Opn ARKANSAS Files.

Once at Camp Robinson, arrangements for logistical support from Camp Chaffee and, by cross-servicing arrangements, from Little Rock Air Force Base were reasonably satisfactory. However, the camp itself was in run-down condition without adequate facilities and there had been little consideration of its use in the prior planning. Many of the Guard officers lacked proper preparations for administrative and logistical tasks. Medical facilities and personnel were inadequate. Complications arose from the fact that normal supply and maintenance facilities for the Guard when under state control could no longer be used when the men were called into the federal service. In their Command Report, Guard officials admitted that they found the circumstances somewhat baffling:

> The logistical problems that had developed were further complicated due to the fact that a "Super Crash" program which was underway was strange to all concerned. Even with the abundance of logistical experience and know-how these problems had no precedence. There was no past experience to base the solutions on.[145]

---

145. (FOUO) (1) Hqs Ark NG Cmd Rpt, Annex D, p. 2. (2) Cmd Rpt, 4th US Army, 1 Sep - 30 Nov 57, pp. 20-21.

Solutions were, nevertheless, worked out with the sympathetic assistance of the Fourth Army support force and of Headquarters, Arkansas Military District, and by the waiving of restrictive regulations by the Department of the Army where feasible and necessary. One step taken by General Walker, in order to provide better maintenance support for Guard vehicles, was to order two ordnance units to join the Alert Force (Headquarters and Headquarters Detachment, 739th Ordnance Battalion, and 176th Ordnance

Company, both Little Rock units). This addition brought the Alert Force to nearly 1,700 men and it remained at this point until after 15 October. Plans were hastily drawn up for the minimum necessary repairs and utilities at Camp Robinson. The Department of the Army waived certain of the regulations pertaining to property accountability enabling the Purchasing and Fiscal Officer to resume his normal functions, substituting active army funds for National Guard funds and for personnel of the Alert Force to be supplied with winter uniforms from Fort Chaffee. Similarly, arrangements were made for paying the Guardsmen through the Finance and Disbursing Section at Fort Chaffee, and this section was augmented by one officer and twelve enlisted finance personnel from Fort Hood.[146]

---

146. (FOUO) (1) On these problems generally see Cmd Rpt, USARMD, Ark, Annex D; Cmd Rpt, Hqs, Ark NG, Annex D; Cmd Rpt, 4th US Army, pp. 4-21. (2) Msg, AKMAR 10-42, CGUSARMD ARK to CG, ARK NG, 4 Oct 57, DA-IN-868988. (3) Msg AKMAR 10-117, CGUSARMD ARK to DEPTAR, 16 Oct 57, DA-IN-875226. (4) Cf. strength figures appearing in Hqs Ark NG Cmd Rpt, 24 Sep - 30 Nov 57, Annex C, App 5, pp. 9-19. (5) Instructions on pay and allotments are contained in DA 572502 to CGUSARMD, ARK, 25 Sep 57 and DA 574351, 2 Oct. (6) On the problem of property accountability see Msg 10-0040, CGUSARFOUR to DCSLOG, 1 Oct 57, DA-IN-867057 and DA 575436 to CGUSARFOUR, 4 Oct 57. (7) Cmd Rpt, 4th US Army, 1 Sep - 30 Nov 57, pp. 8, 16. (8) Cmd Rpt, Hqs, USARMD, Ark, Annex D, pp. 3-5. (9) Cmd Rpt, Hqs Ark NG, Annex D, pp. 2-3.

The most difficult and plaguing problem of all was that of physical and administrative processing of Guard personnel, both those in the Alert Force and those mobilized at home station. This processing, under the actual conditions of the Call, was the responsibility of the National Guard itself under directives issued by Headquarters, U.S. Army Military District, Arkansas, and with the assistance of National Guard advisor personnel from that headquarters. As events turned out, it proved necessary to call on Fourth Army personnel and facilities for extensive assistance. Initial plans prepared at Fourth Army had provided for administrative processing under the provisions of AR 130-10 and SR 130-10-1 on a reduced basis, and these plans were taken over by the Military District. In-processing as originally set up called for two schedules with the units at home station to receive only token processing while alert forces at Camp Robinson received a more complete processing. Under this plan physical examinations would be given only to the personnel of the Alert Force, and because of limited facilities these exams were not to include serology or blood typing. A medical team was assembled at Camp Robinson drawn from the Alert Force and augmented by five medical officers, two dental officers, and necessary enlisted technicians from Fort Chaffee. Approximately 1,380 physical examinations were completed by this team between 27 and 30 September.[147]

---

147. (1) Cmd Rpt, Hqs, USARMD, 24 Sep - 30 Nov 57, Annex A, App 3; Annex D, App 2. (2) Cmd Rpt, Hqs Ark NG, Annex A, p. 2. (3) Cmd Rpt, 4th US Army, 1 Sep - 30 Nov 57, pp. 8, 13.

Meanwhile, in Washington, the whole problem was subjected to review by The Adjutant General's Office, the National Guard Bureau, and other administrative agencies that had not been consulted in the original planning because of the need to keep information on these plans as restricted as possible. A new draft regulation on in-processing of the National Guard and U.S. Army Reserve when called to active federal duty had been in preparation for a long time. At a meeting held in The Adjutant General's Office on 26 September, it was agreed that this draft regulation was sufficiently advanced to be used and that SR 130-10-1 was obsolete. TAG then sent a letter to the Commanding General, Fourth Army, instructing him that the new draft AR 135-300, Reserve Components, - Mobilization of Army National Guard of the United States and Army Reserve Units, would apply in the administrative processing of members of the Army Arkansas National Guard called to active duty. The instructions also stated:

> The draft Army Regulation 135-300 contains many revised procedures for processing reserve component personnel into active military service. The present situation in Arkansas will afford an opportunity to field test these procedures. Comments and recommendations relative to your experience in implementing the regulations are desired.[148]

---

148. (1) Ltr, Actg TAG to CGUSARFOUR, 26 Sep 57, sub: Mobilization of Army NG of US and Army Reserve Units, 26 Sep 57, Tab A to App 2, Annex A, USARMD, Ark, Cmd Rpt, 24 Sep - 30 Nov 57. (2) MR, Col J J Hamlin, Precedent & History Br, TAGO, 30 Sep 57, sub: Federalization & Call of the Ark Army & Air NG into the Active Mil Svc of the US, AGCT 325.3 (30 Sep 57), in file kept by Prec & Hist Br, AGO, on Operation ARKANSAS.

This request for a field test of the regulation changed the initial plans of Arkansas Military District. It was decided that all men of the Arkansas National Guard should have a complete administrative in-processing including a physical examination. In fact, physical examinations on induction and release were statutory requirements applying to either an Order or a Call to active duty.[149]

---

149. Revised U. S. Code, Title 10, Section 3502.

Under the circumstances it was a difficult requirement to fulfill. The Guard units mobilized at home stations were scattered throughout 63 stations in addition to Camp Robinson. To provide for physical examinations for all these scattered units, the state was divided into eight areas with a central point in each area to which Guardsmen should report. Four Teams were formed to give physical examinations, one to remain at Camp Robinson, another at Fort Chaffee, and the other two to move around the state to areas from whence men could not be expected to report to one or the other of the regular stations. To provide medical personnel to carry out the plan, at the request of General Walker the Department of the Army on 1 October granted him authority to order medical officers mobilized at home station with the National Guard to go to any location within the state where needed and to keep them at those stations as long as necessary to complete physical examinations. He was to make sure that no community was depleted of doctors. In this way, a first round of physical examinations covering 7,173 National Guardsmen (including the Alert Force) was completed by 13 October. This, Arkansas Military District reported, completed the program "except for strays and/or those who missed the first round examinations," all of whom would be required to come to Robinson or Chaffee.[150]

---

150. (FOUO) (1) USARMD, ARK, Sit Rep # 26, DA-IN-873983, 15 Oct 57. (2) DCSOPS Journal, items 398, 466. (3) Cmd Rpt, Hqs USARMD, 24 Sep - 30 Nov 57, Annex D, App 2. (4) Msg AKMAR 9-53, CHUSARMD, ARK, to DCSOPS, 30 Sep 57, DA-IN-866598. (5) Msg DA 930424 to CHUSARMD, ARK, 1 Oct 57.

The completion of other steps in administrative in-processing got under way much more slowly. It did not begin for the Alert Force at Camp Robinson until 3 October and was not completed there until 12 October. The plan was to send administrative processing teams, composed of Fort Chaffee personnel, to the other central areas around the state, but actual implementation of this plan had just gotten under way when on 15 October it was decided to release the major portion of the Guardsmen mobilized at home station. In consequence, administrative in-processing for these men was combined with outprocessing in a single operation.[151]

---

151. (1) Hqs USARMD, Cmd Rpt, Annex A. App 2. (2) Fourth US Army Cmd Rpt, pp. 9, 13-14.

The field test of the draft regulation was subjected to severe criticism by all field headquarters involved. Headquarters, Fourth U.S.

Army commented as follows:

Valid tests could not be conducted of draft AR 135-300 due to provisions in the regulation for an "alert period" and "mobilization station," both of which were lacking in the Arkansas operation. Further, confusion existed as to the period of Call and the extent of administrative processing required. Administrative processing that would have normally been accomplished during an alert period had to be accomplished after personnel were already in active service and were engaged in carrying out the mission for which called. Mobilization at widely dispersed home stations and the requirement that inprocessing be accomplished at local armories made effective control and guidance difficult.[152]

---

152. (FOUO) Fourth US Army Cmd Rpt, 10 Sep - 30 Nov 57, p. 21.

Headquarters, U.S. Army Military District, Arkansas, echoed much the same criticisms:

Department of the Army directed that the "Arkansas Situation" be used as a vehicle to "Field Test" draft AR 135-300. The draft regulation obviously envisioned an "Alert Period" during which time local commanders could gather their units and accomplish certain processing. No such warning was given as the National Guard troops were federalized within hours. The referenced regulation further directed that the balance of processing be accomplished at "Mobilization Station," again envisioning some type of installation having facilities and some regular army personnel to direct the personnel conducting the processing. Camp Robinson did not have any facilities or personnel. In addition, the majority of Arkansas National Guard personnel were mobilized at home stations having neither facilities nor qualified supervisory personnel. The validity of such a "Field Test" of regulations is questionable in view of the situation in Arkansas. Future "Field Testing" should be planned for situations more closely resembling the emergencies for which the regulations were prepared.[153]

---

153. (FOUO) Hqs USARMD, Ark, Cmd Rpt, 24 Sep - 30 Nov 57, Annex A, App 2, p. 1.

Headquarters, Arkansas National Guard had this to say:

. . . The (Draft) regulation was confusing, at best, due to the general mixture of terminology contained throughout such as CALL, ORDER,

INDUCTION, MOBILIZATION, AND ALERT PERIODS without clearly defining the action required under the separate methods of bringing the reserve components into the active federal service. This staff section recommends that the various means of bringing the reserve components into active federal service be treated under separate regulations even though some duplication may result.[154]

---

154. (FOUO) Hqs Ark NG Cmd Rpt, Annex A, p. 2.

The basic difficulty was not so much the order for a field test of the draft regulation as the inapplicability of either this new draft or the older SR 130-10-1 to the specific situation in which the Arkansas National Guard was called. The introduction of a new regulation at the last minute nevertheless certainly contributed to the confusion and uncertainty that prevailed in the in-processing. Fourth Army noted that "The late receipt of instructions from Department of the Army and the need to obtain DA approval on any deviations to draft AR precluded timely implementation of administrative requirements." Fourth Army also noted, however, that the state of maintenance of National Guard personnel records and the unfamiliarity of National Guard administrative personnel with procedures seriously militated against smooth in-processing, as did the fact that "due to lack of clearly delineated instructions, administrative assistance provided by National Guard advisor personnel was insufficient during this CALL to active duty."[155]

---

155. (FOUO) Fourth US Army Cmd Rpt, pp. 20-21.

Personnel of the Alert Force were, as the Arkansas National Guard puts it, "pulled from college and high school as students or teachers while others were taken from their jobs with little or no opportunity to make satisfactory arrangements with employers."[156] As noted earlier the

---

156. (FOUO) Ark NG Cmd Rpt, Annex A, p. 1.

---

personnel of the Alert Force felt they had received discriminatory treatment as compared to those who were mobilized at home station. Pressures began to be exerted for release of individuals or groups almost immediately after the Guard was mobilized and continued to mount thereafter. The problem of the students and teachers was brought forcibly to the attention of the Department of the Army on 30 September 1957 by Senator John L. McClellan of Arkansas. Investigation revealed a preliminary count of 153 college students, 222 high school students, 10 college teachers, and 5 high school teachers at Camp Robinson on 3 October, or almost a third of the entire Alert Force as then constituted. Hardship cases were more difficult to identify, since there was some degree of hardship involved for practically all men and most of them would likely claim hardship. "Adversely affected is a matter of degree," remarked General Pachler. "Is $2 a day in the guard rather than $5 in civilian life hardship?"[157] Nonetheless, the

---

157. (FOUO) (1) *Ibid.* (2) Quote fm phone conv w/Gen Wheeler, 4 Oct 57, DCSOPS Journal, item 297 (OUO). (3) Memo, Dir Opns, ODCSOPS for Asst Secy Army (M&RF), 3 Oct 57, sub: HS & Coll Students Now on Duty

w/Ark NG Fces, Journal item 494. (4) Msg AKMAR 10-34, CHUSARMD, ARK, to DCSOPS, 3 Oct 57, DA-IN-868626.

National Guard Headquarters identified about 190 cases of "confirmed hardship," such as owners and managers of business, specialized or skilled workmen, men whose pay would not permit them to support their families, and farmers whose release it felt was justified.[158]

---

158. (FOUO) (1) <u>Ibid</u>. (2) Hqs USARMD, Ark, Cmd Rpt, 24 Sep - 30 Nov 57, Annex A, p. 4.

The problem to be resolved was how to release the students, teachers, and hardship cases without emasculating the Alert Force. On 1 October, General Walker had authorized General Clinger to permit up to 10 percent of duty strength of the Alert Force 10 days of leave "in compassionate or hardship cases" but only on condition that those men were replaced by men from the National Guard mobilized at home stations.[159] This was not enough

---

159. (FOUO) Msg AKMAR 10-2, HQ USARMILDIST, ARK to CG, ARK NG, 1 Oct 57, DA-IN-866856.

---

to take care of the students and teachers. General Clinger recommended that the 153d Infantry be replaced by other units, but General Walker's staff found this unacceptable since the new structure would not be a cohesive one. "Whatever plan is finally accepted," commented the USARMD

G-3, "will require considerable work to figure out. It must be noted that some guard units are nearly all high school students. If all high school students are relieved and replaced, units may be up to strength but will suffer in tactical control."[160] But something had to be done, at

---

160. (FOUO) DCSOPS Journal, item 265.

---

least in regard to the students and teachers, and on 3 October General Walker told General Clinger that he must "take action immediately to replace with other federalized Army National Guard personnel under your command all members of the alert force who are students, teachers, or whose means of livelihood are in jeopardy or are adversely affected by their continued service. Replacements should be on a man-for-man basis insuring that replacement personnel are physically present and qualified to perform the mission." In issuing the call for the two ordnance units to join the Alert Force, General Walker stipulated that students and hardship cases should be replaced by other suitable individuals.[161]

---

161. (FOUO) Quote from Msg AKMAR 10-30, CG USARMILDIST ARK to CG ARK NG, 3 Oct 57, DA-IN-868503. (2) n 159 (3).

The solution was thus a considerable shuffling of personnel between the Guard units mobilized at home and the Alert Force at Camp Robinson. As far as students and teachers were concerned, this solution was approved by the Department of the Army which instructed Arkansas Military District to speed the action. But on hardship cases, the Secretary of the Army ruled there should be no blanket releases, that they should be handled on a case by case basis strictly in accordance with existing regulations. The students and teachers, 398 in all, had been released and replaced by 8 October. Under the case by case review procedure, only 48 hardship cases had been validated and personnel released by 13 October. Nevertheless, the replacement of 446 members of the Alert Force by personnel mobilized at home stations involved a considerable reshuffling of the Guard units at Camp Robinson, a prelude to the greater reshuffling that was to come when the men mobilized at home stations were to be released.[162]

---

162. (FOUO) (1) DCSOPS Journal, items 297, 308, 309, 310, 381, 430. (2) USARMD, ARK, Sit Rep 21, DA-IN-871621, 10 Oct 57; Sit Rep 22, DA-IN-872338, 11 Oct 57 (OUO). (3) Hqs USARMD, Ark., Cmd Rpt, Annex A, p. 4.

A final problem relating to the National Guard involved the use of Camp Robinson. The camp was divided into two parts, a state and a federal section. Pursuant to an Act of Congress the Secretary of the Army in 1950 had transferred 34,000 acres of land at Camp Robinson to the State of Arkansas, under a requirement that the land be used primarily for National Guard and other military purposes under penalty of recapture if the requirement was not fulfilled. The United States also retained the right to recapture the land in case of a national emergency proclaimed by the Congress or the President. The Regular Army units were placed in the federal section of the camp, but the Alert Force of the Arkansas National Guard was housed in the section that had been turned back to the state. Since none of the conditions set forth for recapture existed, this created serious problems. The Judge Advocate General ruled on 25 September that "there would be a liability on the part of the United States for the use of the land and for any damage occasioned by such occupancy."[163]

---

163. (FOUO) (1) Memo, Col Alan B. Todd, Chf Mil Affairs Div, TJAG, for Col Easton, sub: Claims Liability for use of Camp Robinson, App 2 to Annex H (JA), Hqs USARMD, Ark, Cmd Rpt, 24 Sep - 30 Nov 57. (2) Excerpt from deed of land at Camp Robinson to State of Arkansas, Annex D, App 1, Tab A.

The question raised, however, went beyond this. It involved the whole question of whether use of the state facilities was legal without a permit or lease from the state. The necessary rehabilitation program for the camp was delayed while this question was threshed out. On 1 October, Fourth Army requested guidance from the Department of the Army, noting that a plan had been initiated to "obtain permit and/or lease from the State of Arkansas to legalize the use of facilities required by Federal troops," but that this action had been suspended because General Walker thought it might "cause embarrassment and contains considerable political aspects adverse to the national interests."[164] This embar-

164. (1) (C) Msg 1983, CGUSARFOUR to DCSOPS, 1 Oct 57, DA-IN-58878. (2) (FOUO) Memo, Lt Col Marvin G. Krieger, Chf, Lands Div, JAGC, for DCSOPS, 7 Oct 57, sub: Use and Occupancy of Camp Joseph T. Robinson by Federal Troops, DCSOPS Journal, item 351. (3) (FOUO) USARMD, ARK, Sit Rep 20, DA-IN-870984, 9 Oct 57

rassment, put more bluntly, was a fear that if the situation were called to the attention of state authorities "they might summarily evict the Federalized National Guard from that installation."[165]

165. (FOUO) DCSOPS Journal, item 335.

The problem was turned over by DCSOPS to the Deputy Chief of Staff for Logistics and The Judge Advocate General but after some discussion it was agreed that only the Secretary of the Army could resolve it. On 7 October the Secretary directed that "all action on this matter be held up for the time being and further that there be no further discussion or speculation."[166] The solution adopted was simply to go ahead with such

166. (FOUO) (1) Note by Maj R G Benckart on copy of DA-IN-58878, 2 Oct 57. DCSOPS In-Cables Opn ARKANSAS. (2) DCSOPS Journal, items 335, 351, 375.

minimum improvements to the state-owned facilities at Camp Robinson as were essential to the health and welfare of the troops and without any clear legal authorization. As the Arkansas Military District Command Report put it:

>   A formal reply was not received from higher headquarters to the numerous telephone requests, by this headquarters, for guidance in how much R & U support should be provided to this area. By the same token, this headquarters did not submit a formal request to higher headquarters because of the informal ruling by higher headquarters to continue on a status quo basis.[167]

---

167. (FOUO) Hqs USARMD, Ark, Cmd Rpt, 24 Sep-30 Nov 57, Annex D, App 1, p. 1.

The National Guard Command Report simply had this to say:

>   The rehabilitation of facilities was delayed pending a decision from the Department of the Army upon the basis that state owned property was involved without a use permit. Maintenance crews from Fort Chaffee continued to make minor repairs and emergency calls throughout the area. With the supervision of the Fort Chaffee personnel and the National Guard Engineer personnel, the stoves at Camp Robinson were being installed.[168]

---

168. (FOUO) Hqs Ark NG, Cmd Rpt, Pt 1, Annex D, p. 3.

The First Reduction Plan, 4-15 October 1957

In the aftermath of the troubles inside Central High School on 2-3 October, any early action to remove the regular troops from Little Rock or even to phase down operations there seemed in doubt. On Friday, 4 October, however, the situation was relatively quiet and school attendance increased to 1,669, despite numerous suspensions. When the Negro students entered the school there were some scattered cat calls but considerably fewer than previously and there were no incidents during the day.[169] A high

---

169. (FOUO) (1) DCSOPS Journal, items 299, 303. (2) USARMD, ARK, Sit Rep 16, DA-IN-869369, 5 Oct 57.

---

school football game and dance were held on Friday night during which there was one incident involving the guard and an ex-student of the high school who used abusive language to the soldiers and refused to move away from the front of the school when ordered. At the Livestock Exhibition also there was an altercation between city police and two sergeants from the 101st Airborne Division that had little to do with segregation.[170] Otherwise the

---

170. (FOUO) (1) DCSOPS Journal, items 316, 317. (2) USARMD, ARK, Rpt of Investigation, Re The Arrest of Sgt James D. Holt and Sgt Lawrence E. Kunst at the Arkansas Livestock Showgrounds on 4 October 1957; Rpt of Investigation Re Incident on 4 October 1957 Wherein Mr. Robert King, Civilian, Was Allegedly Struck by Private Robert L. P. Warrick in the Performance of Duties Connected with Operation Arkansas. DCSOPS

Investigations file, Opn ARKANSAS.

---

situation remained quiet but with the undercurrent of tension that had existed since Governor Faubus first turned out the National Guard.

General Wheeler returned to Washington over the weekend of 5-6 October and reported directly to the Secretary on the happenings of the previous week. When asked by the Secretary if he foresaw any trouble ahead, General Wheeler said "No, that the main part was probably broken and the tough element under control," but that he could not be sure about "outside interference." The Secretary approved a plan to start phasing the National Guard troops back into the school to work with the airborne units but stipulated that the military command must be sure that everything was under control. The Secretary reemphasized the fact that the safety of the Negro students was a matter of primary concern. The Chief of Staff indicated that the reserve company of the 101st should be kept in the basement of the school.[171]

---

171. (FOUO) (1) Tel Con Gen Wheeler - Gen Walker, 6 Oct 57, DCSOPS Journal item 330. (2) M/R by Lt. Col. George M. Seignious, Mil Asst to SA, 5 Oct 57, sub: Rpt by Gen Wheeler, Journal item 371.

The next school week, 7-11 October, continued to be quiet with school attendance increasing almost to normal. But the attitude of the Governor indicated that there was not the slightest possibility he would come to terms with President Eisenhower. On Monday, 7 October, a letter arrived at General Walker's headquarters from the Governor's Mansion addressed to the "Commanding General Occupation Troops," and was delivered to the headquarters sergeant-major. General Walker immediately asked DCSOPS for instructions and was told to return the letter unopened with a note saying that it was improperly addressed and that he was prepared to receive any communication addressed to the Commanding General, U.S. Army Military District, Arkansas. There was no mystery about the contents of the letter for it had already been released to the press. Governor Faubus charged that the troops on duty inside the school had been peeking in the girls' dressing rooms and suggested the assignment of a WAC detachment to the school. The Army conducted a thorough investigation of every rumor of this sort and found them all unfounded. The Secretary of the Army openly challenged Governor Faubus to furnish proof but the Governor said he did not wish to do so because it would result in teachers being fired, pupils suspended, and soldiers disciplined. This incident appeared to verify that Governor Faubus would not agree to a solution to the problem that involved any concessions on his part. Later in the week he produced a photograph purporting to show General Sherburne and Colonel Kuhn gazing at the bare legs of the high school girls in gym class.[172]

---

172. (1) (FOUO) DCSOPS Journal, items 354, 358, 368, 387, 403, 412. (2) (S) Msg AKMAR 10-80, CHUSARMD, ARK, to DCSOPS, 8 Oct 57, DA-IN-60809. (3) (FOUO) G-2, USARMD, ARK, reported: "The General and party did walk through the playfield area moving from one area of the school to the other in the course of his inspection. This area is open to the public, bounded

by a street on two sides." Item 412.

With Governor Faubus displaying an uncompromising attitude and the President and Secretary of the Army determined that the Negro students must be protected within the school, the time had clearly come for the preparation of some long-term plans for the use of federal troops at Little Rock. The maintenance of the entire Arkansas National Guard on duty was an expensive operation costing an estimated $79,000 a day.[173]

---

173. (FOUO) DCSOPS Journal, item 325.

However, valuable the experience the airborne troops were getting in Little Rock, it was onerous duty and interfered with the 101st Airborne Division's training program intended to prepare the division for a much more vital role in national defense. Military police might be expected to benefit a good deal more from this kind of duty since it was much more clearly related to their primary mission. The operation was also causing interference with normal activities of Fourth Army, particularly those of the training command at Fort Chaffee.

To relieve some of the burden of the duty on the airborne battle group, arrangements were made to permit up to 5 percent of the command to go on two-day pass to Fort Campbell with a C-123 plane leaving Little Rock Air Force Base each Monday, Wednesday, and Friday and returning two days later. The first plane, carrying 42 men, left Little Rock on Monday, 7 October. Arrangements were also made for the use of recreational facilities at Little Rock Air Force Base. Similarly on 12 October, a C-47 was made available on a scheduled weekend run to provide Fourth Army augmentation personnel 32-hour passes to San Antonio. Meanwhile, between 2 and 6 October, Fourth Army returned most of the original provisional support company to Fort Chaffee and replaced it with a transportation detachment from Fort Sill, a Quartermaster Bath Platoon from Fort Polk, a platoon of the 720th Military Police Battalion, and detachments from the 53d and 54th Signal Battalions from Fort Hood.[174]

---

174. (FOUO) (1) Ibid., items 250, 253, 267, 270, 326, 348, 352, 392, 429. (2) Cmd Rpt, USARMD, Annex A, p. 1; Annex D, App. 1 Sit Rep 17, DA-IN-869692, 6 Oct 57; Sit Rep 18, DA-IN-869744, 7 Oct 57; Sit Rep 23, DA-IN-873007, 12 Oct 57. (OUO). (3) Cmd Rpt, 4th U.S. Army, p. 8-9.

Meanwhile, operations at Central High School settled down to a routine basis. In accordance with the plan approved by Secretary Brucker, General Walker began once again to phase the National Guard back into the operation in the interior of the school. On 9 October his headquarters prepared a plan for this purpose. One officer and five enlisted men from the 153d Infantry were to be introduced into the school on the first day and "oriented and trained on the various duties" by the airborne troops. The Guardsmen were to be increased by five men on the following day and then on subsequent days in increments of five "as the situation permits . . . until a sufficient number is on hand to perform the entire mission inside the school."[175] On 10 October General Walker began to implement this plan

175. (FOUO) Memo, G-3 for CG, USARMD, Ark, 8 Oct 57, sub: Concept for Gradual Integration of NG Soldiers w/101st Abn units in Opns in CHS, DCSOPS Journal, item 431c.

and by the 15th had two officers and 21 enlisted men from the 153d Infantry on duty as door guards, hallway patrols, and student escorts. However, there also remained one officer and nine enlisted men from the airborne battle group on this detail, and the reserve company of paratroopers remained in the basement. The airborne commander was responsible for the entire interior operation. The exterior guard, for which the National Guard was entirely responsible, was maintained without much change. The only real reduction in the visible effort lay in the gradual diminution of the number of escorts of Negro students from the military station wagon to the school entrance.[176]

176. (FOUO) (1) USARMD, Sit Rep 23, DA-IN873007, 12 Oct 57 (OUO). (2) Cmd Rpt, Hqs USARMD, Annex C, App 1, p. 6; App 5, p. 2.

All of these were minor steps. The big problem was to cut the cost of the operation, both in terms of money and interference with normal troop training, by tailoring the force in Little Rock more closely to the need. If all the National Guard could not be relieved from the federal service, then at least that part of it could which was not engaged in the actual operation. On 8 October, the Chief of Staff directed that General

Walker have a plan prepared for relieving part of the Guard from duty to reduce costs. At the same time, the 101st Airborne Division became concerned about the loss of training time to the 1st Airborne Battle Group of the 327th and the fact that unless the men were brought back to Fort Campbell they would be unable to qualify for jump pay. If 101st troops were to remain on duty in Little Rock they would either have to be rotated or some area found nearby where they could conduct jump training. By 9 October these two problems -- relief of part of the National Guard and rotation of the airborne battle group -- had become the central points in planning for the future both in Arkansas and the Pentagon. In the end they were to be merged in a single plan for reduction in force.[177]

---

177. (FOUO) (1) DCSOPS Journal, items 382, 392, 431. (C) (2) Notes taken on certain working papers of Lt Col James G. Kalergis, WHD, ODCSOPS.

The problem of setting up an alert force in the National Guard for the long pull was a difficult one. The flurry over students, teachers, and hardship cases indicated that very careful screening would have to be undertaken to provide a force to remain on duty for any considerable length of time. However done, it would **inevitably** result in almost complete loss of unit integrity. In its final form the plan worked out by Arkansas Military District in collaboration with Headquarters Arkansas National Guard called for an active force at Little Rock of 1,800 men, 1,500 for operations and 300 for support, formed around a "hard core" of 1,080 of the existing Alert Force who had no hardship claims. To provide against any unforeseen hardship cases, sickness, and other types of discharge, an additional 1,00 men would be maintained on duty in a reserve replacement pool at home stations to keep the operating force up to strength. The rest of the Air National Guard would be released with the possible exception of General Clinger.[178]

---

178. (C) Staff Study, USARMD, 10 Oct 57, sub: Demobilization of Ark NG, DCSOPS Journal, item 431d.

The first plan for the airborne battle group provided simply for its replacement by another battle group from the 101st Airborne Division. But on the night of 8 October General Eddleman passed on to General Walker the information that military police might be employed for the long pull. General Walker's G-3 considered that "under existing situation and conditions, a trained and oriented 300 man Military Police unit" could assume the mission of the airborne troops at the high school.

    The mission since the first three days of employment of the 101st Airborne Division units has resolved itself into primarily a police type function. The 1st Airborne Battle Group is not trained primarily for such duties and is unable, because of the situation, to conduct training which it needs to maintain a high degree of combat readiness. Actually the longer the 1st Airborne Battle Group remains on this mission, even through it is performing outstandingly, its efficiency as a combat unit is deteriorating. A military police unit with a strength of approximately 300, properly equipped and trained should find duty at Central High School under conditions permitting a phase out of combat troops in line with established military police activities.[179]

---

179. (FOUO) (1) Staff Study, G-3, USARMD, Ark, to CG, 8 Oct 57, sub: Replacement of 1st ABG, 327th Inf; Memo, G-3 for CG, USARMD, Ark, 10 Oct 57, sub: Relief of the 101st Abn Div. DCSOPS Journal, item 431a-b.

(2) Journal, item 382.

The Army staff in Washington agreed. On 9 October Maj. Gen. Thomas J. H. Trapnell, Assistant DCSOPS, visited CONARC and secured a recommendation that the 720th Military Police Battalion at Fort Hood with the organic Military Police company of the 1st Armored Division attached (a total of 587 men) would be the "best trained and best commanded available unit of this type." CONARC said the Military Police Battalion could be ready to move on the fifth day following receipt of orders by that Headquarters to execute the mission.[180]

---

180. (1) (S) M/R, Maj Gen T J H Trapnell, 9 Oct 57, sub: Planning for Replacement of Trps at LR, DCSOPS Journal item 464.

On the night of 10 October General Wheeler returned to Washington bearing the plans of Arkansas Military District. A round of conferences and staff studies followed during the next few days out of which emerged the final reduction plan. The first of these, prepared on 11 October by the Western Hemisphere Division, concluded quite positively that a partial defederalization of the Guard would be desirable and that it should be accompanied either by a gradual phase out of the 101st Airborne Division, or replacement of the airborne troops by a Military Police Unit, with the latter preferable. Meanwhile, on the same day, it was decided in the higher levels in DCSOPS that the 2,800 man National Guard Force proposed by Walker's Headquarters could be reduced to 1,800, 1,000 in the active force, 300 for support, and a 500-man replacement pool. General Wheeler secured General Walker's approval for this proposal in the afternoon. During the weekend the plan was further refined and combined with that to replace the airborne troops with the 720th Military Police Battalion. General Eddleman conferred with officers from Office of the Provost Marshal General who confirmed the readiness of the 720th and added that "it would be desirable experience for them to obtain."[181]

---

181. (FOUO) (1) Memo, Lt Gen C D Eddleman, DCSOPS, for CofS, 12 Oct 57, sub: Use of 720th MP Bn in LR, DCSOPS Journal, item 488. (2) (U) Draft Study on De-Federalization of the Ark NG, 11 Oct 57, Staff Study File, WHD. (3) (C) Notes taken on Lt Col Kalergis Working papers. (4) (FOUO) DCSOPS Journal, items 392, 419, 421, 434, 440.

Action went so far as the investigation of the availability of the new green uniforms for the Military Police personnel. Then on Monday, 14 October, the plan was taken to the White House where the use of the military police battalion was vetoed. Instead it was decided that the 101st Airborne troops should be reduced by half with about 500 to return to Fort Campbell and 500 to remain in Little Rock. As soon as possible after the return of the first 500, however, the remaining contingent of the 1st Airborne Battle Group of the 327th was to be replaced by 500 men from another battle group. Late on the night of 14 October, the Department of the Army officially informed General Walker of the decisions:

It is desired that you prepare a detailed plan for continued operations in the Little Rock area, employing minimum Arkansas National

Guard units and such Regular Army units as are made available. Plan will be based on the concept of utilizing the 153rd Infantry Regiment (-), as the major National Guard operational force. All other elements of the Army National Guard and the Air National Guard would be released from active federal service as soon as necessary transfers of personnel and other administrative arrangements have been completed. . . .

The 101st Airborne Division element will be phased down expeditiously to a strength of approximately 500. Phased replacements of elements of the 1st Battle Group, 327th Infantry from within the 101st Airborne Division is authorized, in coordination with the Commanding General, 101st Airborne Division.[182]

---

182. (1) (C) Msg DA 931128 to CHUSARMD, ARK, 15 Oct 57. (2) (FOUO) DCSOPS Journal, items 452, 454, 458, 459, 463. (3) Info fm Col Williams and Lt Col Kalergis.

The rest consisted of detailed instructions on how to handle the reduction of the National Guard, a big problem that will be dealt with separately.

The above decisions were followed by a nessage on 15 October to both General Walker and General Sherburne of the 101st Airborne Division confirming the arrangement on relief of half of the airborne troops and rotation of the other half. The movement of the increment to be permanently relieved was to be accomplished on 16 October with vehicles loaded to capacity with personnel to move overland, the rest of the personnel and individual equipment to be airlifted. Tactical Air Command would provide eight C-123 aircraft for the movement on the 16th. Then on 17, 19, 21, and 23 October Tactical Air Command was to provide three planes each day to transport the rest of the 1st Airborne Battle Group to Fort Campbell and return an equivalent number from another battle group of the 101st to Little Rock. A press release on 14 October made public the essentials of the reduction plan but nothing was said about the proposed rotation.[183]

---

183. (1) (C) Msg DA 931225 to CHUSARMD, ARK, & CG, 101st ABN DIV, 15 Oct 57. (2) (FOUO) DCSOPS Journal, items 459, 462, 465, 468, 471, 476, 480. (3) (FOUO) There was some misunderstanding about General Walker's being informed of the press release, see Journal items 458, 459, 465, 477.

The movement of vehicles overland loaded with personnel was decided on because of a shortage of aircraft gasoline for training purposes and the differential between complete air and complete motor movement was so small that in terms of cost this seemed the best compromise. The movement was carried out on schedule on 16 and 17 October, 374 men departing by air and 66 men with 33 vehicles by road. But the rotation plan was halted. There was a premature press report stating that all elements of the 101st in Little Rock would be withdrawn and replaced by 500 men of the 502nd Airborne Division. As garbled as this version was it created a strong reaction. In the afternoon of the 16th General Eddleman called Generals Wheeler and Walker and stated that "in view of the press release . . . the phased replacement of the 327th by the 502nd Airborne Infantry Regiment would be stopped immediately." He told General Walker he could replace individuals in the 327th by other individuals in the 327th but there would be no unit replacements, and he told General Wheeler that the higher echelons "did not want a rotation right now." This decision was confirmed by message to the Commanding General, 101st Airborne Division the following day.[184] It was never to be changed and elements of the 327th remained in

184. (1) (FOUO) Ibid., items 509, & 517. See also items 476, 480. (2) (C) Msg DA 931303 to CG 101st ABN DIV, 16 Oct 57, rescinded the part of the directive in DA 931225 relating to the availability of planes but did not rescind that part authorizing rotation of the battle group. (3) (FOUO) On the return movement to Ft. Campbell, see DCSOPS Journal, items 471, 480, 485, 514, 515, 542 and USARMD Sit Rep 27, DA-IN-874665, 16 Oct 57; Sit Rep 28, DA-IN-875428, 17 Oct 57.

Little Rock until the final withdrawal of all airborne troops on 27 November 1957.

Release and Adjustments in the Arkansas National Guard, 15-23 October 1957

There were problems involved in cutting an airborne battle group in half,[185] but they were comparatively simple compared to the adjustments

---

185. (FOUO) DCSOPS Journal, item 459. General Walker stated he was concerned about the fact that it wasn't realized what it means to cut a unit in half under the new type organization. Some rotation in the battle group was carried out later in order to assure that all members qualified for jump pay.

---

that had to be made in the Arkansas National Guard. There were two main problem areas, the first involving the method of organizing the 1,800 man alert force and the second the procedure and mechanics to be used in releasing the rest of the Guard. In many ways the two were interdependent.

Exploration within DCSOPS of the general problem of relieving the National Guard from a Call began on 1 October when hopes were high that the conference between the President and the delegation of Southern Governors would be fruitful. These hopes were not justified, but did engender some preliminary work on means of releasing the Arkansas National Guard and related legal problems. Preliminary drafts of messages to be dispatched to the Chief, U.S. Army Military District, Arkansas, to Fourth Army, and to Governor Faubus effecting the release were drawn up and coordinated with interested staff agencies.[186]

---

186. (FOUO) (1) DCSOPS Journal, items 210, 223, 224, 492. (2) Draft

Summary Sheet and Msgs prepared by Lt Col J D Kalergis in WHD File Draft Msgs. (3) Memo, Brig Gen Bruce Easley, Chf Personnel Div, TAG, for Dir Opns, ODCSOPS, n.d., sub: Relief of Army and Air NG Units from Active Mil Service, item 1 A, Precedents & History Br, Personnel Div, TAG, file on Defed of Ark NG.

Meanwhile, The Adjutant General (TAG) was also working on the preparation of up-to-date instructions on administrative outprocessing. At the time that it had been decided to substitute the draft AR 135-300 on in-processing for older regulations, it was also decided that a new draft AR should be drawn up for out-processing to replace the existing SR 130-22-1, that was also considered obsolete. Between 27 September and 4 October a new draft AR 130-22, Release of Units of the Army National Guard and the Army National Guard of the United States from Active Federal Service and Return Thereof to State Control, was prepared and staffed. DCSOPS by its own decision did not participate in the preparation of this regulation. On 4 October the draft AR 130-22 was forwarded by TAG to Fourth Army with an explanatory letter and instructions, as in the case of draft AR on in-processing, that the Arkansas situation be used as a vehicle for field-testing the procedure.[187]

---

187. (1) MR by Col. J. J. Hamlin, Chf, Prec & Hist Br, Pers Div, TAG, item 3 Prec & Hist Br file on Defed of Ark NG. (2) Ltr, TAG to CGUSARFOUR, 4 Oct 57, sub: Procedures Upon Release of Army NG & Army NG of US from Active Fedl Svc & Return Thereof to State Control, AGAO-CP 325 452 (2 Oct 57)

(3) (FOUO) DCSOPS Journal, item 224.

The early planning was mainly based on the supposition that the entire Arkansas National Guard would be relieved at one time. The decision to relieve part of the Guard only and to make numerous personnel readjustments before doing so added appreciably to the complications.

When Headquarters, Arkansas National Guard, was first asked for a plan to create an alert force to serve for a protracted period, General Clinger again proposed rotation of units, but by 11 October the Guard officials had changed their minds and presented a personnel rotation plan under which the 153d Infantry Regiment and supporting units already on duty at Little Rock would continue as the operating units with personnel being transferred in and out of them as required. The underlying idea in the plan was to spread the burden of service as equitably as possible. The Guard officials wanted to replace the entire Alert Force over a period of 10 weeks at the rate of about 10 percent a week and would start the rotation about 1 November.[188] But this plan proved

---

188. (FOUO) (1) Ltr, Hqs Ark NG to CG, USARMD, Ark, 8 Oct 57, sub: Rotation of NG Units Within Camp Robinson Alert Fce, DCSOPS Journal, item 431a. (2) Memo, Hqs Ark NG for CG, USARMD, Ark, 12 Oct 57, sub: Proposed Rotation Plan, item 38 in papers brought back from Little Rock by Col Crayton, WHD. (3) DCSOPS Journal, items 392, 403, 437, 441.

---

entirely too complicated and the pace too leisurely to satisfy the

Department of the Army once the decision had been made to release part of the Guard. The concept of using the 153d Infantry as a vehicle for personnel rotation was retained, but in the plan as finally adopted rotation was reserved for the more clearly definable hardship cases and the main idea was to create a stable force.

In the conferences held and the staff studies prepared in the Pentagon between 11 and 15 October, the problem of how to handle the reduction in the National Guard was the most troublesome one to resolve. Several drafts of instructions to General Walker were drawn up, and the final draft was agreed on only after several consultations with TAG, The Judge Advocate General (JAG), and the National Guard Bureau. Authority was found in AR 130-10 for the reassignment of National Guard personnel from one unit to the other, and the whole solution was mainly hinged around this provision. The National Guard Bureau suggested that "maximum consideration should be given to obtaining . . . individuals on a voluntary basis for retention in the alert force," but this suggestion was firmly rejected in DCSOPS.[189]

---

189. (FOUO) (1) DF, Chf NGB for DCSOPS Attn WHD, 14 Oct 57, sub: Plan of Opns, Little Rock, DCSOPS Journal, item 479. (2) Draft of msg to CHUSARMD, ARK, DCSOPS Journal item 478. (3) Journal, items 416, 434, 443. (4) Draft Staff Study by Lt Col J D Kalergis, sub: Study on De-Federalization of the Ark NG. (5) Notes taken on certain of Lt Col Kalergis' working papers.

The instructions as finally agreed on were sent to General Walker in two separate messages, the first the general instructions previously mentioned to prepare a plan, and the second a follow-up message containing suggestions on administrative procedures to be used. In the first message, General Walker was instructed that within an overall ceiling of 1,800 spaces, he was to provide for an operational force of 1,000 including the National Guard State Headquarters, one regimental headquarters and headquarters company, and 4 to 6 operational companies of the 153d Infantry, a support force of approximately 300, and a personnel replacement pool of 500 to be held at home stations. The rest of the Arkansas National Guard would be released. The plan was also to provide for detailed organization of the National Guard units retained, for assignment of personnel to be retained to units to be retained and for personnel to be discharged to units to be discharged, for screening out students and teachers, case-by-case review of hardship and compassionate cases, and minimum future disruption of units remaining on active duty. To facilitate the process, National Guard Regulation 15 requiring 50 percent of T/O strength in officers and 25 percent of T/O strength in enlisted men for federal recognition was waived. General Clinger was to be retained on active duty and consulted on the formulation of the plan. Basic authority to release the excess Guard units would be issued by the Secretary of the Army and the draft Ar 130-22 with the covering TAG letter to Fourth Army was to be used as a guide to procedures in effecting release. General Walker was to report as soon as possible his estimate of the time required to complete administrative arrangements.[190]

190. (C) Msg DA 931128 to CHUSARMD, ARK, 15 Oct 57.

Among the detailed suggestions on administrative procedures in the message that followed was a specific citation of AR 130-10, paragraph 12a, as authority for transfers "from one National Guard unit to another within the same state." This device, it was suggested, should be used to maintain unit integrity "by the assignment of individuals retained on active service to units retained on active service, and the assignment of individuals released from active service to units released from active service." Further suggestions were that consideration be given to releasing the Air Staff section of the State Headquarters and such of the Army members of the State Headquarters as might be required for the state administration of units being released; that individuals who could not be released from federal service because they were in hospitals, the guardhouse, and so forth, upon release of their parent unit should not be transferred but continue as members of that parent unit; and that personnel assigned to the replacement pool and stationed in the vicinity of their homes not be authorized per diem.[191]

---

191. (C) Msg DA 931161 to CHUSARMD, ARK, 15 Oct 57.

The plan, as reflected in these two messages, had as its goal the expeditious creation of a relatively stable National Guard Alert Force capable of carrying out the mission of enforcing the court order and releasing the rest of the Guard equally expeditiously. It was as simple a plan as probably could have been conceived under the circumstances, but yet one whose execution would certainly involve many complications and take some time. But in Washington, once the reduction in the Arkansas National Guard had been decided upon, the pressure mounted to see that it was done as quickly as possible in order to cut costs of the operation. From 16 through 23 October this was the primary concern of all staff officers connected with Operation ARKANSAS. The result was a crash program for the execution of the release plan that, though it was successful in achieving the purpose intended, provoked considerable criticism from National Guard authorities.

On the night of 16 October, the Arkansas Military District Plan was threshed out at a conference with Arkansas National Guard officers and forwarded to DCSOPS by General Wheeler in the early morning of the 17th. This plan called for the organization of the Alert Force within five days, to be composed of the Headquarters, Arkansas National Guard, one platoon of the 172d Engineer Company, one platoon of the 39th MP Company, one platoon of Company D, 212th Signal Battalion, the 739th Ordnance Battalion less Company A, 39th Replacement Company, Headquarters 153d Infantry, Headquarters 1st and 3d Battalions, 153d Infantry, and four operational infantry companies. The detailed implementation of the plan was entrusted to Headquarters, Arkansas National Guard, which was to determine the transfers of personnel required, establish criteria for screening the student, teacher, and hardship cases, and submit as rapidly as possible a list of units not being drawn on, which could be released from active duty as soon as medical processing was completed. In addition to the 500-man replacement pool to be included in the 39th Replacement Company, an additional temporary overstrength of 225 would be retained for three weeks to "complete deprocessing procedures after release of parent units of these personnel."[192]

---

192. (C) (1) Msg AKMAR 10-121, CHUSARMD to DCSOPS, 17 Oct 57, DA-IN-60394. (2) Msg AKMAR 10-125, CHUSARMD, ARK, to DEPTAR, 17 Oct 57, DA-IN-875824.

General Wheeler approved the plan in principle for the Department of the Army. In so doing he warned General Pachler that many delays would stem from "complicated and incomplete processing procedures." The draft AR 130-22 had just been received in Little Rock from Fourth Army on 15 October. Out-processing under this draft AR would have to begin while in-processing under the other draft AR had not yet been completed. Even the induction physical examinations previously reported completed for over 7,000 men, General Wheeler said, had actually been completed only for about 2,500. The rest were incomplete mainly because of clouded X-Ray plates and unuseable urine and blood specimens. The processing and de-processing procedures in the draft ARs, he continued, were being field-tested by Fourth Army and were "most complicated and time-consuming." General Wheeler suggested the elimination of all non-essential processing steps as the only means by which the designated Guard units could be released expeditiously. He also raised the question as to the proper procedure to be followed in the retention of General Clinger on active duty.[193]

193. (C) <u>Ibid</u> (2).

In connection with the problems raised by General Wheeler, it is worth noting that the G-1, Arkansas Military District, at a staff meeting on 14 October estimated that there were still about three weeks' work involved in processing the National Guard to on-duty status.[194]

194. (FOUO) Notes by Lt Col Crayton on USARMD, Ark, Staff Mtg, 14 Oct 57. Item 45 in file of documents brought back from Little Rock.

Before these problems of processing could be intelligently considered, the question had to be settled as to the way in which the order for releasing part of the Guard should be handled at the highest level. The General Counsel for the Secretary of Defense held that, under the President's Executive Order, the relief order would have to be issued by the Secretary of Defense, not by the Secretary of the Army. The first draft of this Secretary of Defense Order provided that all units should be released on the same date. It was soon recognized that under this system all units would have to be completely processed before any one of them could be released and that this would probably mean two weeks of delay. The Department of the Army pressed for more flexibility whereby units could be relieved as their processing was completed, and on 17 October the Secretary of Defense signed an order providing for such a flexible system by granting the Secretary of the Army authority to specify the actual date of release of each unit. This Secretary of Defense Order provided for the release of a long list of "units, parts of units, and members thereof" of the Army and Air National Guard of the State of Arkansas with the proviso that:

> The relief from active military service provided by this order shall take effect, for particular units or parts of units, and the members thereof, at the earliest practicable time, as determined by the Secretary of the Army.
>
> All other steps in connection with the relief from active military service under this order shall be taken by the Secretary of the Army and the Secretary of the Air Force, as the case may be.[195]

---

195. (FOUO) (1) Sec Def Order signed 17 Oct 57, DCSOPS Journal, item 545. (2) Original draft w/MR by Brig Gen F T Pachler stating DCSOPS objection, Journal, item 526. (3) Journal, items 504, 511, 517, 554, 560. (4) Memo by Lt Col Crayton on telcon w/Col R C Williams, 161550 Oct 57, item 65 in documents brought back from Little Rock.

This list included 102 Army National Guard units selected by General Walker for release and all of the Air National Guard units called to service.

While this big issue was being settled, the effort to eliminate the administrative bottlenecks was proceeding apace. In the planning that attended the drafting of the AR 130-22, it had been the assumption of TAG officers that out-processing would be the responsibility of the Arkansas National Guard itself in order to save regular army personnel. In the planning carried on at Arkansas Military District, the assumption was much the same, that out-processing would be carried out much as the in-processing had been, under the supervision of the Military District with the assistance of Fort Chaffee personnel. In anticipation of rendering some additional assistance, Fourth Army on 16 October sent six more enlisted finance specialists from Fort Hood to Fort Chaffee.[196] This proved to be only the

---

196. (FOUO) (1) DCSOPS Journal, Items 224, 492. (2) Cmd.Rpt, 4th US Army, 10 Sep - 30 Nov 57, p. 9. (3) Cmd Rpt, Hqs USARMD, Ark, Annex A, App 3, p. 1.

---

beginning of Fourth Army participation. Department of the Army decided that Fourth Army was best prepared to handle out-processing and that that headquarters should be made responsible rather than U. S. Military District, Arkansas. On 17 October, before official orders had gone out to this effect, General Eddleman called Lt. Gen. John H. Collier, Commanding General, Fourth Army, and told him of the urgency of getting the excess Guard personnel out, saying that "anything he wants he should ask for and that if he does not have sufficient personnel within his own resources to let us know and the personnel or resources will be shipped in." On information from General Collier that he had just dispatched a message to the Adjutant General recommending "certain short cuts in deprocessing," General Eddleman called The Adjutant General and told him to approve any recommendations Fourth Army made.[197] On the following day, 18 October, after approval of the Secretary

---

197. (FOUO) DCSOPS Journal, item 530. Apparently no message was received from Fourth Army by TWX, but the matter was discussed with TAG by telephone.

of the Army, the text of the Secretary of Defense order was transmitted to Fourth Army and followed by formal official instructions that that headquarters should "take necessary action in coordination with the Chief, US Military District, Arkansas, to process for release from the active service of the United States" the units of the Army National Guard listed in the Secretary's order.[198]

---

198. (FOUO) (1) Msg DA 579624 to CGUSARFOUR, 18 Oct 57. (2) Msg DA 931391 to CGUSARFOUR, 18 Oct 57 (OUO). (3) See also DCSOPS Journal, items 512, 513, 519, 531.

Meanwhile, at the urging of DCSOPS, TAG set out on 17 October to determine the steps prescribed in the draft AR that could be safely eliminated in the interests of speeding out-processing. TAG recommendations were approved by all interested staff agencies except the National Guard Bureau, which protested against the elimination or abbreviation of certain forms pertaining to the establishment of claims for veterans' benefits. Despite the Bureau's objections, the decision was to proceed with the plan for eliminating these steps in the out-processing, and TAG dispatched an authorization to this effect to Fourth Army on 18 October.[199]

---

199. (FOUO) (1) Msg DA 580058 to CGUSARFOUR, 18 Oct 57. (2) MR, Prec & Hist Br, Personnel Div, TAGO, sub: Background of DA 580058, item 19 Prec & Hist Br file on Defed Ark NG. (3) DCSOPS Journal, item 624 contains a convenient summary of steps required in both in-processing and out-pro-

cessing furnished by TAGO. (4) Memo, Brig Gen Bruce Easley, Chf Personnel Div, TAG for Brig Gen F T Pachler, 25 Oct 57, sub: Streamlined Deprocessing of Ark Army NG, contains list of steps omitted. DCSOPS Journal, item 671.

The other questions to be threshed out included whether Governor Faubus was to be officially notified, how the release of the Air National Guard would be handled, and how General Clinger, the Air Guard officer commanding the Army National Guard as State Adjutant General, could be retained. The Secretary of the Army settled the question about notifying Governor Faubus very positively, stating that "the Governor was not in the chain of command and that he did not intend to send any message to the Governor."[200] Fourth Army was instructed to follow the draft of SR 130-22

---

200. (FOUO) MR by Maj Benckart, 18 Oct 57, sub: Briefing for Secretary of Army 1145 hours 18 Oct 57, DCSOPS Journal, item 560.

---

and notify the Adjutant General of the State of Arkansas of the effective date of release for each unit as set by the Secretary of the Army. This raised some question as to who this Adjutant General was since General Clinger and his staff were to be retained in the federal service. It was finally decided that this was no problem since the Governor still had an Adjutant General's Office staffed with some civilians and would have a partially staffed office upon release of the excess National Guard. Accordingly, the State Adjutant General's Office was notified of the release by Headquarters, Arkansas Military District, acting under direction of Fourth Army.[201]

---

201. (1) (C) DA 931391 cited n 198 (2). (2) (FOUO) DCSOPS Journal, items 561, 569, 575.

The release of the Air National Guard and the retention of General Clinger were handled by a single action. In listing the units to be released, the Secretary of Defense Order had included all the Air National Guard units, but since General Clinger was not in any of them, it was decided he constituted a separate case by himself. On 18 October, the Secretary of the Army addressed a memorandum to the Secretary of the Air Force citing the Secretary of Defense order and the fact that General Clinger was specifically exempted from it:

> The effective date of release from active military service for particular units and parts of units and the members thereof will, in accordance with the memtioned order, be determined by me.
>
> It is requested that all Air National Guard units and the members thereof, except Major General Sherman T. Clinger, be processed immediately for release that you furnish me the earliest projected release date for each unit. In accordance with the order of the Secretary of Defense, I will then furnish you the effective date of release for each paricular unit and members thereof.[202]

---

202. (1) Memo, Sec Army for Sec AF, 18 Oct 57, sub: Release of Ark NG Units fm Active Service of the US, DCSOPS Journal, item 550. (2) See also Journal, item 560. (3) (C) AF orders on deprocessing are contained in msg AF-OOP-OC-R 51737 to COMCONAC, 18 Oct 57, DA-IN-63854.

Acting on instructions received and the representations of urgency from the Department of the Army, both Fourth Army and U.S. Army Military District, Arkansas, moved quickly to set up the necessary system for rapid out-processing. For a day or so after issuance of orders to Fourth Army to do the processing there was considerable confusion about the channels of responsibility and reporting. General Walker had at first expected to handle it directly with the Department of the Army with the necessary Fort Chaffee support personnel working under his orders, and he was somewhat surprised by the Department of the Army action assigning responsibility to Fourth Army. Fourth Army assigned the Commanding General, Fort Chaffee, the task of accomplishing the out-processing. In the end misunderstandings were cleared up by a three-cornered coordination among the Department of the Army, Fourth Army, and Arkansas Military District. DCSOPS decided that Fourth Army could still issue orders to General Walker wearing his old hat as Chief of the U.S. Army Military District, Arkansas, while the Department of the Army continued to issue him orders in his role as essentially a task force commander in charge of Operation ARKANSAS. Fourth Army therefore assigned to General Walker responsibility for the out-processing of National Guard personnel to be carried out by the Commanding General, Fort Chaffee. The process worked generally as follows. Under the direction of General Walker, Arkansas National Guard Headquarters made the necessary re-arrangements in personnel and reported to Arkansas Military District when each individual Army National Guard unit was ready for processing. The necessary processing was then carried out by mobile teams working at and out of Fort Chaffee, and General Walker reported to Fourth Army and to DCSOPS when this processing was completed. Fourth Army then made a final report to the Department of the Army of units ready to be released and the Secretary of the Army issued orders prescribing the effective date of release. The personnel were then discharged and Fourth Army reported the action to the Department of the Army. For the Air Guard, the processing was carried out through Air Force channels and readiness reported to the Secretary of the Air Force, who then asked the Secretary of the Army to prescribe effective dates of release.[203]

---

203. (FOUO) (1) Msg OR 2013, CGUSARFOUR to CHUSARMD, ARK, 18 Oct 57, DA-IN-63771. (2) DCSOPS Journal, items 561, 562, 569, 570, 571, 572, 577, 583. (3) Cmd Rpt, 4th US Army, 10 Sep - 30 Nov 57, pp. 10, 14. (4) Cmd Rpt, Hqs, USARMD, Ark, Annex A, App 3, p. 1.

The place of U.S. Army Military District, Arkansas, in this chain of command was maintained mainly to provide a speedier channel of reporting to the Department of the Army of readiness of units for discharge. The actual out-processing work was done by or under the direction of Fort Chaffee personnel, though the plans used were, with certain modifications, those originally drawn up by the Military District staff. The same system that had been used in the abortive in-processing was adopted, that is, the dispatch of mobile processing teams to the eight regional centers around the state. This time, however, the teams were heavily augmented with Fourth Army specialists. On 18 October, 10 officers and 69 enlisted men from Fort Sam Houston, Fort Hood, Fort Sill, and Fort Polk were rushed in to the

Personnel Center at Fort Chaffee to act "as supervisors of National Guard administrative personnel and as working members in the out-processing." On the same day, 42 sedans and 53 drivers arrived at Fort Chaffee to provide round-the-clock transportation for the de-processing teams.[204]

---

204. (FOUO) (1) Cmd Rpt, 4th US Army, 10 Sep - 30 Nov 57, pp. 9-11, 14. (2) Cmd Rpt, Hqs, USARMD, Ark, Annex A, App 3.

On 19 October, the Commanding General of Fort Chaffee dispatched teams to the designated processing areas, assembled unit clerical personnel and records, and commenced outprocessing. To resolve the confused status of in-processing, incomplete steps were simply combined with the modified out-processing steps authorized and the whole administrative procedure completed in one single action. The medical processing was speeded by acceptance of induction physicals for discharge where the individual would sign a statement that there had been no change in his physical condition. The field test of the regulation was cancelled in practice if not by explicit order. U.S. Army Military District, Arkansas, Command Report comments that "If such field testing was conducted, the validity of such a test must certainly be questioned."[205]

---

205. (FOUO) (1) *Ibid*. Quote fm USARMD Cmd Rpt, Annex A, App 3, p. 2. (2) DCSOPS Journal, items 525, 532, 571.

Once under way the administrative out-processing was completed rapidly. On 20 October Fourth Army reported two units ready for release and on the following day four more. These six units were released at midnight CST 21 October. Processing of the remaining units was completed during the next two days, and fifty were released at midnight CST 22 October, the remaining 46 at midnight CST, 23 October. The eleven units of the Air National Guard were all released at the same time, at midnight CST 23 October. Fourth Army reported that a total of 6,114 Army National Guardsmen had been released by the terminal date. Personnel were not released from active duty prior to a completed physical examination or receipt of a medical certificate signed by the individual stating that his condition had not changed. If there was doubt as to physical condition, or if the individual was not available to sign the certificate prior to the release of his unit, the individual was transferred to the 39th Replacement Company for further review and subsequent processing at Fort Chaffee. This created an "administrative hold" of men who were discharged later when processing could be completed. The strength of units available for duty at Little Rock was effectively reduced to 1,800 as of 23 October. However, as late as 30 October, total strength of the Arkansas National Guard on active duty, including the administrative hold, was 2,023. The Alert Force as of that date was made up of the following twelve units plus General Clinger and part of his headquarters staff:

        Hq. and Hqs. Co., 153rd Inf. Regt.
        Hq. and Hqs. Co., 1st Bn., 153rd Inf. Regt.
        Co. C, 153rd Inf. Regt.
        Co. D, 153rd Inf. Regt.
        Hq. and Hqs. Co., 3d Bn., 153rd Inf. Regt.

        Co. K, 153rd Inf. Regt.
        Co. L, 153rd Inf. Regt.
        Svc. Co., 153rd Inf. Regt.
        Med. Co., 153rd Inf. Regt.
        Hq. and Hqs. Det., 738th Ord. Bn. (Inf. Div.)
        Co. B, (Rear), 739th Ord. Bn. (Inf. Div.)
        39th Replacement Co. (Div.)

The use of Fourth Army personnel and the rapidity with which the release of the entire group of units was effected obviated the necessity for holding the pool of clerical personnel as long as had been initially contemplated.[206]

---

206. (1) Sections of Cmd Rpts cited n 204. (C & FOUO) (2) Following Fourth Army messages are pertinent: DA-IN-64077, 64224, 877747, 878108, 878418, 878881, 878869, 879445. (3) Following USARMD messages are pertinent: DA-IN-64076, 64085, 64120, 877330, 877453. (4) Signed authorizations for release by Secretary of the Army are in special file in WHD, ODCOPS. (5) Authorizations by Secretary of the Army to Fourth Army for release are contained in DA 580206, 21 Oct 57, DA 580554, 22 Oct 57, and DA 580986, 23 Oct 57. (6) On the release of the Air National Guard see DA-In-64364, 22 Oct 57, and DA-IN-877453, 21 Oct 57; DCSOPS Journal items 591, 608-11, 599, 614. (7) On the administrative hold see Journal items 612, 634, 649, and Cmd Rpts cited above.

The hasty release of the National Guard units had several repercussions. Governor Faubus at first issued a statement saying he did not know that he would take the National Guard back unless all of them were returned at one time. There was also some doubt about who would be the State Adjutant General as long as General Clinger remained in the federal service. A review of pertinent statutes, however, revealed that the Governor had no legal basis for his stand, and in the end he took the Guard back and appointed General Clinger's Assistant, Lt. Col. William O. Page, as State Adjutant General (as Major General in the state service but not federally recognized as such).[207]

---

207. (FOUO) DCSOPS Journal, items 586, 604, 638, 640, 648, 697, 726.

Meanwhile, there was evidence of dissatisfaction among National Guard officials in Arkansas and even in the National Guard Bureau over the way in which releases had been handled. General Clinger inquired pointedly of General Walker by what "abbreviated process" it had been done, and through Air National Guard channels obtained an Air Force authorization for a visit to the National Guard Bureau in Washington to discuss the matter. The National Guard Bureau reported "grumbling" in the State of Arkansas over the manner in which the Army deprocessed the National Guard units and compared it unfavorably with the manner in which processing of Air Guard units had been handled by the Air Force.[208]

---

208. (FOUO) (1) Ibid., items 614, 617, 626, 640. (2) MR, Lt Col J H Robinson, Prec & Hist Br, Pers Div, TAGO, 24 Oct 57, item 29 in Prec & Hist Br file on Defed Ark NG.

DCSOPS secured the cancellation of General Clinger's visit by strong representations to the National Guard Bureau that it would be impolitic at the time. On 25 October TAG was queried in regard to the criticisms and a message drafted in cooperation with TAG asking Fourth Army to review the deprocessing operation "with a view of uncovering any loopholes or inequities that may have developed in the process," and to obtain officially the views of General Clinger and other State National Guard authorities.[209]

---

209. (FOUO) (1) Memo, Lt Gen C D Eddleman, DCSOPS for CofS, w/addendum thereto, n. d., sub: Proposed Contact w/State Authorities Ark NG and/or Major General Clinger, DCSOPS Journal, items 649-50.. (2) Msg DA 581446 to CGUSARFOUR, 24 Oct 57. (3) MR cited n 208 (2). (4) MRs on subject in Hist & Prec Br, Personnel Div, TAGO, file on Defed Ark NG, item 30. (5) DCSOPS Journal, items 619, 626, 639, 640, 679.

Brig. Gen. Bruce Easley, Chief of the Personnel Division of TAG, assured General Pachler that the abbreviated processing procedures involved no injustice to individual Guardsmen:

> . . . it appears that all administrative steps directed by the Department of the Army were accomplished prior to release from active duty. . . .
>
> no statutory requirement was waived and no step essential to the welfare or entitlement of the individual guardsman was modified. In effect, the forms and steps eliminated were either inappropriate or were niceties which can not be justified in view of costs and the urgency of the deprocessing operation.[210]

---

210. (1) Memo, Gen Easley for Gen Pachler, 25 Oct 57, DCSOPS Journal item 671. (2) For drafting of this memo see MR cited n 203 (2).

Fourth Army's reply was also reassuring:

... It is the opinion of this Headquarters that the release of National Guard members and units was accomplished in a proper manner. ... The processing followed very closely the normal processing through our transfer section. No modifications or exceptions were made other than those directed by Department of Army. All necessary administrative detail, to include medical processing for release, was accomplished prior to release of any member or unit. All administrative details were completed on personnel prior to release of unit. No known loopholes or inequities developed during the process of release.[211]

---

211. Msg CGUSARFOUR to TAG, 31 Oct 57, Adv Copy, DCSOPS Opn ARKANSAS In-Cables, No. 166.

Fourth Army, however, objected to the requirement to consult General Clinger saying it would serve no useful purpose since his views while on duty might be completely contrary to views he might express later when relieved.[212]

---

212. (FOUO) (1) DCSOPS Journal, items 639-40. (2) MRs cited n 209(4). (3).

General Clinger's views were, however, obtained before he was relieved from active duty. They contained both a criticism and a compliment:

a. The crash program was distasteful from an administrative point of view, i.e., mistakes from this rush operation will doubtless show up in individual records for many months to come.

b. The Out-Processing personnel from Fort Chaffee, Arkansas, should be commended for their considerable effort in accomplishing the release of the Arkansas National Guard from active military service.[213]

---

213. Ltr, Maj Gen Sherman T Clinger, USAF, to Maj Gen Edwin A Walker, 18 Nov 57, sub: Arkansas National Guard in Operation "Arkansas", WHD Opn

ARKANSAS File.

The Command Report of the Arkansas National Guard shows a similarly mixed reaction:

> Out-processing was combined with the remaining in-coming processing and placed under the initial guidance of Major Combs, Arkansas Military District, who did a most outstanding job considering the confusion created by piece-meal processing under a guinea pig status created by the issuance of a second /Draft/ AR 130-22. . . .
>
> All processing was reduced where possible to delete those records not considered essential by the Department of the Army. The future results of the reduced administrative processes as to the violations of the rights of the individual, if there should be such, cannot be determined at this time and such violations of rights, if any, must be justified by the Department of the Army.[214]

---

214. (FOUO) Cmd Rpt, Hqs Ark NG, 24 Sep - 30 Oct 57, Pt 1, Annex A, p. 2.

These comments were made later. At the time the whole episode served to bring General Clinger's status once more into the limelight. On 25 October General Walker informed General Wheeler that though General Clinger's Headquarters had been useful in the past and his rank and position appropriate for the command of the National Guard force prior to reduction, the existing size of the force was insufficient to warrant his retention and his headquarters had become an unnecessary link in the chain of command. The feeling in the Department of the Army, however, was that General Clinger should be retained for some time longer. On 26 October, General Wheeler informed General Walker that:

In my opinion, General Clinger should be retained on Federal service for the present. He understands the problem and his rank is appropriate to the importance of the mission. He has informed me that he feels the National Guard can eventually do the job without regular Army assistance. Since this situation may well eventuate, I consider it prudent to retain him in the chain of command.[215]

---

215. (1) (C) Msg DA 931826 to CHUSARMD, ARK, 26 Oct 57. (2) (C) Msg AKMAR 10-184, CGUSARMILDIST ARK to DEPTAR, 25 Oct 57, DA-IN-65458, Excl fm General Walker to Gen Wheeler. (3) (FOUO) DCSOPS Journal, items 617, 626, 639, 640, 652.

This was not the only reason. There was strong feeling in the Department of the Army that General Clinger should put in writing his views on many aspects of Operation ARKANSAS, including the processing for release of the National Guard, while he was still in the active military service of the United States.

Reduction in Operations and the Second Reduction in Force, 23 October - 9 November 1957

While the relief of part of the National Guard was proceeding, operations continued on a routine basis at Central High School. There was an epidemic of flu and school attendance fell drastically. No incidents of note occurred though on 16 October an AWOL U.S. Seaman was apprehended trying to take pictures inside the school and on 18 October there was some excitement when a National Guard officer allegedly searched a white student and confiscated a rubber band and paper clip ammunition. Dispositions of the military guard remained basically unchanged with the Arkansas National Guard responsible for the exterior guard and the airborne battle group for that in the interior of the school. However, from 15 October onward the National Guard also furnished the major portion of the active guard in the interior, 3 officers and 21 enlisted men as opposed to only one officer and nine men furnished by the airborne. The airborne battle group continued to maintain one platoon as an interior reserve in the school basement, a company on 30-minute alert at the Little Rock Reserve Center and part of a company on 60-minute alert at Camp Robinson. The only reduction in the visible effort accomplished during this period was in the escort of the Negro students from their vehicle to the school steps. From 18 October onward this was accomplished by one National Guard officer.[216]

---

216. (FOUO) (1) DCSOPS Journal, items 474, 490, 507, 522, 537, 543, 553, 564, 566, 594. (2) Memo, Maj Gen Earle G Wheeler, Asst DCSOPS, for Col Taylor, OSA, 21 Oct 57, sub: 1st Airborne BG Opns in Little Rock,

DCSOPS Journal, item 590. (3) USARMD Sit Reps, 15-23 Oct 57. (4) Hqs, USARMD, Cmd Rpt, 24 Sep - 30 Nov 57, Annex C, App. 5.

Certain additional troop adjustments were made. The four specialist personnel with their gas dispenser returned to Fort Myer on 21 October, General Walker foreseeing no further need for them. Fourth Army augmentation and support personnel, whose numbers had reached a peak of 44 officers and 310 enlisted men during the crash program to release the National Guard, were also reduced. The additional personnel assigned to Fort Chaffee to assist in the de-processing returned to home station when it was completed. On 29 October one platoon of the 163d Transportation Company returned to Fort Sill. By 29 October, Fourth Army support in staff augmentation and support personnel had fallen to approximately 30 officers and 140 enlisted men. The remaining units were:

> Bath Platoon, 1st Quartermaster Battalion (Fort Polk)
>
> Detachment, 163d Transportation Company (Light Truck) (Fort Sill)
>
> 2d Platoon, 720th Military Police Battalion (Fort Hood)
>
> Detachment, 53d Signal Battalion (Fort Hood)
>
> Detachment, 54th Signal Battalion (Fort Hood)[217]

---

217. (FOUO) (1) Msg AKMAR 10-146, CHUSARMD to DCSOPS, 19 Oct 57, DA-IN-876996. (2) Msg AFOOP-OS-T 34655, HQS USAF to COMTAC, 20 Oct 57, DA-IN-877052. (3) DCSOPS Journal, items 475, 502, 573, 585. (4) Cmd Rpt, 4th US Army, 10 Sep - 30 Nov 57, p. 11. (5) USARMD Sit Rep 35, 23 Oct 57, DA-IN-878953.

This support force and the remaining elements of the Airborne Battle Group (approximately 29 officers and 469 enlisted men) made up a total of 650 regular troops in addition to the 1,800 National Guardsmen in the Alert Force. With cold weather approaching some arrangement had to be made both for winter clothing and adequate quarters. National Guard troops were sent to Fort Chaffee in increments of 200, drew winter clothing and returned to Little Rock. Men of the 1st Airborne Battle Group, 327th Infantry, were flown to Fort Campbell in increments of 85 to secure their winter clothing. The problem of winterizing quarters, however, raised the old vexing question of the status of the state section of Camp Robinson. Both because of this and because of a desire on the part of the Department of the Army to keep rehabilitation costs low, the winterization program conducted at Robinson was largely confined to the installation of heating equipment and minimum necessary repairs in the state section. The Department took the view that Little Rock Air Force Base could be used for about 300 of the airborne troops, though this solution was not entirely satisfactory to either General Walker or Colonel Kuhn.[218]

---

218. (FOUO) (1) Cmd Rpt, USARMD, 24 Sep - 30 Nov 57, Annex D, pp. 3-6; App 1, p. 2 & tabs D & E. (2) USARMD Sit Rep 30, 19 Oct 57, DA-IN-876713; Sit Rep 34, 23 Oct 57, DA-IN-878287. (3) DCSOPS Journal, items 502, 509, 570, 590.

From every standpoint the most desirable solution seemed to be to reduce further the force at Little Rock, working toward the goal of removing first of all the regular troops and then the National Guard. Any sudden removal of all of them at one time seemed clearly ruled out for there was every indication that unless some form of federal protection continued means would be found to remove the Negro students from the school, whether by mob action or subtle pressure. But both General Walker and General Wheeler, who had returned permanently to the Pentagon on 18 October, agreed that the existing force was excessive.

General Wheeler advanced a concrete reduction plan on 23 October. His general concept was:

> Diminish progressively over-all military operations, concurrently decreasing operations of the 1st Airborne Battle Group, 327th Infantry and increasing those of the 153d Infantry Regiment. At an appropriate time, withdraw the bulk of the 1st Airborne Battle Group, 327th Infantry from Little Rock and reduce the number of National Guard troops on active duty.

The first specific steps, General Wheeler said, should be to relocate the bulk of the 1st Airborne Battle Group at Little Rock Air Force Base with the remainder at the Reserve Armory and Camp Robinson and to "progressively turn over all operations to the National Guard." Then the transport and escort of the Negro students to and from the school should be modified with the goal the use of civilian vehicles, but Walker was to be guided by "the fact that it is considered of paramount importance that safety of the Negro students is insured." In similar manner, the escort and interior guard within the school should be progressively reduced. Finally, General Walker was to prepare a plan for reducing the airborne element to a total of 200-225 men and the Arkansas National Guard to 900--500 in the operating force, 200 in the support force, and 200 in the replacement pool. The timing of these operations, Wheeler said, should be carefully considered since each step would be "in fact a test of public attitudes and possible reactions." General Walker was authorized to discuss the program with General Clinger and the Superintendent of Schools, Mr. Blossom, and to seek again the cooperation of the city police.[219]

---

219. (1) (C) Msg DA 931623 to CHUSARMD, 23 Oct 57, General Wheeler to General Walker. (2) (FOUO) DCSOPS Journal, items 598, 603, 605.

On Thursday, 24 October, General Walker began a program to carry out Wheeler's ideas. He eliminated the military escort from the vehicle to the school, reduced the hallway guard from 30 men to 16, (the four officers remained) removed all door guards except for two at the main entrance, and reduced the exterior guard to five two-man details, two one-man details and a three-man motor patrol. On that day for the first time since 2 October, the Negro students walked from the curb to the school building without a single military guard. And within the school, six of the nine agreed to the elimination of their personal escorts.

The participation of the airborne troops was diminished, that of the National Guard increased. The 153rd Infantry, in addition to furnishing the entire exterior guard, now provided 13 of the 16 enlisted hall guards, and placed a platoon in the basement alongside the airborne platoon for orientation in the duties of the interior reserve. In an accompanying move, the rifle company of the 1st Airborne Battle Group at the Reserve Armory was placed on a one-hour alert rather than a thirty-minute one, and the company at Camp Robinson placed on a two-hour alert. The rest of the airborne troops moved to Little Rock Air Force Base where Company E was used as a vehicle for rotating men to Fort Campbell for winter clothing and prescribed jump training.

These moves provoking no incident, on the following day, 25 October, the Negro students came to the school for the first time in civilian vehicles driven by their parents with military surveillance reduced to the operation of a motor patrol along their route. This too worked successfully and soon became a regular routine.[220]

---

220. (FOUO) (1) DCSOPS Journal, items 607, 613, 616, 625, 627, 628, 630, 632, 635, 636, 640, 643. (2) USARMD Sit Rep 35, 23 Oct 57, DA-IN-878953; Sit Rep 36, 24 Oct 57, DA-IN-897578; Sit Rep 37, 25 Oct 57, DA-IN-880303. (3) Cmd Rpt, USARMD, 24 Sep - 30 Nov 57, Annex C, App 5.

General Walker was not, nevertheless, ready to proceed full speed with the reduction plan. He accepted Wheeler's general concept but urged a gradual approach and he thought any relocation of the airborne troops to Little Rock Air Force Base, beyond any increment destined soon to return to Fort Campbell, unnecessary. The airborne strength, he thought too, should be reduced gradually over a four-day period. On 26 October he submitted a plan in response to General Wheeler's instructions, providing for maintenance at Little Rock of one rifle company plus support elements from the 1st Airborne Battle Group, a total of 200-225 men, and a National Guard force of 900-960 organized as follows:

```
One Infantry Battalion Headquarters (Reinforced); includes
      task force                                      150-160
```

Commander; medical section; service section	
Three rifle companies - 155-165	460-490
Support Troops; one company (reinforced)	140-150
Includes Military Police Section; Ordnance Section; Engineer Section; Signal Section	
Replacement pool; 39th Replacement Company	150-160
Includes Headquarters Arkansas National Guard personnel 20-25	
TOTAL	900-960

General Walker thought that "under existing conditions" these forces would suffice for his mission, but that no further reductions would be desirable.[221]

---

221. (C) (1) Msg AKMAR 10-179, CHUSARMD to DCSOPS, Gen Walker to Gen Wheeler, 24 Oct 57, DA-IN-65249. (2) Msg AKMAR 10-191, CHUSARMD to DCSOPS, Gen Walker to Gen Wheeler, 26 Oct 57, DA-IN-65793.

General Walker's cautious attitude was more than matched in the Office of the Secretary of the Army. No action was to be taken on Walker's plan for more than a week. The explanation for this caution, both in Washington and Little Rock, lay in the political situation in the latter city. Little Rock was changing over from a Mayor-Council to a City Manager form of government and elections were scheduled to choose the seven members of the new City Council on Tuesday 5 November. This new City Council was to choose a temporary Mayor from among its members to replace Mayor Woodrow Wilson Mann who, in opposing the change in the city government, had been decisively defeated in an earlier election. The candidates were generally divided into two groups, those sponsored by the Little Rock Good Government League and those supported by the Capital Citizen's Council, a segregationist organization. While the Good Government League candidates were not necessarily in sympathy with the integration program they were generally in favor of order and some degree of cooperation could be hoped for if they were elected. On the other hand, if the segregationist candidates were chosen they might be expected to take a more hostile attitude toward the presence of Negro students in Central High School.

Further, the Chief of Police, Marvin Potts, was planning to retire on 16 November. He was to be temporarily succeeded by his assistant, Eugene Smith, pending the choice of a new Chief of Police by the new City Council. In compliance with his instructions from Washington, reiterated several times, General Walker undertook a new approach to the city police to interest them in taking over the task of preserving order at Central High School. The results he reported on 24 October as follows:

. . . police officials have refused to patrol the interior of the school, to participate in escorting negro children to the school, to patrol the school area other than in their normal city patrolling procedure which is presently five (5) patrol cars for the entire city.

The police officials' refusal to participate jointly with the army is predicated by their admission upon the uncertainty of the outcome of the election of a new city council on 4 Nov, the uncertainties surrounding the selection and designation of a new chief, and limited manpower. . . .

. . . In addition the present Chief of Police, has on several occasions, firmly stated that under no circumstances would he use his force to escort the negro students to and from school or within the school proper. His policy is to provide them the same protection as any other students and no more.[222]

---

222. (C) (1) Msg AKMAR 10-182, CHUSARMD to DCSOPS, Gen Walker to Gen Wheeler, 23 Oct 57, DA-IN-65418. (2) (C) Msg DA 931669 to CHUSARMD ARK, 23 Oct 57, Gen Wheeler to Gen Walker. (3) (FOUO) DCSOPS Journal,

items 618, 625, 628, 630, 640, 646, 647, 667.

Another discouraging note was struck in a USARMD conference with the Central High School authorities. The school officials, Walker reported, accepted the program for reduction, but felt that it should be executed with caution. They pointed out that though the majority of the students would cause no trouble there was a small group who would take every opportunity to discourage the Negro students from attending the school if the airborne troops were withdrawn. This group, Mr. Blossom thought, could be controlled through the school disciplinary program if they were not stimulated by parents and adult anti-integration organizations. The school authorities also pointed out that the attitude of the students toward the National Guard was one of indifference and disrespect, quite in contrast to that toward the paratroopers, and they expressed concern over the possibility of adverse action on the part of the students when the airborne troops were removed.[223]

---

223. (FOUO) (1) Msg AKMAR 10-191, CHUSARMD, ARK to DEPTAR, 25 Oct 57, DA-IN-880413. (2) DCSOPS Journal, item 628.

The only other hope seemed to lie in legal action against specific offenders who had participated in the September disturbances at the school. Some 56 people had been arrested on various charges, but the local police court judge had deferred the cases until the week of 22 November. The Justice Department and the local U.S. District Attorney, Osro Cobb, seemed reluctant to bring any federal cases. The whole situation seemed stalled, as General Walker put it, on "dead center."[224]

---

224. (FOUO) DCSOPS Journal, items 625, 652, 658, 677.

Considering all these factors, the Secretary of the Army on 28 October decided to hold off troop reductions for a time. General Walker, meanwhile, began to push for further reductions in the active guard at Central High School. On 30 October, and again the next day, he suggested to General Pachler that the interior detail might be cut by 30 per cent and two outside patrols eliminated entirely. While the DCOPS, General Eddleman, approved both this plan and General Walker's larger reduction plan, Secretary Brucker decided to defer any action at all until after the Little Rock election.[225]

---

225. (1) (FOUO) Ibid., items 656, 677. (2) (C) Memo, Lt Gen C D Eddleman for CofS, 30 Oct 57, sub: Opns and Reduction of Fces in Little Rock, Ibid., item 688. (3) (FOUO) For USARMD reduction plan see Cmd Rpt, 24 Sep - 30 Nov 57, Annex C, App 5, Tab A.

In that election, on 5 November, the Good Government League candidates won a victory by a narrow margin. Six of the seven men chosen were sponsored by the League, while the seventh was a man who had repudiated Capitol Citizens' Council support. Despite the small margin of victory, on the morning of 6 November, the Secretary decided to move and General Walker was immediately informed that his "recommendations with regard to reductions of troop strength and operations in and around Central High School" were "generally approved." He was to commence phasing back airborne elements to one rifle company reinforced plus support units, and subsequently to phase out National Guard elements in accordance with his plan. Remaining airborne troops would be billeted at Camp Robinson. The Secretary also authorized Walker to reduce guard operations in the interior of the school by approximately 30 per cent and to reduce walking posts outside.[226]

---

226. (1) (FOUO) Memo, Brig Gen F T Pachler for CofS, USA, 6 Nov 57, DCSOPS Journal, item 743. (2) Results of election summarized item 751. (3) (FOUO) See also Journal, items 718, 720. (4) (C) Msg DA 932339 to CHUSARMD, ARK, & CGUSARFOUR, 6 Nov 57.

The second reduction plan was placed into effect expeditiously. On 8 November AF planes returned 175 men to Fort Campbell, and on the following day a land tail of 40 vehicles and 81 personnel departed the Little Rock area. On 10 November there remained in Little Rock a small task force of 11 officers and 219 enlisted men from the 101st Airborne Battle Group, organized as a reinforced rifle company in five platoons of 35 men each and a small headquarters detachment.[227]

---

227. (FOUO) (1) DCSOPS Journal, items 741, 748. (2) Msg AFOOP-OS-T 39062, Hqs USAF to COMTAC, 6 Nov 57, DA-IN-886279. (3) (C) Msg AKMAR 11-26, CHUSARMD, ARK to CGUSARFOUR, 8 Nov 57, DA-IN-69606. (4) Cmd Rpt,

101st Abn Div., 12 Sep - 27 Nov 57, p. 7. (5) Cmd Rept, USARMD, 24 Sep - 30 Nov 57, Annex D, p. 6; Annex C, App 1, p. 7.

Colonel Kuhn, Commanding Officer of the Battle Group, accompanied the troops to their home station. Colonel Kuhn's relief from duty in Little Rock had been held up after the first reduction in airborne strength because of a petition filed in the Federal District Court by a member of the Mothers' League asking an injunction against him and General Walker, and challenging the constitutionality of the federal statutes under which the troops were sent to the area. Department of the Army felt that Colonel Kuhn must remain in the area in case he was compelled to testify. However, Judge Ronald Davies dismissed the suit out of hand on the ground that no substantial constitutional issue was involved. Though the petitioners appealed this decision, it was decided Colonel Kuhn could depart and prepare to take over a new assignment with the Military Advisory Assistance Group in Iran.[228]

---

228. (FOUO) (1) For material on suit see USARMD Cmd Rpt, 24 Sep - 30 Nov 57, Annex H, p. 5 & Apps 7 & 8. (2) DA 932339 cited n 226 (1). (3) DCSOPS Journal, items 536, 555, 729, 730, 739.

Six of the twelve National Guard units were selected for release. This time processing was carried out at Camp Robinson, a team of three officers and 12 enlisted men being dispatched from Fort Chaffee for the purpose. Processing was completed in time to effect the release of two

units at midnight CST 9 November and of the other four at midnight 10
November. On 12 November Fourth Army reported that 848 men had been
released, 498 with the six units returned to state control, 350 as
individuals from the 39th Replacement Company, and that 40 had been
reassigned to Fort Chaffee to be released when medically qualified.
The second reduction in the Guard Force, like the first, was used as
a convenient occasion to release men with hardship claims.[229]

---

229. (1) Sec Def Order transmitted to Fourth US Army by DA 586086,
7 Nov 57. (2) Sec Army Order prescribing effective date of release
transmitted to Fourth Army by DA 586373, 8 Nov 57. (4) Fourth Army report
on readiness is DA-IN-888013, 9 Nov 57. (5) (C) On selection of units by
USARMD see DA-IN-69606, 8 Nov 57. (6) (FOUO) Cmd Rpt, USARMD, Annex C,
App 1, p. 7; Annex A, App 3, p. 2. (7) (FOUO) Cmd Rpt, 4th US Army,
10 Sep - 30 Nov 57, p. 11. (8) (FOUO) Msg 11-0740, CGUSARFOUR to DEPTAR,
12 Nov 57, DA-IN-888591. (9) (FOUO) Cf figures in Sit Rep 54, USARMD,
12 Nov 57, DA-IN-888157.

The other regular army units at Little Rock were also cut back at
approximately the same time. The bath platoon returned to Fort Polk on
8 November. A considerable reduction in the staff augmentation for Headquarters, Arkansas Military District, was also carried out, and on 12
November General Walker reported that remaining TDY strength at that headquarters was 13 officers and 23 enlisted men. By 12 November the total
Fourth Army support force and staff augmentation personnel assigned to

Operation ARKANSAS had been reduced to 16 officers and 117 enlisted men, making a total regular army force especially assigned to Operation ARKANSAS of approximately 366 men, including the remaining airborne task force. The total Arkansas National Guard personnel reported on active duty on 13 November was 895, organized into six units:

    Headquarters and Headquarters Company, 1st Battalion, 153d
        Infantry Regiment
    Company C, 153d Infantry Regiment
    Company D, 153d Infantry Regiment
    Company K, 153d Infantry Regiment
    Company B, 739th Ordnance Battalion
    39th Replacement Company

In addition General Clinger also remained as Commander of the Arkansas National Guard.[230]

---

230. (FOUO) (1) Cmd Rpt, 4th US Army, 10 Sep - 30 Nov 57, pp. 11-12. (2) (C) DA-IN-69606 cited n 226 (3). (3) Msg AKMAR 11-33, CHUSARMD, ARK, to DEPTAR, 11 Nov 57, DA-IN-888150. (4) Msg AKMAR 11-37, 12 Nov 57, DA-IN-888466. (5) DCSOPS Journal, item 780, gives troop strengths for 13 Nov 57. (6) (FOUO) Cmd Rpt, USARMD, 24 Sep - 30 Nov 57, Annex C, App 1, p. 7. (7) (C) Msg AKMAR 11-17, CGUSARMD, ARK, to CGUSARFOUR, 6 Nov 57, DA-IN-68983.

Withdrawal of the Last Airborne Elements, 11-27 November 1957

Meanwhile, General Walker was also carrying out his design for reducing the scope of operations at Central High School. On 6 November he presented a detailed plan to DCSOPS, its essential features being the complete removal of airborne troops from the school and a considerable reduction in Arkansas National Guard operations. The plan was approved and carried out during the following week. On 7 November USARMD cut the hallway guard inside the school from 16 men and four officers to 11 men and one officer and the outside guard to three walking 2-man patrols, a 3-man motor patrol, and a 2-man guard post on the school employees' entrance. On 13 November, the 2-man guard post was eliminated. The individual escort for the three Negro students who had requested it was also discontinued.

On 11 November, Walker relieved the 1st Airborne Battle Group of responsibility for operations in the interior of the school and the reserve platoon of paratroopers was withdrawn from the school basement. One officer and three enlisted men of the battle group remained as liaison in the school for two days longer but on 13 November the last of the paratroopers departed, leaving complete responsibility for operations at Central High School with the Arkansas National Guard. The five platoons of the Airborne Battle Group were placed in reserve, two at Camp Robinson and three at Little Rock Air Force Base. One of the platoons at Camp Robinson stayed on on a constant 30-minute alert to move back to the school if an emergency required it.

As of 13 November, the day the last airborne elements were withdrawn, the National Guard troops at Central were disposed as follows. During school hours, one officer and 11 enlisted men were on duty inside the school with three posts on each of the three floors, one post in the school cafeteria, and another in the band tower. One platoon at reduced strength (2 officers and 25 men) constituted a reserve in the basement. Outside three two-man walking patrols covered the three sides of the school facing 16th, 14th, and Park Streets respectively. A three-man motor patrol in a jeep operated in the area adjacent to the school. A Counterintelligence Corps motor patrol in unmarked cars maintained a general surveillance over the routes which the Negro students traveled to and from the school in private automobiles. At night and on weekends and holidays, the dispositions were approximately the same, except that the motor patrol was eliminated, and no guard posts were manned inside the school though the reserve platoon remained in the basement. In addition to the airborne reserve, a rifle company of the 153d Infantry remained on 60-minute alert at Camp Robinson at all times.[231]

---

231. (1) (C) Msg AKMAR 11-19, CHUSARMD, ARK, to DCSOPS, 6 Nov 57, DA-IN-68982. (2) (FOUO) DCSOPS Journal, items 764, 770, 778, 780, 782, 798, 828, 829. (3) (FOUO) Ark NG, Cmd Rpt, 24 Oct - 30 Nov 57, pp. 5-6. (4) (FOUO) 101st Abn Div, Cmd Rpt, 10 Sep - 1 Dec 57, p. 7. (5) (FOUO) USARMD Cmd Rpt, 24 Oct - 30 Nov 57, Annex C, App. 5, p. 1 & Tab A.

These dispositions remained in force until 24 November when USARMD made further reductions, cutting the interior guard during school hours to one officer and eight enlisted men. And while the reserve in the school basement remained at 2 officers and 25 enlisted men during school hours, at night, on weekends and holidays, it was reduced to one officer and six men. Moreover, a two-man interior patrol and a two-man guard post on the school employees' entrance substituted for the full exterior guard during these hours. The alert forces at Camp Robinson remained the same.[232]

---

232. (FOUO) (1) DCSOPS Journal, item 835. (2) ARK NG, Cmd Rpt, 24 Oct - 30 Nov 57, p. 5.

No incidents of serious enough consequence occurred during November to delay these reductions in the scope of operations. The Arkansas National Guard, in reporting on the month, stated that "several incidents occurred at Central High School in which one or more of the Negro students were involved, none of which were considered of a serious nature."[233] The

---

233. (FOUO) Ark NG Cmd Rpt, 24 Oct - 30 Nov 57, p. 4, Intell. Annex.

---

only one of any import reported to DCSOPS was on 12 November when a white boy struck one of the Negro boys in the locker room and knocked him to his knees. The school authorities took proper disciplinary measures and characterized the case as "nothing to get excited about." There were the usual run of rumors, and on 18 November three of the Negro girls reportedly received telephone calls stating there would be a lynching the following day. But on the whole the situation seemed under control.[234]

234. (FOUO) (1) DCSOPS Journal, items 765, 766, 770, 771, 773, 808, 860. (2) Msg AKMAR 11-41, CHUSARMD, ARK to DEPTAR, 14 Nov 57, DA-IN-889223.

Nevertheless, the old question of how to liquidate the operation and withdraw the Army entirely remained as difficult and troublesome as ever. Governor Faubus' attitude remained unchanged and the newly elected city government seemed as unwilling as the old to take on the entire burden of protecting the Negro students. And there undoubtedly were a sufficient number of dissident or irresponsible individuals inside and outside Central who would seek to compel the Negro students to depart if federal protection were removed. Even before the city elections, General Walker had come to the conclusion that the troops ought to be withdrawn as soon as possible; the development of any practical program for this purpose was, however, a frustrating exercise.

The goal of withdrawal was one to which all responsible military authorities in Washington subscribed, but they had, in every case, to count the costs and keep constantly in mind the fact that no situation could be allowed to develop in which the Negro students would be forced to withdraw by any form of physical violence. The Western Hemisphere Division of DCSOPS prepared a study early in November based on the concept of returning "the responsibility for enforcing the orders of the Federal District Court . . . to the local Federal and city law enforcement agencies," with a military force to be retained at Camp Robinson as a reserve. Under this concept, the National Guard was to be reduced to 250 men by approximately 1 December, the 101st to be replaced by a military police company from Fort Hood (one platoon of the company was already there) approximately 10 December, and if "politically feasible" the balance of the National Guard released around 15 December, leaving the Military Police Company at Camp Robinson as a reserve until such time as the situation seemed sufficiently under the control of law enforcement agencies to permit its removal.[235]

---

235. (FOUO) Draft memo, Dir Opns for Actg DCSOPS, n. d., sub: Proposed Course of Action for Withdrawal of Federal Forces from Little Rock, DCSOPS Journal, item 763.

This approach was never to be used and the bases of the staff study were changed before it was ever presented to the DCSOPS. On 14 November, General Walker recommended that the airborne company be released for return to home station between 21-23 November "in anticipation of the situation continuing as it is or better." He said that the Military Police Platoon he already had would be a sufficient reserve of regular troops, and should it become necessary an additional Military Police Platoon could be readied for movement. There seemed to be no situation, he said, which would justify returning 101st Airborne troops to Little Rock upon release of the company remaining there.[236]

---

236. (1) Msg AKMAR 11-45, CGUSARMD, ARK, to DCSOPS, 14 Nov 57,

DA-IN-889907. (2) See also DCSOPS Journal item 783.

Based on Walker's recommendations and following a conference in General Wheeler's office, Western Hemisphere Division prepared a revised study on 14 November, stipulating that the remaining elements of the 101st should be returned to Fort Campbell on 23 November 1957, that the regular army Military Police Platoon would remain on duty in Little Rock as a reserve, and that the National Guard force should be cut to 450 "at the time of the initiation of the acceptance of responsibility for the mission by the Federal Marshal." The study recommended that the Secretary of the Army initiate a request to the Secretary of Defense that the Attorney General assume responsibility for the enforcement of the court order. A preliminary investigation by the Judge Advocate, attached to the staff study, established the fact that the use of marshals was legal and that a United States Marshal could deputize individuals "without limitation as to numbers." There was, however, one thorny point in the JAG opinion. Once troops had been removed it would require a new Presidential Proclamation and Executive Order to bring them back.[237]

---

237. (1) (C) Draft Memo, Actg DCSOPS for CofS, n. d., sub: Proposed Course of Action for Withdrawal of Federal Forces from Little Rock, Arkansas, DCSOPS Journal item 788. (2) See also Journal items 783, 789, 791.

This study too was abortive. On 15 November, General Wheeler conferred with the Secretary of the Army and the latter suggested a bolder approach. Secretary Brucker wanted to remove all Regular Army elements from Little Rock except General Walker and his headquarters, putting out a press release ahead of time to this effect. Instead of using Federal Marshalls or even maintaining a military police reserve, he wanted to get the local authorities to accept responsibility. The course of action he suggested, Brucker thought, would have the psychological effect of forcing the local authorities to take on a greater portion of the burden of maintaining order. He would follow sometime in December by withdrawing the National Guard. The Secretary, evidently reflecting the opinion of the Justice Department, said that he did not want to use Federal Marshals both because they were untrained for this type work and because using them would still provide federal protection and would not require the local people to stand up and be counted.[238]

---

238. (FOUO) (1) Notes by Maj Coates on Conf w/Gen Wheeler, 1400 15 Nov 57. (2) DCSOPS Journal, items 796, 801, 804.

Western Hemisphere Division, at General Wheeler's request, drew up yet another staff study outlining the advantages and disadvantages of several courses of action and concluded once again that gradual withdrawal of troops and the substitution of Federal Marshals would be best, but the Secretary's decision stood.[239]

239. (FOUO) (1) Draft Staff Study, 16 Nov 57, DCSOPS Journal, item 799. (2) n 238 (1).

The course of action finally determined was to withdraw the regular army units at Little Rock by 27 November, the day before Thanksgiving, except for minimum forces required for support of the National Guard and to issue a press release preceding the withdrawal in accordance with the Secretary's views. Just how and when the National Guard forces would be reduced or withdrawn was left for future decision when the reaction to the withdrawal of the 101st could be determined. The plan thus conformed closely to the pattern of earlier reductions, each of which had provided for a careful test of public reaction in Arkansas before further steps were taken. And the whole process by which it was arrived at emphasized the pitfalls that lay in the way of any course of action that provided for precipitate or complete withdrawal of all military protection for the Negro students at Central High School.

Unfortunately, the information on the withdrawal of the 101st again leaked to the press prematurely on 18 November before the official press release was made and before General Walker had been officially instructed to carry out the withdrawal plan. There was considerable consternation and an intensive investigation was launched to determine the source of the leak. However, after General Walker had hastily secured Mr. Blossom's reaction and learned that he had no objection to withdrawal of the regulars, the Secretary decided to proceed on the course planned.[240] On 20

240. (FOUO) DCSOPS Journal, items 804, 805, 806, 807, 810, 817.

November, Department of the Army instructed General Walker that all elements of the 101st Airborne Division were to be relieved and returned to their home station on 27 November, reverting to the control of the Commanding General, 101st Airborne Division, on departure from Little Rock; that the detachment from the 720th Military Police Battalion was to be returned to Fort Hood on the same date; and that other Fourth Army support units would simultaneously be reduced to the maximum extent possible. Movement of the last elements of the 101st to Fort Campbell was to proceed according to the same plan used in the two earlier reductions, vehicles to move overland loaded to capacity with personnel and the rest of the men with their individual equipment to move by air in planes furnished by Tactical Air Command.[241]

241. (C) Msg DA 932937 to CHUSARMD, ARK and CG, 101st ABN DIV, 20 Nov 57.

The withdrawal was carried out on 26 and 27 November as planned. The overland convoy of the 101st consisting of only three jeeps and two trailers, departed on 26 November; the rest of the airborne troops moved out on 27 November in six C-123 aircraft furnished by Tactical Air Command. Concurrently, the detachment of the 720th Military Police Battalion returned to Fort Hood, the remaining part of the 163d Transportation

Company to Fort Sill, and the rest of the Fourth Army support units and augmentation to Headquarters Arkansas Military District were reduced to a minimum. On 30 November the total of this staff augmentation and support personnel from Fourth Army on duty in Little Rock was ten officers and 18 enlisted men, a reduction from a figure of 16 officers and 117 enlisted men on 12 November. Most of these were signal personnel necessary to maintain the communications system. As an operating force for enforcement of the court order at Central High School there remained 894 officers and men of the Arkansas National Guard.[242]

---

242. (FOUO) (1) DCSOPS Journal, items 818, 819, 826, 850, 852, 855, 856, 858. (2) Cmd Rpt, USARMD, Annex C, App. 1, p. 7. (3) Cmd Rpt, 101st Abn Div, p. 7. (4) Fourth Army, Cmd Rpt, Opn ARKANSAS, 1 Sep - 30 Nov 57, p. 13. (5) DCSOPS Journal, item 863.

The Third Reduction in the National Guard, 27 November - 18 December 1957

The reaction to the withdrawal of regular forces was watched closely in Washington. Secretary Brucker directed a step-up in CIC reporting on the general situation in Little Rock and asked for a daily briefing by the Director of Operations, General Pachler. The whole effort produced little that was new. The situation was generally frozen with Governor Faubus adamanant in his stand that he would not guarantee the Negroes' right to attend Central High School, extremists in Little Rock and elsewhere determined to get the Negro students out of the school, the supporters of Negro rights equally determined to keep them in, and the great mass of citizens of Little Rock apparently in favor of law and order but opposed to integration and unwilling to take the necessary actions to repress the extremists. The neutral attitude of the mass of the citizenry was reflected in the approach of the new city government. On 20 November, General Walker and General Pachler, the latter on an official visit to Little Rock, met with the Acting Mayor and another member of the new City Council and found them not yet ready to take any more positive steps to assume responsibility, though they seemed to appreciate the problem of the military authorities.[243]

---

243. (FOUO) (1) MR, Lt Col R B Crayton, sub: Telecon w/Lt Col G Seignious, 21 Nov 57, DCSOPS Journal, item 824. (2) There is no record in DCSOPS Journal of this conference with the school officials. Information here was gleaned from reference to another contact in memo, Maj Gen Edwin A Walker for Col Reaves, 14 Jan 58, sub: "Operation Arkansas."

Meanwhile, the withdrawal of the airborne troops provoked few incidents, though on 27 November, the day they departed from Little Rock, one Negro girl had a chair shoved into her back by a white student and another was kicked in the leg while coming out of assembly hall. An unidentified student threw a rock at a National Guard soldier. Rumors were rife of a plan fostered by the League of Central High School Mothers to promote a march on the school on Monday, 2 December, the first school day after the Thanksgiving holidays, but it proved to be a false alarm. The Guard troops took special precautions that day, but when no trouble materialized restored the usual routine on 3 December.[244]

---

244. (1) (C) Memo, Asst DCSOPS for CofS, 2 Dec 57, sub: Demonstration by High School Mothers League, Political & S/A Briefing Book, Opn ARKANSAS, WHD, ODCSOPS. (2) (FOUO) DCSOPS Journal, items 860, 862, 866, 867, 868, 869, 870, 872, 873, 874, 875, 876, 879, 880, 881.

The National Guard Command Report summed it up:

There is still a small element of students at Central High School who persist in making an outward show of defiance towards military personnel. This is evidenced by the rock throwing incident and conversation that can be overheard in the building and on the grounds. . . . Apparently this defiance is aimed at any of the military and not just the Arkansas National Guard.[245]

---

245. (FOUO) (1) Hqs, Ark NG, Cmd Rpt, 24 Oct - 30 Nov 57, p. 4, Intell Annex. (2) See also DCSOPS Journal, item 843.

This analysis simply illustrated that the divisions among students in Central High School closely paralleled those among the population in general. In this situation the prospects were that there would continue to be minor incidents as long as the Negro students continued in Central, but the general opinion was that the school authorities could and would keep the situation under control if outside agitation could be curbed. Curbing the outside agitation was another problem. It appeared to be more a threat than a reality as long as federal troops remained on duty, whether it be the airborne or the Arkansas National Guard, but the major question was what would happen when troops were removed. In any case, it seemed reasonably clear that the transition to complete responsibility of the National Guard had been successfully made. The problem was how next to proceed in the general direction of removing all federal forces engaged in enforcing the court order at Little Rock.

For the Army staff as well as for the school authorities a central issue continued to be the extent of Justice Department participation either through the assignment of marshals to protect the Negro students or through active prosecution of individuals who took overt actions in defiance of the court order. On 28 November, Mr. Blossom passed to General Walker, with the request that he pass them on to Sherman Adams, Assistant to the President, several points that the Little Rock School Board wished to make in this regard. These were:

    a. When is the Justice Department going to act in terms of indictment of the fringe groups? (Fringe groups are segregationist organizations such as Citizens Council and High School Mothers League).

        (1) It is the opinion of the board members that the resistance to the integration problem has increased.

(2) They think that the failure of the Justice Department to act has materially strengthened the opposition.

b. The new city government is unable, not necessarily unwilling, to assume their full responsibilities.

c. That information regarding the situation should be secured direct from the Board or through me (Mr. Blossom) and not from outsiders with no responsibility.

d. Under present conditions they think they need continuous use of Federalized National Guard on an indefinite basis and there is no way to foresee when it would be discontinued unless the Justice Department acts.

e. Nothing hurts operations of school more than to have the news media know of troop reductions or changes prior to school officials knowing it.[246]

---

246. (FOUO) Memo for Rcd, Maj G C Viney, 28 Nov 57, sub: Little Rock, Polit & SA Briefing Book.

This message was passed to Secretary Brucker but was not, at least through military channels, passed to Sherman Adams. However, the information contained in it, that the school authorities did not feel that the new city government was ready to take over and that they desired the maintenance of federal troops until such time as the Justice Department took action to prosecute individual violators, had its effect in delaying any further moves to liquidate Operation ARKANSAS. The local U.S. District Attorney, Osro Cobb, apparently doubted that he had sufficient basis for federal action against those who participated in the September riots in Little Rock. The fact that the hearing of the cases in the local Municipal Court produced no stern punishments, in fact practically no punishments at all, made it seem futile to the local police to make arrests. "Veteran police officers feel," a DCSOPS report on 27 November read, "that because of the light sentences in yesterday's trials, agitators will not hesitate to take action against them in future incidents."[247] All in all, the

---

247. (1) (C) Intell. Sum. No 5, 28 Nov 57, Polit & SA Briefing Book. (2) (FOUO) DCSOPS Journal, items 816, 831, 846, 853, 877, 890. (3) Telecon between Gen Walker and Gen Wheeler, 291100 Nov 57, Polit & SA Briefing Book.

---

possibility of removing the last of the military forces in Little Rock seemed as remote in early December as ever.

General Wheeler proposed to proceed by cutting the National Guard to the "irreducible minimum" capable of maintaining law and order in the area while seeking approval once again for the phasing in of Federal Marshals at the appropriate time. Some staff work was done on such a plan.[248] How-

---

248. (FOUO) DCSOPS Journal, item 968.

---

ever, the Secretary of the Army continued opposed to the idea of using marshals and so it once again went into discard. With Mr. Blossom and the School Board insisting that federal protection must be maintained in one form or another, the only possible course seemed to be to proceed along the old line of piece-meal reduction of military force and careful observation of reaction to each move. On 5 December, General Pachler asked General Walker by phone for his recommendations on further reductions.

The following day, G-3, Arkansas Military District, presented a reduction plan, also by telephone, including recommendations on pass and leave policy for the Christmas holidays. General Walker proposed, prior to 18 December, to reduce operations by cutting the strength of the guard inside the school by from 12 to 6, by removing the walking patrols outside the school, and limiting the stationing of guards in the hallways to the periods 0800-0915, 1515-1545, and at lunch hour. He would maintain the reserve in the basement at its current strength of 2 officers and 25 enlisted men. During the Christmas holidays he proposed to remove all troops from the school, leaving the responsibility for the school building in the hands of the school authorities, and to grant Christmas leaves or passes to 70-75 percent of the Arkansas National Guard personnel on active duty. The National Guard could, he said, before Christmas be reduced to an aggregate strength of 435-450, and he presented a reduction plan, worked out by Guard officers, for this purpose. He proposed that the reduction be effected before 20 December, "since Fourth Army personnel who would be engaged in processing units for release will begin to take leave on 20 December 1957."[249]

---

249. (FOUO) (1) Ibid., items 882, 889, 905. (2) (C) Item 909.

The Secretary of the Army, perhaps influenced by Mr. Blossom's views, was reluctant to proceed with another precipitate reduction of the National Guard. He held up approval of General Walker's plan for further decrease in the scope of operations at Central High School and suggested a different plan for "nominal reduction of the strength of the National Guard on active duty prior to 25 December 1957" by releasing "ineffectives" in groups of five to eight at a time with no attendant publicity. He thought the total number to be released under this plan should be on the order of 100 to 200 and directed a survey on a need-to-know basis to determine the feasibility of such a system of release. He indicated that he did not want to "move too quickly" in making further reductions.[250]

---

250. (1) (C) Memo, Dir Opns, ODCSOPS for CofS, USA, n. d., sub: Future Actions Concerning the Mission in Little Rock, Arkansas, DCSOPS Journal, item 909. (2) (FOUO) DCSOPS Journal, items 911, 916. (3) (FOUO) On exploration of problem of releasing small isolated groups see DCSOPS Journal, item 926.

Both General Walker and the military staff in Washington opposed the Secretary's plan. They foresaw that publicity could hardly be avoided and that legal and administrative complications would result since the Secretary of Defense would have to issue separate orders for the release of each small group, unless it was to be considered legal simply to release individuals after transfer to the 39th Replacement Company as had been done with the administrative hold. General Walker, somewhat reluctantly, made the survey but ended with a recommendation that about 465 men be released at one time rather than in small groups. He was particularly opposed to the use of the word "ineffectives," which he said "could cause resentment and result in adverse publicity," suggesting instead the use of the phrase "personnel not necessary to the mission." He did not feel that there could be any meaningful selection of personnel for release on this basis since "there is no known group of personnel in the active service guard who could be classified as ineffective in the sense that they are individuals not capable of efficient performance of duty." General Walker believed that the screening process by which the National Guard had previously been reduced was the only valid and practicable basis for further reduction. The criteria used he defined as follows:

1. Personnel hardship cases including:
   a. Dependency - illness in family where presence and care are required.
   b. Where military pay is insufficient to meet bills and family requirements.
2. Seasonal occupation requirements such as Christmas season, business, harvest, etc., require individual presence.
3. Occupational hardship where the job or position is in jeopardy due to absence, example, a company hires replacement and reassigns individual to another area.
4. Where a critical requirement exists by employees in federal, state, or city agencies.
5. Retain personnel in MOS's required in organization to perform the mission.
6. Political interests and effects.
7. Considering all the above, release the lesser qualified in any specialty and retain the better qualified.
8. Considering all the above the individual's desire affects his thinking and ability to do the job.[251]

---

251. (FOUO) DCSOPS Journal, item 919, M/R on Little Rock Telecon, 8 Dec 57.

General Walker's arguments were persuasive and the Secretary finally accepted his plan to reduce Guard strength by 50 percent at one time "in principle." He also approved the 70-75 percent Christmas leave policy for the National Guard, with the proviso that strength for duty be in camp by 0001, 2 January 1958. With regard to reduction in the scope of operations, his approval was less positive:

> The employment of troops at Central High School can be gradually reduced. However, the entire program is not to be implemented until after 2 January. In addition, no reduction in outside patrols is authorized. Also, the surveillance inside the school is to be continued even though a reduction in numbers is authorized. In effect, this decision delays any drastic reduction or change in the school until after 2 January.

These decisions were made about 9 December with implementation to be held until the Secretary of the Army gave the word.[252] It was clear from

---

252. (C) Memo, Dir Opns, ODCSOPS for CofS, USA, n.d., sub: Future Actions Concerning the Mission in Little Rock, DCSOPS Journal, item 909. This memo is undated in Journal. The date can probably be established as 9 December from a telephone conversation between General Pachler and General Walker on that day in which General Pachler stated that "there is no question on your big plan." DCSOPS Journal, item 920. Moreover, there was no further discussion of the problem of "ineffectives" after that date.

---

their nature that the "bold approach" urged in November had given way once again to a most cautious one.

The Secretary held up final approval for the reduction of the Guard for several days, apparently because of some uncertainty about the reaction of Mr. Blossom, then absent from Little Rock on a visit to Washington and New York. He finally agreed to dispatch of orders for the reduction on 13 December. Instructions to General Walker on that date stipulated the National Guard on active duty should be reduced to approximately 430 prior to 18 December 1957, and approved his plan for the organization of the units to be retained. Fourth Army was instructed to carry out the processing of

Guard personnel to be released following the now routine procedures. On the same date, the 70-75 percent Christmas pass and leave policy was given formal official approval.[253]

---

253. (FOUO) (1) DCSOPS Journal, items 939, 942, 943, 944, 945, 960, 962, (2) MR on Telecon between Gen Walker & Gen Pachler, 031756 Dec 57; MR on telecon Gen Walker and Gen Pachler, 041201 Dec 57, Polit & SA Briefing Book. (3) DA 933976 to CGUSARFOUR, 13 Dec 57. (4) (C) DA 933977 to CHUSARMD, ARK, 13 Dec 57. (5) (C) DA 933987 to CHUSARMD, ARK, 13 Dec 57.

The effective date of release for four of the six remaining units of the Arkansas National Guard on active duty was set at midnight CST, 18 December, and the release was carried out smoothly. On that date U.S. Military District, Arkansas, reported that a total of 404 men had been released either in the designated units or as individuals and that 21 men remained in the administrative hold at Camp Chaffee. There remained on active duty at Little Rock only two units, Company D of the 153d Infantry Regiment organized into five platoons, and the 39th Replacement Company in which was included the Task Force Headquarters, the Replacement Pool, an ordnance section, and a medical one. The total personnel remaining in the Alert Force was 435.[254]

---

254. (FOUO) (1) Copy of Sec Def Order, 13 Dec 57, DCSOPS Journal, item 967. (2) Sec Army Order setting effective date in Special WHD, ODCSOPS File of these Orders pertaining to release of Ark NG. (3) DA

934060 to CGUSARFOUR, 16 Dec 57, sets effective date of release of units. (4) Msg 12-1109, CGUSARFOUR to CHUSARMD, ARK, 13 Dec 57, DA-IN-604848. (5) Msg 12-1196, CGUSARFOUR to CHUSARMD, (6) Msg AKMAR 12-41, CHUSARMD, ARK, to CGUSARFOUR, 17 Dec 57, DA-IN-606285. (7) Msg 12-1515, CGUSARFOUR to DCSOPS, 19 Dec 57, DA-IN-607921. (8) USARMD Sit Rep 91, 18 Dec 57, DA-IN-607176. (9) DCSOPS Journal, items 909, 951, 955, 958, 993.

While the guard was being reduced, operations at the school continued on the same pattern as they had since 24 November and without major incidents. Of some significance, however, were reports that the school Board was considering petitioning the Federal Court to allow removal of the Negro students because they were unable to adjust to the school environment. It was established that at least three of the students were somewhat "incompatible." Headquarters, Arkansas National Guard reported bluntly that

>   Most of the incidents that have occurred at Central High School have involved the same three (3) colored students. Indications are that these three (3) students, to a large extent, responsible for these incidents as a direct result of their own antagonistic attitudes.[255]

---

255. (FOUO) (1) Hqs ARK NG, Cmd Rpt, 24 Oct - 30 Nov 57, p. 4, Intell Annex. (2) DCSOPS Journal, items 944, 954, 960.

Even if there was some bias in the Guard report, some substantiation of it was given on 17 December when one of the "incompatibles" spilled some chili on two white students in the school cafeteria and was suspended from school.[256] The question of the "incompatibles" and whether indeed the school

256. (FOUO) DCSOPS Journal, items 975, 976, 981, 982, 987, 989, 992.

authorities might try to rule all nine Negro students incompatible at the end of the first semester and remove them added another element of uncertainty to the entire situation as Central High School closed for the Christmas holidays on 18 December, not to re-open until 2 January.

The only further step toward reduction taken before Christmas was a decision that during the holidays the military guard would be entirely withdrawn and the security of the school building entrusted to city police and special school guards. This step was significant in two ways. First, it could possibly establish a pattern whereby the military force would eventually give up responsibility for building security, something the National Guard Headquarters had recommended on several occasions. Second, during discussions held in December with local school authorities, it had been seriously suggested that the City School Board might hire civilian guards to replace the troops, and the use of such special guards constituted a step in this direction. Further development of any plan for reducing the scope of operations, or for removing the troops, remained in abeyance, however, pending the resumption of school after the New Year.[257]

257. (FOUO) (1) Ibid., items 971, 972, 973, 991, 994, 999, 1006. (2) Hqs, Ark NG, Cmd Rpt, 24 Oct - 30 Nov 57, p. 5.

The Release of General Clinger

From 25 October 1957, when General Walker indicated he had no further need for the services of General Clinger, formerly Arkansas State Adjutant General and commander of the Arkansas National Guard, until early January 1958, his relief remained an unsettled issue. At that time, General Wheeler had indicated that General Clinger ought to be retained because of his understanding of the problem and the fact that his rank was appropriate should the National Guard be called on to carry out the mission at Little Rock without regular army assistance. Since Colonel Page, General Clinger's former assistant, had been made a temporary major general and designated as State Adjutant General by Governor Faubus, there was some concern that General Clinger's position with the state authorities might be undermined in his absence and that he might not get his old job back. At the time Colonel Page was appointed, Secretary Brucker indicated to the National Guard Bureau that he did not desire that General Clinger be hurt in his status in Arkansas by remaining on active duty during the Little Rock situation. As a result, the National Guard Bureau apparently followed the situation in the Arkansas National Guard closely to detect any indications that General Clinger might lose his position.[258]

---

258. (FOUO) Memo, Maj Gen Winston P Wilson, Chf Air Force Div, NGB, for Sec Army, 7 Jan 58, sub: Adjutant General, State of Arkansas, DCSOPS Journal, item 1075.

At the time of the second reduction in the National Guard Alert Force in early November the question of relieving General Clinger was revived, and General Walker again indicated that the size of the remaining Guard forces did not justify Clinger's continuation on duty. Generals Pachler and Wheeler agreed, and prepared a memorandum for the Chief of Staff recommending the General's release as soon as practicable "with the exact date to be determined by Chief, US Army Military District, Arkansas." But the memorandum was never sent, though its contents were discussed with General Taylor.[259]

---

259. (FOUO) (1) Draft memo, Asst DCSOPS for CofS, USA, n.d., sub: Cmd Structure, Ark NG in Fedl Service, DCSOPS Journal, item 777. Note initialled by Gen Wheeler says "Do not forward. Has been discussed w/CSA." (2) DCSOPS Journal, items 732, 747, 757, 764, 770, 774.

The Secretary of the Army, meanwhile, indicated that he wanted to provide General Clinger adequate opportunity to express himself in an official report before his release. Accordingly, on 14 November 1957, General Walker asked Clinger for a "personal statement" of his views on the operation by 18 November, indicating that he wanted them for use in a military analysis to determine how it might have been improved.[260]

---

260. (1) (C) Ltr, Gen Walker to Gen Clinger, 14 Nov 57, Incl 1 to memo DCSOPS for CofS, USA, 26 Nov 57, in WHD Files on Opn ARKANSAS. (2) (C) Msg AKMAR 11-39, CHUSARMD, ARK to DEPTAR, 12 Nov 57. (3) (C) Msg

DA 932675 to CHUSARMD, ARK, 14 Nov 57. (4) (FOUO) DCSOPS Journal, items 772, 775, 776, 777, 779.

General Clinger's reply, dated 18 November 1957, commenced:

I do not believe that it would be fitting for me, while still on active duty, to comment on the political implications of this operation. However, it seems highly probable that such considerations did have a decided bearing on the method of employment of the Arkansas National Guard. In no other way can I explain, to my own satisfaction at least, the many departures from the normal principles of operation.

General Clinger then went on to cite certain of these departures and to make some obvious criticisms of the operation insofar as it affected the National Guard. Mostly they centered on the crash programs employed both in the Call and the release of the Guard, the use of excess personnel, and the retention of control in Department of the Army "of the most minute decisions." He also thought that General Walker should have included National Guard officers on his staff and that the "mission assigned to troops to protect school property during the hours when school was not in session should have been . . . the responsibility of the school board." Perhaps his most telling criticism was on the point of excessive force: "All units of the Arkansas National Guard were called into active federal service though it should have been apparent that only a small percentage of that number would be needed. . . . Troop missions assigned were at no time considered to be beyond the capabilities of the alert force assembled at Camp Robinson." In citing the lack of an alert period during the Call he also noted: "It would seem that time was not a critical item, since elements of the 101st Airborne Division were already en route to Little Rock by air."[261]

261. (FOUO) Ltr, Gen Clinger to Gen Walker, 18 Nov 57, sub: Ark NG in Opn "Arkansas", Incl 2 to memo, DCSOPS for CofS, USA, 26 Nov 57, WHD files on Opn ARKANSAS.

DCSOPS forwarded General Clinger's letter to the Chief of Staff on 26 November, noting that it contained only "mild objective criticisms," and recommended that he be released from active duty.[262] But no action

262. (FOUO) Memo, DCSOPS for CofS, USA, 26 Nov 57, sub: Ltr Rpt from Maj Gen Sherman T Clinger, Ark NG, WHD Files on Opn ARKANSAS. Memo and comments also in DCSOPS Journal, items 838, 841, 847, 864.

was taken for more than a month. The Air Force pointedly suggested General Clinger's release on 27 November, citing the fact that no other Air Guardsmen remained on duty, but no action was taken on this request either. When the third reduction of the National Guard took place, General Walker again recommended the release of General Clinger but to no avail.[263] The situation continued in status quo until 7 January when Maj.

263. DCSOPS Journal, items 861, 1001, 1027, 1041.

Gen. Winston P. Wilson, Chief, Air Force Division of the National Guard Bureau, informed the Secretary of the Army that he had been advised that "certain developments are taking place in the State which will eliminate General Clinger from his position as Adjutant General of the State of

Arkansas if he is not released from active duty." General Wilson went on to say that he had been further advised that General Clinger would probably be retained as Adjutant General if he could be released in the next ten days. This information seems to have been the final spark that touched off the long delayed action to release General Clinger. That release was effected by the usual chain of orders pertaining to the relief of National Guard units and individuals on 8 January 1958 with the release effective midnight CST on that date. On his release, Governor Faubus restored him to his position as Adjutant General of the State of Arkansas, and Colonel Alton Balkman was designated as commander of the remaining task force of the Arkansas National Guard.[264]

---

264. (1) DCSOPS Journal, item 1075, 1056-57, 1060-64, 1066-67, 1069, 1072. (2) Msg DA 302550 to CGUSARFOUR, 8 Jan 57.

Phase Out Plans, School Incidents and Dynamite Scares, January 1958

The Christmas holiday period passed quietly in Little Rock. The city police and special school guards, most of whom were themselves off-duty policemen, encountered no difficulties in guarding the school property. General Walker spent the holidays in Texas, and his Chief of Staff exercised command in his absence. Before leaving for Texas, General Walker expressed some impatience with the delays in the further reductions in guard operations which he hoped would be the prelude to phasing the military out of the situation. The particular point at issue was the question of permanently removing the military guard at night, on weekends, and on holidays. General Walker thought that this guard should not return after the holidays but was informed by General Pachler that the Secretary of the Army wanted to maintain the status quo for at least a few days after the beginning of the New Year. This was quite possibly because of concern expressed by Mr. Blossom over what might happen on the re-opening of school and again on 20 January 1958 when the second semester began. Arkansas Military District officers felt there was "no intelligence information to substantiate Mr. Blossom's concern" and that the School Superintendent should not be allowed to influence Army policy, that if he had his way the troops would remain at Central indefinitely.[265]

---

265. (FOUO) DCSOPS Journal, items 999, 1001, 1003, 1004, 1006.

This feeling typified the growing sense of frustration that Army officers concerned with Operation ARKANSAS, both in Little Rock and in the Pentagon, were feeling. General Walker's belief that the Army had done its job and now should be relieved was shared by all concerned. Yet there seemed no way to remove the troops and still assure that the purpose of the whole exercise, the assurance of the right of the nine Negro students to attend Central High School peaceably, could be carried out. There appeared to be no new move in the offing by either the federal or local law enforcement agencies to take over the burden the Army was carrying. In a press interview on 27 December, the newly appointed Attorney General, Mr. Warren P. Rogers, had "no comment" about the possibility of troops being removed from Central High School and said that the Justice Department had not even considered sending Federal Marshals to Little Rock. On 27 December 1957 the Fifth Circuit Court of Appeals at New Orleans reversed the decision of a lower court ordering the schools in Dallas, Texas, to integrate at mid-semester and granted the school authorities there more time. If this ruling had no application to Little Rock, it clearly raised some speculation as to whether the same ruling might have been applied there, and created some resentment that may have played a part in making the new city government reluctant to move any further toward taking over responsibility for enforcing a federal court order. A Special School Board Committee was set up to study the decision.[266]

266. (FOUO) Ibid., items 1005a, 1015, 1034, 1042.

At 0700, Thursday, 2 January, the military guard resumed its posts at Central High School in exactly the same pattern that had been followed since

217

24 November. A small crowd (estimated at 11 women and 5 men) stood across the street when the eight Negro students arrived (one girl was still suspended for the chili spilling incident), but they apparently came simply to satisfy themselves that the military guard was back on duty, and soon dispersed.[267] Shortly after 1000 CST, an anonymous call was received on the

---

267. (FOUO) Ibid., 1017-1020, 1022-25, 1028, 1039.

---

school switchboard saying that a bomb had been placed in the school set to go off at 1015 CST and "they had to get the people out. . ."[268] Mr. Blossom

---

268. (FOUO) Ibid., item 1026.

---

called General Walker and after consultation decided to continue school as usual. The bomb scare proved to be a false alarm, the first of a long series of such scares that soon began to assume a rather definite pattern of harassment.[269]

---

269. (FOUO) Ibid., items 1026, 1028.

This pattern did not show clearly for another two weeks. On 2 January, none of the incidents was considered serious and it was judged that Mr. Blossom's first danger date had been passed safely. During the day, Arkansas Military District presented to DCSOPS its plan for a gradual phase-out of the active guard at the high school and its removal to Camp

Robinson as a reserve. There were six steps in the proposed plan:

a. Remove and discontinue the use of troop guard at night at Central High School.

Explanation: This can be done and is recommended immediately. There has been no troop guard on the school during the past holiday nights. There is no difference in the situation on those nights from any other nights. School employees can perform watchman duties. Should they need assistance they have an arrangement with the city police for support. Troop support would assist where warranted.

b. Reduction of three two-man patrols around school.

Explanation: Substituting a relay of jeep motor patrols in the area assuming responsibility as the two-man patrols are reduced -- this over a two to five day period. The procedure visualized reducing two man patrols to a point where a patrol may be coming out of the basement and walking around the school two or three times at odd intervals while a jeep patrol is in the area surveying the school when the other patrol is not visible.

c. Gradually removing hall guards and reducing them to four men.

Explanation: This visualizes the guard being visible at certain periods in the hallways to include beginning of school, lunch period, and end of school. At other times the guard would be in a reserve status in a school office on call and it is hoped in time in the basement on call. It is further anticipated that while the time of visibility is reduced the number of guardsmen is also reduced by four to six men.

d. Reduce the present reserve in the basement until it is finally removed to a new location at Camp Robinson.

Explanation: This visualizes reduction of present reserve to approximately 20 men gradually in phase with reducing inside and outside the school. It anticipates the present interior guard of the school becoming the reserve and the jeep patrols outside the school keeping the school under surveillance from the outside either being able to call on the other where necessary.

e. Withdraw the last reserve and all troops inside the school maintaining a reserve at Camp Robinson.

Explanation: This anticipates all troops being removed from inside the school and from the school grounds proper -- surveillance being carried on by the jeep patrols as previously established in the school area.

f. Withdrawal of all troops to Camp Robinson as a reserve.

Explanation: This anticipates the removal of surveillance by jeep from the school area and leaving it up to the school administration to call for any assistance desired. At this time a reserve platoon could be moved to the reserve center each day in order to be more quickly available -- should it be deemed necessary at that time.

The Military District proposed no time schedule beyond proposing that the first step be taken immediately.

The intricacies and relationships of the above steps . . . and the timing of their becoming public information makes a time schedule impossible or useless. It certainly would not appear that the above could be accomplished in less than two or three weeks and there is nothing definite at this time that assures the final point could be accomplished at Little Rock at any foreseeable designated time. However, without such efforts this particular time may never be brought closer unless it is by actions beyond military control.[270]

---

270. (FOUO) Ltr, Hqs USARMD, Ark, to DCSOPS, 2 Jan 58, sub: Recdns for Reduction in Strength at CHS, in papers filed with DCSOPS Journal. The plan was first sent in by telephone on 2 Jan 58.

Both DCSOPS and the Secretary of the Army studied the implications of these steps and on 3 January, the Department of the Army informed General Walker that:

Steps No. 1 through No. 4 are approved in principle. Implementation does not have to be consecutive but this HQ will be notified at least 48 hours in advance of implementation of each step. Notification will include a statement as to whether or not the contemplated action has been coordinated with school and local authorities.

It is desired that you submit recommendations concerning Steps 5 and 6 after effect of implementing the first four steps has been determined. Recommendations should include your views on the timing of these steps and the conditions under which they should be implemented.[271]

271. (1) (C) Msg DA 934784 to CHUSARMD, 3 Jan 57. (2) (FOUO) Papers on reduction plan filed with DCSOPS Journal.

Military guard on the night and weekend scale remained at Central High School on Saturday and Sunday, 4 and 5 January 1958, but on Friday, 3 January, General Walker informed DCSOPS that he wanted to implement step one and remove these guards on the night of Monday 6 January. He was authorized to proceed subject to two conditions: first, that proper authorities, including the police, take responsibility; and second, that a small alert force be kept at Camp Robinson for emergency purposes. General Walker accepted these conditions and the night guard was removed on schedule. School authorities took full responsibility for the security of the school during the night and weekends, establishing a civilian guard with two reliefs of three men each, manned by two night watchmen who had been in the employ of the school for years, supplemented by off-duty policemen hired as special guards. One rifle platoon of the task force of the 153d Infantry remained on 30-minute alert at Camp Robinson during these periods and two platoons on 60-minute alert.[272]

272. (FOUO) DCSOPS Journal, items 1027, 1037, 1041, 1044, 1046, 1049, 1050, 1052, 1070.

There were no immediate repercussions to the implementation of step one, and on 8 January General Walker notified the Department of the Army that he intended to start implementing step two on 10 January. There was no objections, and accordingly on the designated date the regular three-man patrols were discontinued and one two-man dismounted patrol and the two jeep patrols substituted for them. The dismounted patrol covered the area at irregular intervals; the two jeep patrols ranged over an area within two blocks of the school during periods when the Negro students were traveling to and from school and watched for gatherings or other possible troubles.[273]

---

273. (FOUO) (1) Ibid., items 1053-55, 1087. (2) Troop Dispositions, 17 Jan 57, Gen Theimer Book, WHD Files, Opn ARKANSAS.

At this point the reduction plan again stalled. As the end of the first semester approached, there was a renewed outbreak of incidents at Central High School, none of them serious in themselves, but reflecting in their entirety a possible new effort to nullify the effects of the federal court order. Whether these incidents were simply the spontaneous and sporadic action of individuals or whether they were part of some plan concocted by an organized group, the Army could only conjecture. There was at least a peculiar coincidence between their occurrence and other efforts by segregationist organizations and by Governor Faubus to keep public attention centered on the continued presence of federal troops at Little Rock. This public attention had declined rapidly after the launching of the Russian Sputnik claimed the headlines of the nation's press. The absence of incidents at Central High School and the withdrawal of regular troops in late November led many people to believe that the Little

Rock Incident had been closed. Congress gave it little attention after convening for the 1958 session, and the hearing on the confirmation of Mr. Warren P. Rogers as Attorney General on 23 January before the Senate Judiciary Committee passed without any reference to the use of federal troops at Little Rock. To Governor Faubus and to the segregationist leaders in the South, Little Rock remained very much alive. As early as 30 December the Governor announced he might provide "new thought on the integration problem" in a speech to be delivered in Little Rock before the Independent Magazine Wholesalers of the South on 18 January. And on the night of 14 January, the Capital Citizens' Council of Little Rock was the scene of a series of talks delivered by segregationist leaders from other southern states - Roy V. Harris of Augusta, Georgia, editor and publisher of the Augusta Courier; Robert P. Patterson, Executive Secretary of the Citizens' Council of Mississippi; and John U. Barr of Louisiana. In general these men criticized President Eisenhower and the federal courts, praised Governor Faubus, and encouraged the citizens of Little Rock to continue their resistance to integration in their public schools.[274]

---

274. (FOUO) DCSOPS Journal, items 1016, 1092.

It was in this atmosphere that the new series of incidents took place. The first occurred on 10 January when a white girl pushed a Negro girl in the hallway. The school authorities suspended the white girl from school. Her parents demanded a hearing before the School Board. This hearing, closed to the public, was held on 22 January, at which time the School Board decided the girl could return to school on 27 January.[275]

---

275. (FOUO) Ibid., items 1076, 1094, 1127, 1137.

On 15 January, eight or ten girls appeared at the school dressed in black dresses adorned with stickers depicting soldiers with bayonets at the backs of two girls and bearing the caption "Remember Little Rock." General Walker called DCSOPS around mid-day and warned that he thought he perceived a "general trend" toward an effort to aggravate the situation. He said he believed that the Capital Citizens' Council and the Mothers' League were endeavouring to organize a group within the school to continue to cause incidents. Though he indicated that he did not believe that the threat of increasing incidents was due to reduction of troops,[276] it is quite apparent

---

276. (FOUO) Ibid., items 1091, 1095.

---

that with this pattern developing he had necessarily to delay any implementation of step three of the reduction plan.

The trend predicted by General Walker began to show itself the next day, 16 January. A white male student who was apparently about to be suspended for academic failure dumped a bowl of soup on a Negro girl, allegedly because she had called him "poor white trash" the day before. He was suspended though apparently for academic reasons rather than because of the soup spilling incident. He was allowed to return to school on Monday, 27 January.[277]

277. (1) (FOUO) Ibid., item 1099. (2) Arkansas Gazette, 17 Jan 58.

In the evening, following the soup spilling incident, the first of a series of bomb scares occurred. At 1645 CST, Mr. Blossom appeared at General Walker's Headquarters and told him that Marcus George of the Arkansas Democrat had received a long distance call from Atlanta, Georgia, advising him that something serious, "similar to what happened at Nashville prior to the opening of schools," would happen at Little Rock Central High School at 2200 hours. The man purported to be someone who worked in the office of the Governor of Georgia. Mr. Blossom told General Walker he would take full responsibility for the protection of the school and would put his own guards and city police on it but requested additional assistance from the Army. At approximately the same time, the city police, newspapers and radio stations received calls from excited women alleging that someone from out of town was going to blow up the school. The city police responded with alacrity and the alert platoon was dispatched from Camp Robinson to aid in the search of the school property. They found nothing, and a check on the purported identity of the caller from Georgia revealed no such person in the Georgia Governor's office. A further indication that the whole thing was a hoax, deliberately perpetrated to provoke a military reaction, was the fact that the local radio announced the dispatch of troops to Central High School one hour before General Walker issued any orders for the move.[278]

278. (FOUO) (1) DCSOPS Journal, items 1100, 1109. (2) USARMD Sit Rep 108, 17 Jan 57, DA-IN-621575.

January 16 was the last regular attendance day of the first semester at Central High School. The following day the interior guard patrolled the school despite the absence of regular classes. When school re-opened for the second semester on 20 January, other bomb scares and other incidents followed in rapid succession. On 20 January a local radio announcer informed the FBI he had received an anonymous call stating there were two sticks of dynamite in a locker in the school basement. City police conducted a search and found one stick of dynamite, uncapped. On 21 January, school authorities reported another anonymous telephone call on the school switchboard stating that another stick of dynamite had been placed in the school and that the stick was capped. School custodial personnel undertook an immediate search and found this too to be a hoax. A similar anonymous call on 23 January resulted in another search; this time a package of firecrackers was found in a locker with a cigarette attached, presumably as a device for firing them. The cigarette had been lit, but the fire had gone out before reaching the fuze. Later in the day one of the guards found and extinguished a small fire buring in a locker. On the last day of the week, Friday, 24 January, there was another anonymous call and another fruitless search.[279]

279. (FOUO) (1) DCSOPS Journal, items 1111, 1113-19, 1121, 1128-29,

226

1135-36. Summary of incidents of this period, items 1131-32. (2) USARMD Sit Rep 111, 20 Jan 57, DA-IN-622480; Sit Rep 112, 21 Jan 57, DA-IN-623211; Sit Rep 114, 23 Jan 57, DA-IN-624564; Sit Rep 115, 24 Jan 57, DA-IN-625349.

Concurrently, the harassment of the Negro pupils increased. Available evidence indicates that they were completely isolated within the school and that because of pressure from student segregationists even white students who were inclined toward friendliness did not dare to associate with them. The increased harassment, therefore, appeared to be another step in a concerted campaign to force them from the high school. On 20 January a Negro student reported he had been struck in the mouth by a white boy whom he identified by name and indicated that another white boy was also involved. The school authorities investigated but took no action. Then on 27 January, the beginning of the second week of the new semester, a white boy was observed by a National Guardsman to be walking behind a Negro girl making derogatory and obscene remarks. The guard instructed the boy to accompany him to the Principal's office, but was refused. The guard was joined by the Sergeant of the Guard and one of the other guards who, happening by, noticed a disturbance. The boy then threw his books on the floor and dared any of the guards to lay a hand on him. None did. The Sergeant went to the school office, and the Assistant Principal took the boy into custody. However, school authorities took no disciplinary action on assurances from the boy's father that he would take care of the boy for he had an excellent academic record.[280]

280. (FOUO) (1) DCSOPS Journal, items 1116, 1138. (2) Sit Rep 118, USARMD, 27 Jan 57, DA-IN-626360.

Three days later, on 30 January, an even more serious incident occurred when a white student already suspended for academic reasons, kicked the Negro girl who had been insulted three days before and apparently made an effort to use a jack knife on her. The incident was reported by General Walker as follows:

> Sergeant Roy D. Blackwood had witnessed incident from his usual vantage point, a second story window, overlooking the entrance to the school. After school he noticed a crowd of boys and girls, which is not normal these days, and he felt something was wrong or would happen . . . (a white student earlier suspended for academic reasons) followed 5 colored girls to their car. He had a pocket knife in his hand which was not open. A teacher, Mrs. Brandon, had observed . . . /his/ actions and grabbed the boy before he could open his knife (which he attempted to do). Mr. Powell, principal for boys, also grabbed the boy and took knife away . . ./the boy/ had kicked the girl . . . several times during the fracas.
>
> Sergeant Blackwood ran down from the second floor and took 2 soldiers with him. When they arrived at the scene Mr. Powell and Mrs. Brandon had boy under control, and military help was not needed. . . .[281]

281. (FOUO) DCSOPS Journal, item 1148.

There seemed to be grounds for criminal prosecution against the boy, but on the following day the Pulaski County Prosecuting Attorney decided against taking any legal action despite the urging of the girl's mother.[282]

282. (FOUO) DCSOPS Journal, items 1154, 1165.

On 31 January three white boys were apprehended starting a fire in a trash basket in one of the school hallways. When questioned they also admitted starting the fire in the basement locker the previous week and explained that both were in fire-proof areas and that they had started both fires only to add smoke to the excitement and confusion in the school. The City Fire Marshal, like the County Prosecutor, was lenient on this youthful exuberance, according to a report submitted to DCSOPS:

. . . Captain Throckmorton, City Fire Marshal, informed the boys in the presence of Mr. Matthews that he would not submit charges against them. This was based on the fact that all three of the boys have excellent academic records and have no disciplinary records. Their names will be placed in the City Fire Department records, and if at any time in the future there is a fire of suspicious origin, in the school or where they have been known to have been, they will be apprehended and questioned.

The school authorities, however, suspended the three boys from school for three days and stipulated they could not return until they and their parents met with Mr. Blossom.[283]

---

283. (FOUO) DCSOPS Journal, item 1164.

This series of bomb scares and incidents was disturbing. General Walker nevertheless tried hard to keep them from interfering with the plan for orderly withdrawal, insisting that the responsibility for policing teenagers lay with the school and local authorities and was not a military function. Yet he had to keep in mind the fact that a similar crisis on 2 and 3 October had produced such a reaction at high levels that his original program for phasing out the military operation had been set back indefinitely.[284] Thus his course continued to be cautious and to

---

284. See above, section on the Second Crisis, 30 Sep - 3 Oct.

---

the end of January he made no effort to implement step 3 of his reduction plan. He also kept military reaction to the incidents at a minimum. The reserve platoon was sent to Central High School on the occasion of the first big bomb scare on the night of 16 January and from 21 through 23 January the military guard inside the school was temporarily bolstered by six men, but in general General Walker's policy was to let the local school and city authorities take the responsibility.[285]

---

285. (FOUO) Hqs, USARMD, Ark., Cmd Rpt, 1-31 Jan 58, p. 2.

This policy could be termed only a partial success. If the bomb scares had been intended to force the Army to return its off-hours security guard to Central High School, they failed in their purpose. The school guards and the city police showed marked concern and responded with alacrity when there seemed to be a serious threat of property damage to Central High School. To this extent then, step one of the reduction plan had been carried out successfully and local authorities had accepted and fulfilled their responsibility for the protection of the school building. But this was in reality only a side issue. The real crux of the matter lay in their accepting responsibility for affording protection to the Negro students and taking positive steps to assure their right to attend Central High School. And on this issue the prospects seemed no better than before. On 9 January

1958 General Walker launched an inquiry through intermediaries as to the position the new City Government would take. The reply came back from the Acting Mayor that:

. . . no conclusion had been reached; that he is not prepared to take over the responsibility of law enforcement at CHS; that he has not and will not issue any instructions to the police to do so; that under no circumstances would the police be sent inside the school; that if trouble developed outside the school, the police would do what they can with what they have.

General Walker noted that this represented "no change nor does it indicate that there will be any at this time regarding local responsibility in the integration problem at CHS."[286]

---

286. Memo, Maj Gen Edwin A Walker for Col Reaves, 14 Jan 58, sub: Operation Arkansas, WHD Files.

In his press conference on 2 October the President had stipulated that the troops could be withdrawn only if one of two conditions were met, the first that the Governor of Arkansas give "unequivocal assurances" that the court order would be obeyed, the second the development of conditions under which local authorities would be themselves able and willing to maintain law and order.[287] Any chance that the first condition would be

---

287. See above, section on Second Crisis, 30 Sep - 3 Oct.

---

met seemed long past and any remaining doubts were resolved by Governor Faubus in his speech before the Independence Magazine Wholesalers of the South on 18 January. The one new idea introduced was the suggestion that

231

integration matters should be submitted to the popular vote of the communities concerned. The Governor defended state and local rights, quoted from Thomas Jefferson, and attacked the legal basis of the President's action in sending federal troops to Little Rock.[288] The President himself,

---

288. (1) Text of speech in Arkansas Gazette, 19 Jan 58. (2) (FOUO) DCSOPS Journal, items 1106, 1108, 1112.

---

in a press conference on 15 January, had shown no hope of agreement with the Governor and indicated that his main reliance was on development of the second condition stipulated in his 2 October statement. When asked what the "wisest next step" in the Little Rock situation would be, he replied:

> Well, I would hope that the local officials in Little Rock could soon express their confident intention of maintaining order and peace in their town. That having been expressed, I see no reason for keeping any of the National Guard.[289]

---

289. Quoted in Arkansas Gazette, 16 Jan 57. DCSOPS Journal, item 1105.

It was in the light of this statement that the continuing inconclusive attitude of the new city government and the failure of the city and county authorities to take any real punitive action in the jack-knife case and the setting of fires in Central High School had to be viewed.

A further disturbing factor was a seeming lack of the determination formerly shown by the school authorities in disciplining students involved in integration disturbances. On 29 January General Walker held a conference with Mr. Blossom and Mr. Wayne Upton, one of the members of the Little Rock School Board, at which he attempted to urge on them, in diplomatic fashion, more drastic action to control the situation. "There was discussion," General Walker reported:

over the point that punishment and discipline are still being handled like it would be in a case which was strictly a first incident in some other school where the integration problem was not involved. It was pointed out that this was unrealistic and will not accomplish the results where the incidents are . . . organized against integration and are in most cases from repeated offenders. This view was discussed and apparently was recognized.

    I pointed out that the situation and the deficiency it is causing in the educational system is by approximately 1% of the student body, and while it is a disgrace it is to the disadvantage of the school board, staff, faculty and this command to be harrassed by such a small percentage who are interfering with integration and at the most bordering on defiance of the court order.

Nevertheless the school officials insisted that they could only act on specific instances, and inherent in their every response was their feeling of a lack of community support for any strong disciplinary program. General Walker assured them of his whole hearted cooperation but also reminded them "of the objective, admitted by them to be for the good of all, to get the troops out of the school."

Throughout the meeting, Mr. Blossom referred to what had now become the dominant motif in his thinking - "That the whole problem was left with the school board and the military, that the Justice Department had not done its part."[290] There was ample evidence from the meeting that the School

---

290. (FOUO) MR by Maj Gen Walker, 29 Jan 57, sub: Mtg between Mr. Blossom and Mr. Upton, DCSOPS Journal, item 1161.

Board and the school officials generally were feeling the same sort of frustration that Army officers were and were tiring of their role as pioneers in carrying out integration that circumstances had forced upon them.

In Washington, meanwhile, every move toward getting a high level decision that would result in liquidation of Operation ARKANSAS was also stymied. In this pattern of events, the new series of incidents in Little Rock also played its part. A staff study prepared in DCSOPS on the choice of a reserve of regular troops to stand ready to move to Little Rock should trouble develop after removal of the National Guard died on the vine, for the new outbreak of troubles indicated there was little prospect of removing the Guard. Efforts to get the Justice Department to take a larger role in enforcement of the court order all seemed to run up against roadblocks. General Hickman, The Judge Advocate General, in mid-January suggested an approach to the Attorney General of the United States by the Secretary of the Army. He suggested stating bluntly that the use of troops in Little Rock was a temporary expedient, that incidents since the initial period had been of a minor nature, and that other civil law enforcement agencies available to the Attorney General should be employed to carry out the mission currently assigned the Army. In urging this approach, General Hickman stated that he feared that the Secretary of the Army might have to appear before a Congressional Committee and justify the retention of troops in Little Rock over so long a period and he indicated some uneasiness about whether this course of action could be legally justified. Col Kelsie B. Reaves, Acting Director of Operations in the absence of General Pachler then on a world-wide inspection trip, demurred. It would, be contended, place the Secretary in the position of declaring that he did not want to continue a mission assigned him by the Secretary of Defense on the President's Executive Order and suggested instead an informal meeting with the Presidential Assistant, Mr. Sherman Adams, with Adams to present this proposal to the Attorney General. LT. COL. George Seignious, Military Assistant to the Secretary, also urged an approach much like that supported by Colonel Reaves. In the end, however, the Secretary decided on neither a formal letter nor a presentation to Mr. Sherman Adams.[291] Instead an informal contact was made with Justice

---

291. (FOUO) DCSOPS Journal, items 1083, 1089, 1138.

Department officials and a channel of liaison, something that had previously not existed, established between The Judge Advocate General and that department. The Justice Department apparently agreed to review old cases and study the possibilities of action against offenders but made no promises of definite legal action.

This channel was soon tested. Despite his anxiety to avoid involvement of Army troops in the incidents that were occurring at Central High School with such distressing frequency, General Walker was quite perturbed about what action the National Guard soldiers were actually authorized to take against students. The case in which a boy had defied the soldiers to lay a hand on him raised serious questions as to whether they could actually do so if necessary in pursuance of their mission. The attempted

use of the jack knife by the white boy on the Negro girl heightened this
concern. On 29 January, following the knife-brandishing incident, General
Walker asked for a decision from the Judge Advocate General on this issue
and suggested that The Judge Advocate General go to the Attorney General
for a ruling. He also suggested that an injunction should be sought
against the students who were causing the difficulty in the school. General
Hickman thought such a legal act to enjoin a specific group of specifically
named individuals possible and on 30 January consulted the Justice Department
contact on this point, but reported that he "received little or no
satisfaction."[292] No action was taken on General Walker's request for an

---

292. (FOUO) Ibid., items 1147, 1148, 1150, 1154, 1157, 1158.

---

injunction, and the whole question of the legal rights of the Guardsmen in
relation to troublesome students remained unsettled. Thus despite the
implementation of steps one and two of General Walker's reduction plan, at
the end of January the Army's responsibilities at Little Rock appeared as
heavy as ever.

Hesitant Reductions - 1 February - 4 April 1958

One of the Negro girl students left Central High School early on Friday, 31 January, at her own request, stating that she could no longer stand the harassment in gym class. However, she was back with the other eight Negro students on Monday, 3 February, and the old routine was resumed. The same pattern of school incidents continued through the first three weeks of the new month. There were anonymous telephone calls communicating bomb threats on six occasions, one each on 4, 7, 9, and 20 February and two on 6 February. The search of the school by custodial personnel became almost a regular routine and in no case were explosives found. On two other days, 12 and 18 February, devices such as a railroad flare and a railroad torpedo were found in the school. The harassment of the Negro students continued apace, with incidents reported almost daily. There was pushing, spitting, and on one occasion snowballing of the cars in which the Negro students came to school. On 13 and 14 February, lockers of several of the Negro students were broken into and two books reported stolen. The more ardent segregationists among the white students passed out various sorts of inflammatory cards and slips. The most hectic day of incidents was 6 February, the day on which there were two bomb scares. On that day one Negro girl reported that she had been kicked by white students and another was involved in two incidents, the first an altercation with a white girl who ended by throwing her purse at the Negro, and later another soup spilling incident with a white boy who had been involved in previous trouble.[293]

293. (FOUO) DCSOPS Journal, item 1166, 1180, 1184, 1187, 1190-92, 1198, 1199, 1205, 1208, 1212, 1214, 1216-18, 1221-23, 1225, 1244. Summary of incidents in items 1194, 1202, 1260. (2) See also USARMD Sit Reps and Summaries of local press reports, 1-20 Feb 58, WHD Opn ARKANSAS In-Cable File.

General Walker continued to view these incidents as the primary responsibility of the school authorities and felt that soldiers should not intervene unless they observed an overt incident or were requested to act by these authorities. Despite the continuing pattern of harassment, he determined to push ahead with the phase-out plan. On 4 February, he notified the Department of the Army of his intention to commence carrying out Step 3 on Thursday, 6 February. The Secretary, after some hesitation, finally gave General Walker word to go ahead. Step 3 entailed reducing the interior guard on duty by four to six men, making the guard visible only at certain periods when the students were moving around, and maintaining it in reserve at other times, first in the school office and later in the basement. The first action, on 6 February, involved no reduction in the size of the interior guard (one officer and 8 men), but this guard was removed from the halls to the school office except during the opening of school, the lunch hour, and the closing of school. At the end of the day, General Walker reported to the Department of the Army that "because of the manner in which this change in the guard has been made it is doubtful if the student body was aware of any change."[294]

---

294. (FOUO) DCSOPS Journal, items 1178, 1181, 1182, 1183, 1185, 1197. Quote from item 1197.

Gradually during the following days, Walker carried out most of the other essential parts of Step 3. By 25 February the pattern was as follows:

    3. a. Inside School on school days
        (1) Guard personnel
            1 officer and 4 EM in school office with 4 supernumeraries in basement. Two of the 4 guards stationed in the school office go out into the halls at irregular intervals, at an average of once each hour.

        (2) Reserve
            2 officers and 25 EM in basement of school.

    b. Outside school on school days
        (1) Dismounted posts
            A 2-man walking patrol is maintained. The patrol covers the front and sides of the school at irregular intervals, at an average of once each hour.

        (2) Motorized jeep patrols
            Two 3-man motorized jeep patrols cover an area within two blocks of the school between 0700 and 1600 hours. . . .

    4. Patrol system for surveillance of students:

    a. The jeep patrols listed in paragraph 3b(2) above observe an area within two blocks of school during periods when negro students are traveling to and from the school. These patrols watch for gatherings or other possible trouble but do not maintain direct surveillance of Negro students.

    b. Intelligence personnel conduct sporadic unscheduled surveillance rather than personal surveillance.

The reserve at Camp Robinson remained as it had been.[295] While in the

---

295. (FOUO) Ibid., 1272.

---

midst of executing Step 3, on 11 February, USARMD, Arkansas, proposed moving into Step 4 on the required 48-hour notice. This step involved the gradual withdrawal of the reserve from the basement and its removal to Camp Robinson. In contrast to Step 3, which involved mainly a reduction in the visibility of the guard, it entailed a drastic curtailment in the number of soldiers physically present at the school. It was the last step on which General Walker had been authorized to proceed with the sole requirement that he give 48 hours notice to the Department of the Army and indicate whether or not the school authorities approved.

The Department of the Army proved unwilling to move quite so fast as General Walker desired, and Step 4 was not in fact to be carried out for seven weeks after this initial request. Against the obvious advantages of pushing toward liquidation of the operation had to be weighed all the complicated factors of possible reaction by the school administration in Little Rock, the public, other levels within the Administration, and the Congress. The increased harassment of the Negro students could not, in fact, be ignored. DCSOPS took the position that there was little point in moving ahead with Step 4 until more fundamental policy issues were resolved and General Walker was denied immediate permission to proceed.[296]

---

296. (FOUO) Ibid., 1206, 1211.

General Pachler, Director of Operations and Walker's main point of contact in the Pentagon, then turned to seek such a fundamental policy decision. On February 10, he had a memorandum prepared by the Western

Hemisphere Division staff, designed to be forwarded by the DCSOPS to the Chief of Staff. This memorandum suggested that there were three possible courses of action: (1) to proceed vigorously with the execution of the six-step reduction plan "directing all efforts to force the school authorities to accept responsibility for actions of the students within the school" (i.e. General Walker's solution); (2) to accept the status quo "informing high Federal Government agencies that the military contribution to this problem only insures a reasonable climate for a solution at political levels"; (3) to revise the downward trend in Army participation and double efforts to reduce incidents. The memorandum concluded that the Army was charged with removing obstruction to the court order but not within

finding a solution to the problem and recommended what was in effect the second course. The Chief of Staff should "advise the Secretary of the Army that action other than military should be taken to permit removal of troops" in view of the obvious fact that "the present situation cannot continue indefinitely." Meanwhile, the Army should complete Step 3 of the phase-out plan and then maintain the status quo "until the situation warrants otherwise."297

---

297. (C) Memo, Brig Gen F T Pachler for CofS USA, 10 Feb 57, sub: Little Rock, DCSOPS Journal, item 1197.

This effort to seek a solution at the highest government levels proved as abortive as had all earlier ones. The Director of Operations' memorandum was held up by General Eddleman while on 13 and 14 February, General

Pachler and General Hickman went to Little Rock to confer with General Walker, get a first-hand view of the situation, and particularly to solicit the views of Superintendent Blossom and the other school authorities. Both reported to the Secretary on their return in a somewhat similar vein. The gist of their findings was that there was ample evidence that the harassing activities within the school were directed from outside with the students paid in some cases to instigate trouble, that the school authorities were reluctant to see any further reduction in troops and equally reluctant to take any strong action against the ring leaders in the troubles without stronger public support, and finally that they were bitter about the failure of the Department of Justice to take any action to deter the outsiders. In contrast they found General Walker's view to be that the only way Mr. Blossom and the School Board would completely accept responsibility was to face them with continuing withdrawals.[298]

---

298. (1) (FOUO) Memo for Sec Army, sub: Rpt on Trip to Little Rock, Ark by BG Pachler, DCSOPS Journal, item 1232. (2) (C) Memo, Maj Gen George W Hickman for Sec Army, 17 Feb 58, sub: Inspection Trip of Little Rock, Arkansas, DCSOPS Journal, item 1251. (3) See also item 1211.

Contrary to Walker's view it seemed at the Department of the Army level that the key to disentangling the Army lay in action by the Department of Justice rather than in forcing the entire burden on the school administration. On learning that Secretary Brucker was to confer with

Mr. Sherman Adams on the Little Rock issue on 18 February, General Hickman suggested that he should urge that the Department of Justice get a new injunction on which to act since the "present injunctions are admittedly inadequate." He also again raised the old question of using marshals in Little Rock.[299]

---

299. (C) Memo, Maj Gen George W. Hickman for Sec Army, 17 Feb 58, sub: Incidents at Little Rock, DCSOPS Journal, item 1252.

There is no record of the conference between Mr. Brucker and Mr. Adams, but the results are apparent. Following the meeting the Secretary himself talked to General Walker and apparently told him that in the existing situation no further steps should be taken toward reducing Army participation. On the following day, 19 February, General Wheeler told General Walker: ". . . They don't want to take a chance on mass withdrawal up here and then run the risk of having to move back in. . . . Until the Department of Justice takes some action, we have to stay put. Secretary wants to drift for a while. At the time being there is no move you can make. . . . The thing they are concerned about is this: If things go along the same line, we might have to take more precautions, not less."[300]

---

300. (FOUO) DCSOPS Journal, items 1238, 1240. Quote from 1238.

In this situation, the Pachler memorandum of 10 February was outdated and no specific action was taken on it by the Chief of Staff. The decision to maintain the status quo did not go without protest from General Walker. ". . . We are going to have incidents regardless of the number of soldiers," he said, "The incidents are not because of the lack of soldiers. Instead, they are to insure that soldiers are kept at the school."[301]

---

301. (FOUO) Ibid., items 1240 & 1308.

Meanwhile, Mr. Blossom and the School Board were seeking their own way out of a dilemma that was even more difficult for them than for the Army. Three of the white boys who had been involved in several incidents and had generally bad records were expelled from school for the rest of the year. Perhaps to balance this action the most volatile and troublesome of the Negro students, a girl, was also expelled on 17 February, ostensibly for the latest soup-spilling incident. Another white boy and a perennial trouble-maker among the white girls were suspended for three days, apparently in part for distributing cards reading "one down and eight to go" in connection with the expulsion of the Negro girl.[302] The School Board

---

302. (1) (FOUO) Ibid., items 1201, 1205, 1209, 1223-26, 1229, 1264, 1270. (2) (C) Item 1241.

---

also published, on 17 February, a statement in the local newspapers explaining its disciplinary policy:

This statement is made in order that all residents of the District may fully understand what the policy of the board has been and will continue to be with respect to disciplinary action as applied to all students.

A large majority of the students, under the proper guidance of their parents, are to be commended for their interest in education and their willingness to conduct themselves in such a way as to enable the District to educate them and all other students.

There is a small group of students whose conduct is such that they make it impossible to obtain an education for themselves and they create conditions which interfere with the efforts of those who are endeavoring to take advantage of the educational opportunities afforded them by the District.

The Directors of the District feel that they must, in the interest of all students, take such action as may be necessary to insure the preservation of an education program for those who desire to learn and are willing to conduct themselves properly.

The duty of the District through its educational staff, is to pass on knowledge to all students and that in itself is a major responsibility and such duty can not effectively be performed when a small group of students impair their own and educational opportunities of others.

Each student will be judged on his or her conduct. Whether the student is for or opposed to integration will not be considered in determining where disciplinary action should be applied. Any student whose conduct is unsatisfactory will be expelled.

We strongly desire to avoid any decision which will deprive any student of his or her educational opportunities and we sincerely appeal to all students to refrain from that kind of conduct which will call for expulsion and to all adults to refrain from encouraging students to follow such course of conduct.[303]

---

303. *Ibid.*, item 1227. See also item 1256.

Three days after this announcement, on 20 February, the School Board indicated its own weariness and discouragement with the existing situation by filing a petition in the U. S. District Court for the Eastern District of Arkansas requesting reconsideration of the court's decrees ordering integration in the Little Rock schools. After a long review of the way in which the trouble had arisen at Central High School, the School Board argued as follows:

9. The opponents of integration in the district, in the state of Arkansas and other states are continually implanting in the minds of the residents of the district by all types of inflammatory publicity the idea that a federal court order to integrate is a nullity; that the officials of the district are betraying the interests of the residents of the district in adhering to their oaths of office and endeavoring in good faith to comply with the order of this court; and they are proclaiming that nowhere in the South has a plan of integration been put into effect except where the schools officials have supinely acquiesced under the theory that the Federal Courts have the power to compel integration in the public schools. A large majority of the pupils in Central High School have exhibited the highest type of citizenship in their daily scholastic activities, but a small group, with the encouragement of certain adults, has absorbed the prevailing spirit of defiance and has almost daily created incidents which make it exceedingly difficult for teachers to teach and for pupils to learn. The existing pupil unrest, teacher unrest, and parent unrest, likewise make it difficult for the district to maintain a satisfactory educational program.

10. In Brown V. Board of Education it is stated that one of the factors to be considered in determining when integration should start is the "revision of local laws." Implicit in the opinion of the Supreme Court of the United States is the assumption that states would bow to the ruling and repeal state laws which are in conflict with the new interpretation of the Fourteenth Amendment to the Constitution of the United States. Instead of revising local laws to bring them into conformity with the Federal Law, the state of Arkansas has enacted several laws which tend to defy the Federal Law and obstruct compliance by the district with the order of this court.

11. The district now finds itself in a most difficult position in providing satisfactory education for its pupils. It has the responsibility of operating under the phase plan of integration as directed by this court, and yet it has no power to enforce the provisions of the plan.

12. The present state of affairs is due to several factors:
(A) The Federal Government, except for having placed troops around the school grounds, apparently is powerless to enforce compliance with this court's order of integration and suppress the interference now being encountered by the officials of the district. Federal officials have not applied penal sanctions to any of the persons who formed into groups near the school grounds, defied this court's order, and interfered with the plan of integration therein specified. They have stepped aside and placed on the district the full responsibility of compliance.
(B) The Judicial Branch of the Federal Government has not aided the district by preventing or attempting to prevent interference with the plan which the officials of the district, in a sense of duty, are endeavoring to apply in the operation of the schools within the district.

(C) There has been no effort on the part of the Congress of the United States to strengthen old or provide new, judicial procedures which will guarantee enforcement of the Civil Rights of the Negro minority.

(D) The district, in its respect for the law of the land, is left standing alone, the victim of extraordinary opposition on the part of the State Government and apathy on the part of the Federal Government.

13. The principle of integration runs counter to the ingrained attitudes of many of the residents of the district. For more than eighty years its schools have been operated on a basis of segregation, and except for Brown V. Board of Education the question of integration would never have been discussed by the officials of the district. The transition involved in its gradual plan of integration has created deep-rooted and violent emotional disturbances. Any change in the attitudes of the residents of the district will come from educating them as to their obligations as American citizens and a concurrent extension of enforceable Civil Rights to the Negro minority, but such change will be slow in arriving.

In the meantime, the concept of "all deliberate speed" should be re-examined and clearly defined by the Federal Courts, and in the absence of an understanding on the part of its residents as to their obligations to the Federal Government and a strengthening of the Federal Government's powers of enforcement short of the use of Federal troops, the district should not be required to submit to unjustifiable persecution of its officials and the destruction of its educational standards by outside interference.

Wherefore, petitioners ask that the plan of integration heretofore ordered by this court be realistically reconsidered in the light of existing conditions and that in interest of all pupils the beginning date of integration be postponed until such time as the concept of "all deliberate speed" can be clearly defined and effective legal procedures can be obtained which will enable the district to integrate without impairment of the quality of education it is capable of providing under normal conditions.[304]

---

304. Text communicated in AKMAR 2-79, CHUSARMD, ARK to DSCOPS, 20 Feb 58. DA-IN-639894.

The Department of the Army took the position that this School Board move did not affect the Army's mission if and until the federal courts took some action upon it and General Walker was so informed.[305] In the

305. (FOUO) DCSOPS Journal, items 1242, 1245, 1247-51, 1254, 1259, 1274.

event this action was to be delayed until after the end of the school year.

Whether as a result of the petition and other actions of the School Board or not, the situation in Little Rock became quieter during the last ten days in February and no significant incidents were reported during this period. This new quiet, however, failed to convince the Secretary that the time had come to take any further steps toward reducing the Guard in the school despite continued urging from General Walker. On 25 February, General Walker persuaded General Pachler to sound out the Secretary on executing Step 4 but was rebuffed. The next day General Walker officially requested authority to go ahead with Step 4 citing evidences of the eased situation such as the absence of incidents and the seemingly stricter and more effective policy of the school authorities. He spelled out in detail what reduction would be accomplished indicating that when the step was completed, two or three officers and eight enlisted men would remain in Central High School. When Walker's arguments were presented to the Secretary, the latter again demurred and adhered to his previous decision to maintain the present position. He felt that the existing calm was "not indicative of what will happen," that it was either the result of "a plan" or confusion following "the bursting of a boiler." The Army, he said, "must do nothing that could be considered to be the spark that set off a chain of events which might result in jeopardy of its mission or the embarrassment of the Administration." Mr. Brucker indicated that this did not constitute a flat denial of General Walker's recommendations but merely "a delay of a few days." He suggested that Walker continue to furnish a day-by-day analysis of the situation so that he might "have evidence on which to furnish judgment."[306]

---

306. (1) (FOUO) DCSOPS Journal, items 1265, 1275, 1279, 1280, 1284, 1285, 1290, 1295. (2) (C) Msg AKMAR-C 2-108, CHUSARMD, ARK to DCSOPS, 26 Feb 58, DA-IN-96089. (3) Msg AKMAR 2-109, CHUSARMD, ARK to DCSOPS, 26 Feb 58, DA-IN-96096 (SECRET).

The requested day-by-day analysis was soon to give General Walker a new opportunity to press his case. Meanwhile, the purported stricter disciplinary policy of the School Board was to receive a serious test in the case of the girl suspended for three days on 17 February. At a school board meeting on 21 February, this suspension was extended to two weeks. Almost immediately, the girl's parents began to threaten legal action to force the return of their child to school. In a very real sense, this case was a test of the School Board's determination. She had been involved in integration troubles from the start and had been specifically identified by Mr. Blossom to General Hickman as one of those white students in contact with outsiders who wanted to stir up trouble. On the night of 26 February, she appeared at a hearing before the school board after which, according to Mr. Blossom's testimony, she and her mother "viciously and physically attacked Miss Huckaby /Assistant Principal for Girls/ as she started out of the meeting."[307] The following night the School Board expelled the girl

307. (FOUO) Ibid., items 1263, 1264, 1270, 1272.

for the rest of the year. Her father then threatened to bring her to school anyway on Monday 3 March and force the school authorities to allow her to enter. This threat he failed to carry out, announcing instead on Sunday, 2 March, that his daughter was in a disturbed emotional state and he would not allow her to submit to further humiliation. On the night of 4 March the child appeared on a well-advertised local television show along with the Attorney for the Capital Citizens Council, in what proved to be a bitter attack not only on the school authorities but also on the local police. On 7 March, the girl's father appealed to the local court to order the re-admission of his daughter to school, thus posing the threat of a test in a state court of the School Board's disciplinary policy. This move created considerable apprehension on the part of Mr. Blossom who evidently feared the case might be lost. The final upshot was anticlimactic. Before the case could be heard, a compromise was arranged through an intermediary. The girl appeared before the School Board on 11 March and on her promise that she would conform to the rules was reinstated at Central High School. The result was thus more of a stand-off than a victory for either the School Board or the segregationists. But it is a matter of record that the child's subsequent behavior was vastly improved.[308]

308. (1) Ibid., items 1283, 1287-88, 1296, 1297, 1303, 1305, 1320, 1329, 1332, 1334. (2) Msgs from USARMD, Ark., to DCSOPS, 7-12 Mar 58, DA-IN-647833, 648309, 648323, 650316, 650327, 650285.

While this case was in process Governor Faubus on 5 March announced his candidacy for a third term as Governor subject to the Democratic primary to be held in July. At the school there was a new high of five bomb scares on 5 March; otherwise the harassing of the Negro students seemed to have diminished. Yet there seemed to be heavier tension than ever, partly as a result of the case of the expelled white girl. Mr. Blossom's life was threatened and a shot was fired at his car while he was driving home at night on 8 March.[309]

---

309. (1) On these incidents see DCSOPS Journal, items 1306, 1309, 1314, 1321, 1329.

General Walker, undeterred in his course, sent in an analysis on 6 March with the familiar arguments that the new school disciplinary policy was working and that the only way to get the school authorities to accept complete responsibility was to thrust it upon them. He coupled these with a new argument that retaining troops at the school was playing into the Governor's hands, since it gave him the best possible issue in the coming election.[310]

---

310. (C) Msg AKMAR 3-21, CHUSARMD, ARK, to DCSOPS, 6 Mar 58, DA-IN-98328.

There was no indication in this analysis that General Walker had the consent of the school authorities to any further reduction in force, and the Department of the Army's reply was a forceful reminder that this consent would be required before he could reduce any further. By cable on 7 March, General Walker was told that "in view of the absence of specific assurance from appropriate school authorities . . . it is believed that it is not appropriate to place Step 4 into effect at this time," that the disposition of the troops would remain in status quo. He was also admonished to avoid political speculation in his analyses as not pertinent to his military mission.[311] This cable was accompanied by specific in-

---

311. (C) (1) Msg DA 938217 to CHUSARMD, ARK, 8 Mar 58. (2) For DCSOPS analysis of Walker's message used in briefing the Secretary of the Army see Journal, item 1316.

---

structions from the Secretary of The Army as to the timing of further reduction steps. These instructions, given by General Pachler over the telephone on 8 March, were to the effect that hall guards and the reserve in the basement could be removed (Step 4) "as soon as the appropriate school authorities specifically express their willingness to accept full responsibility for control of all student activities within Central High School." The Secretary stipulated that he must be informed in advance of any such move. He expressed the hope this could be done by Easter, 6 April 1958. Further, the Secretary said that the dismounted and jeep patrols outside the school could be removed as soon as an agreement could be obtained from the local city authorities, and that when all troops had been removed from the school to Camp Robinson they would remain on duty status there until released by direction of the President.[312]

---

312. (FOUO) DCSOPS Journal, items 1324, 1326.

These quite positive instructions had the desired effect of easing the pressure from General Walker to move toward further reductions. And during the lull, the Army's policy in Little Rock was subjected to a new attack from the NAACP, the object of which apparently was to force the military to take stronger measures to protect the Negro students. On 10 March, Mrs. Daisy Bates of the Arkansas NAACP made a call at the Office of the Secretary of the Army and talked with his Military Assistant. Mrs. Bates asserted that in at least two incidents the National Guardsmen had not offered the protection she felt was necessary to the Negro children at Central High School, one of these being the case of the kicking of the girl by a white boy on 29 January and the other the snowballing incident of 14 February when she said the Negro children were mercilessly pelted with snowballs, some with rocks in them. Mrs. Bates further stated that she had received word that a planned riot was scheduled between 15 and 28 May in a final effort to drive the Negro children out of school before the end of the term, and that she expected a special effort to intimidate the only senior in the Negro group to prevent him from graduating with his class.[313]

---

313. (FOUO) Ibid., item 1333.

The Department of the Army made no direct reply to Mrs. Bates. DCSOPS reviewed the two incidents concerned as well as of the instructions given to military personnel within the school, and drew up an answer stating that "proper measures were taken by military personnel upon arrival at the scene of the incidents," and that the instructions in effect insured that military personnel would intervene in any incidents which involved a threat to the safety of the children. "Further," the reply read, "all military personnel conducted themselves in such a manner as to not interfere with the exercise of control and discipline by school authorities who were present at the scene of the two incidents." After some debate however, it was decided that Mrs. Bates should have addressed herself to the school authorities in Little Rock and that the reply should come from them. Mr. Blossom conveniently agreed to deliver it.[314]

---

314. (FOUO) Ibid., items 1335, 1338, 1341, 1347a, 1357, 1398, 1407, 1343.

This round-about reply to Mrs. Bates evidently did not satisfy her and did not end the NAACP inquiry. On 14 March, Mr. Roy Wilkins, Executive Secretary of the NAACP, wrote the Secretary of the Army making even broader charges that the National Guard troops at Little Rock were under orders to do nothing in case of a disturbance except to observe it. Mr. Wilkins asserted that there had been 42 incidents in the 80 school days between 2 October 1957 and 6 February 1958 involving 30 white students. He declared it to be the NAACP's belief that it was the responsibility of the troops to protect the rights of the Negro students to whatever extent was necessary to enforce the court order. "We believe," he said, "that the order contemplated not merely the bare admission of Negro students physically to the premises of Central High School, but the protection of their declared right to education without segregation as to race." He, like Mrs. Bates, expressed the opinion that there would be a major disturbance at Central High School during the latter weeks of the school year.[315]

---

315. Ltr, Roy Wilkins, Ex Sec, NAACP to Hon Wilbur M. Brucker, 14 Mar 58, in WHD NAACP File, Opn ARKANSAS.

The Secretary ruled that a direct written reply had to be made to Mr. Wilkins, but it was decided that this reply should be signed by John W. Martyn, the Secretary's Administrative Assistant. The reply, dispatched on 21 March, denied that the troops at Little Rock were operating under orders "to do nothing in case of a disturbance except to observe," and assured the NAACP head that "adequate provisions exist in the instructions issued by the Army to the troops on duty to insure necessary action in the performance of their mission. . . . Military personnel on duty in and about the school have been and will continue to be prepared to intervene as necessary to assist the school authorities and to carry out their other instructions." But Mr. Wilkins was reminded that "It must be understood that the school authorities are directly responsible for the control and discipline of the students within the school.

Accordingly, the troops at the high school have conducted themselves in such a manner as not to usurp or interfere with the responsibilities of the school authorities."[316]

---

316. Ltr, John W. Martyn, Adm Asst, SA, to Roy Wilkins, 21 Mar 58, WHD NAACP File.

Mr. Wilkins on 28 March wrote a second and stronger letter to the Secretary of the Army, charging in effect that the system under which the Army was operating did not provide adequate protection for the Negro students. He asserted that the language of Martyn's reply was "subject to the interpretation that the troops have initiated no move in cases of overt action by white students against Negro students, and that they have waited 'to assist' the school authorities presumably on the request of the latter." He charged that there was no record of action by National Guardsmen since the withdrawal of the paratroopers, and that the school authorities who failed to exercise the authority at their disposal were "as guilty of hindering the court order as are those who commit overt acts of obstruction." He insisted that the Army should take "affirmative action" to effect the purpose of the Court order and that Army responsibility did not end with the safe conduct of the students to the doors of the school. He closed with the assertion that unless the Army took more positive action "we are confronted with the incredible spectacle of the government of the United States placing the burden of enforcing the orders of its Courts upon the slender shoulders and the young hearts of eight teen-age Negro students."[317]

---

317. Ltr, Wilkins to Hon Wilbur M Brucker, 27 Mar '58, WHD NAACP File.

Mr. Martyn's reply to this appeal simply referred the head of the NAACP to the Army's position as set forth in the previous letter.[318]

---

318. Ltr, Martyn to Wilkins, n. d., WHD NAACP File.

Meanwhile, as the month of March wore on and incidents, while they continued to occur,[319] remained at a minimum, the Secretary himself

---

319. (FOUO) On these incidents see (1) DCSOPS Journal, items 1358, 1375, 1378 and (2) USARMD Ark Sit Reps for period 10-20 Mar 58.

---

finally decided to move along into Step 4 as General Walker wished. On 17 March General Walker informed General Pachler that Mr. Blossom had expressed a willingness to take out all but one officer and ten men after about two weeks, a period when the School Principal would be absent. General Walker, however, doubted how far he could move in view of the message of 8 March that had instructed him to maintain the status quo. To resolve his doubts on this point, the guidance given by the Secretary of the Army on 8 March was repeated by cable on 19 March and General

Walker was asked for his written recommendations on carrying out Step 4.[320]

---

320. (1) (FOUO) DCSOPS Journal, item 1347a, 1349, 1352. (2) (C) Msg DA 938684, to CHUSARMD, Ark, 18 Mar 58. (3) (C) Msg DA 938690 to CHUSARMD, Ark, 19 Mar 58.

From this point onward events moved swiftly toward fulfillment of Step 4, the only question being the extent and pace of the proposed reduction. On 20 March General Walker reported that though Mr. Blossom was "not ready to accept full responsibility for the control of all students within Central High School if all troops are removed from the interior of the school," he had agreed "in word and spirit" that reduction of troops was "in the best interests of all" and to a further gradual reduction down to not less than ten soldiers. General Walker proposed to carry out this gradual reduction. The Secretary approved and, on 20 March 1948, General Walker was told that he could go ahead, starting on 24 March.[321]

---

321. (1) (C) Msg AKMAR 3-78, CHUSARMD ARK to DCSOPS, 20 Mar 58. (2) (FOUO) For General Walker's report on his conference with Mr. Blossom on 19 Mar 58, see DCSOPS Journal, item 1437. (3) DCSOPS Journal, items 1359-60. (4) (C) Msg DA 938813 to CHUSARMD, ARK, 20 Mar 58.

Next day Secretary Brucker met with General Walker at Fort Benning, Georgia, and there agreed to General Walker's plan to reduce the number of men in the interior of the school to four.[322] Pursuant

---

322. (FOUO) (1) A memo for the record by Lt Col G M Seignious on the meeting with Gen Walker at Ft Benning is found in DCSOPS Journal, item 1394. (2) See also items 1365-67, 1377.

---

to this plan, on 26 March the force in the school office was cut to one officer, four enlisted men, and two administrative non-commissioned officers with one officer and 8 enlisted men in the basement. Four enlisted men were withdrawn from the school basement on 31 March and the remaining one officer and four enlisted men on 2 April, eliminating the basement reserve entirely and leaving only one officer and 4 enlisted men on active guard duty inside Central High School. General Walker had originally intended to post the troops removed from the school as a reserve at the Little Rock Reserve Center but on the night of 27-28 March they were withdrawn to Camp Robinson where they were constituted as a reserve on immediate alert. The two-man foot patrol which had been covering the area around the school at irregular intervals, working out of the school basement, was discontinued on 2 April; in lieu of this patrol the two remaining motorized patrols were instructed to halt at Central High School at irregular intervals with the men to dismount and walk around the school. The small guard remaining in the interior was stationed in the school office and continued to appear in the hallways at irregular intervals as previously. All these changes had been effected by the time Central High School closed for the Easter Holiday on 3 April.[323]

---

323. (1) (C) Msg AKMAR 3-90, CHUSARMD, ARK, to DCSOPS, 21 Mar 58, DA-IN-102728. (2) (C) Msg AKMAR 3-98, 24 Mar 58, DA-IN-103234. (3) USARMD, ARK, Sit Reps, 24 Mar - 3 Apr 58. (4) (FOUO) Fact Sheets, Sub: Use of Troops in Little Rock, 31 Mar & 14 Apr 58. Filed in Opn ARKANSAS Black Book at Tab I.

Step 4 had thus finally been carried out after a long period of hesitancy, but still in time to meet the Easter target date set by the Secretary. It is worth noting, however, that the Secretary's requirement that the "school authorities specifically express their willingness to accept full responsibility for control of all student activities within Central High School" had not been completely met. General Walker had reported only that Mr. Blossom was willing to go along with the reductions and did not ever indicate that the School Board had adopted any position on this issue. In giving the same kind of reluctant consent as he had to earlier reductions, the School Superintendent clearly indicated that he was opposed to a complete withdrawal of troops to Camp Robinson "since there was no assurance of or can he trust their continued and inevitable retention for this Little Rock duty."[324]

---

324. DCSOPS Journal, items 1390 & 1437. Quote from item 1437.

On the other hand, there were other indications that at least some members of the School Board were willing to take greater risks. The timing of the final execution of Step 4 was closely related to a meeting between Mr. Sherman Adams and Mr. Wayne Upton, a member of the Little Rock School Board. As Mr. Adams related this conversation to Secretary Brucker on 27 March, Upton expressed the opinion that the School Board was approaching the point where it would not seriously object to the withdrawal of troops within the school if no public announcement were made, if the city police would indicate willingness to offer a somewhat higher degree of support, and if the troops could be held in readiness close by to assist in case of serious trouble.[325]

---

325. (FOUO) Ibid., items 1384 & 1394.

Out of this conversation and other indications of a similar sort came new moves to work with the city police. General Walker was instructed to inform the City Police Chief, Mr. Gene Smith, in advance of changes in his troop dispositions as a means of beginning the process of persuading the city police to assume more responsibility.[326]

---

326. (FOUO) Ibid., items 1385-87.

Total strength of the troops engaged in Operation ARKANSAS remained almost stationary during February and March 1958, and the reduction in the scale of guard operations entailed no corresponding reduction in overall strength. At the beginning of February there were 420 Guardsmen on duty and by 31 March this number had declined to 408 -- mainly the result of normal attrition due to expiration of enlistments though there were also a few hardship discharges. The number of USARMD personnel, assigned and attached, involved in Operation ARKANSAS also remained relatively constant throughout the period and stood at 14 officers and 17 enlisted men on 31 March 1958. Of these, 6 officers and 11 enlisted men were on temporary duty from Fourth Army.[327]

---

327. See fact sheets at Tab I in Opn ARKANSAS Black Book, WHD.

Final Withdrawal - 4 April - 29 May 1958

The late date of the final execution of Step 4 left little time for further moves toward final withdrawal of Army troops from Central High School before the end of the school year on 28 May 1958. If the school authorities, city government, and the police showed some signs of increased willingness to take responsibility, their attitude remained at best uncertain. No assurances of the sort the Secretary of the Army had stipulated as necessary before the troops could be finally withdrawn across the river to Camp Robinson were forthcoming. Nor had Governor Faubus, engaged in a campaign for a third term as governor, changed his position.

In this situation, the drama was played out to the end with the Army mainly maintaining a reserve but with its presence at the school seemingly still indispensable to continued enforcement of the court order. In a conversation with General Pachler on 7 April, the Secretary expressed the opinion that troop strength at the school was now at an irreducible minimum (one officer and four men in the school, six men engaged on motor patrols).[328] Within DCSOPS, this was accepted as a new

---

328. (FOUO) DCSOPS Journal, items 1397-98, 1418.

---

order to maintain the status quo and await further agreement with the school and city authorities before making any additional move. In a very real sense, the only vital question remaining seemed to have become not whether the troops should be removed before the end of the school year but whether they would have to be maintained on duty through the summer in order to be available the next school year, 1958-59.

General Walker favored final withdrawal at the end of the school year and pushed during the interim for further reduction in the scope of his operations in order to hand the responsibility for preserving law and order over to the local civil officials before the withdrawal took place. On 7 April, in a telephone conversation with General Wheeler, he submitted recommendations that all National Guard troops on active service be released between 28 May and 6 June and that the Army's mission at Little Rock be terminated when this release was complete. On the same day, he submitted for General Pachler's consideration a program for progressive reduction. He recommended that enlisted personnel on duty at the school be cut from four to two on 14 April, subsequently to one, than phased out altogether. When the men were removed Guard officers would continue telephone contacts with the Principal and intermittent visits to the school, but before the end of school would also discontinue these. Meanwhile, the patrol time of the two jeep patrols in the school area would be gradually reduced until finally neither motorized patrol would appear in the school area, and responsibility for law and order would be left in the hands of the police who could call on the troops at Camp Robinson for assistance when needed. Similarly, once the guards had been removed from within the school, the school authorities could call for military assistance "when necessary."[329]

---

329. (1) (C) Msg AKMAR 4-28, CHUSARMD, ARK, to DCSOPS, 7 April 58, DA-IN-106859.

General Walker's proposals were received without enthusiasm in DCSOPS. Insofar as the dismissal of the Guard and discontinuance of the mission at the end of the school year were concerned, decision would have to await guidance from higher authority. And on the proposed interim reductions, the Secretary's dictum on irreducible minimum seemed to bar them until further notice.[330]

---

330. DCSOPS Journal, items 1402, 1404, 1408, 1412.

The month of April meanwhile wore on with only one or two incidents of any significance. On 16 April General Walker reported that Mr. Blossom had agreed the day before to a proposal to reduce the number of men on duty inside the school from four to two and the general stated he proposed to carry this reduction out on 21 April "provided there had been no change in the present conditions of quiet now prevailing." This proposal DCSOPS viewed as a first step in carrying out the plan presented by General Walker on 7 April and in a presentation before the Secretary of the Army opposed it, arguing that the Army must instead be prepared to take additional precautions in view of the possibility of increased disturbances during the last weeks of school. Nevertheless, the Secretary decided in favor of General Walker this time, saying that "he was willing to accept the risk involved in the initial step of General Walker's plan . . . and further that, at irregular intervals, all military personnel would be withdrawn temporarily from the school and that Mr. Blossom would be notified in advance of these withdrawals.

The complete withdrawals were to be only one day at a time and the personnel withdrawn would remain within a ten minute travel radius of Central High School."[331]

---

331. (1) (C) Msg AKMAR 4-53, CHUSARMD ARK to DEPTAR, 16 Apr 58, DA-IN-109040. (2) (FOUO) DCSOPS Journal, items 1416, 1420, 1422-25, 1459. Quote from 1459.

The reduction to one officer and two men in the school was accordingly carried out on 21 April and on the 24th the troops were temporarily withdrawn entirely - the first day since 24 September 1957 when Army troops had not been physically present. The day passed without incident. Despite this favorable result, no further experimentation with withdrawals was carried out. This was largely because experimentation seemed futile with the approach of the end of the school year and the almost certain fact that the troops would have to remain on duty in the area until that time. By the end of April, a final decision on what should be done at the end of the school year seemed more important than prosecution to the bitter end of the gradual withdrawal plan. Moreover, there was a marked increase in incidents again, beginning on 25 April when a Negro girl was hit on the leg with a rock and a scientific experiment prepared by a Negro boy was broken up. On three occasions between 1 and 14 May another boy was kicked, shoved, or struck; there was a veritable rash of cases of breaking into the Negro students' lockers; on 8 and 21 May there was trouble outside the school between Negro and white teenagers, mainly from other schools; on 13 May a group of white junior high school students from outside exploded firecrackers in Central High School. This increase in incidents during the first two weeks of May had to be considered in the light of continuing rumors and warnings from various sources of trouble during the last week of school and during the graduation ceremonies, culminating in an effort to prevent Ernest Green, the only Negro senior, from graduating.[332]

---

332. (1) DCSOPS Journal, items 1448, 1451, 1453, 1454, 1456, 1463, 1475-76, 1479, 1482-85, 1488, 1494-95, 1497, 1500, 1502, 1505, 1509, 1513-14, 1517, 1529, 1533, 1535, 1541. (2) USARMD ARK Sit Reps for period 21-25 Apr 58.

Thus two big problems remained for solution. The first, and most important, involved the central issue of what should be done at the end of the school year, the second what special measures should be taken to care for any contingencies that might arise during the closing weeks of school and particularly during the graduation cermonies. In connection with the first problem there were several pertinent factors to be considered. There were to be no Negroes at Central High School during the summer session since this session was not financed with state funds but by contributions of the attending students. Thus if the National Guard troops were to be maintained over the summer they would be without a mission and simply a financial drain on the federal government. Yet there was ample room for speculation that troops might be required the following

September if the order of the district court were not modified by that time. The local NAACP gave notice of its intent to push for further integration, including integration of Hall High School and Technical High School in Little Rock. Mr. Blossom expressed the opinion that probably a few more Negro students would be enrolled at Central the following year and perhaps one or two at Hall and Technical, since he did not believe that under the court-approved integration plan qualified colored students could be denied admission to these schools. There were possibilities, of course, that the court might approve the School Board's petition for postponement of integration or that Governor Faubus might be defeated, or once he had achieved his third term, might change his attitude.[333]

---

333. (FOUO) *Ibid.*, item 1390.

The decision could not be taken by the Army, but had to be made at higher levels. The problem was given increased urgency by pressures that began to arise from Arkansas with regard to the necessity for the use of Camp Robinson for a Boys' and Girls' State Encampment scheduled to begin on 31 May 1958, almost immediately after the close of school, and run for two weeks. This was an annual event sponsored by the American Legion for the purpose of promoting good citizenship and knowledge of government among the youth of Arkansas. It required facilities for an encampment of 600 boys for one week and 600 girls the next. While there was obviously room at the camp to accomodate the few hundred Guardsmen remaining and the Boys' and Girls' State Encampment too, it involved some difficult arrangements since the Guard had not contracted the space it was occupying in proportion to the reductions in its strength. Arkansas officials for the most part insisted that the encampment could not be held unless the Guard moved out and members of the Arkansas Congressional delegation made representations to both the Department of the Army and the President requesting that facilities be made available.[334]

---

334. (FOUO) Ibid., items 1420, 1429, 1431, 1433, 1436, 1438-41, 1446-47, 1449, 1466-67, 1471, 1474.

Any definitive answer to these representations was held in abeyance while the major question of eventual troop withdrawal was debated. After a talk with Mr. Sherman Adams on 23 April 1958, the Secretary of the Army asked DCSOPS to prepare a paper on the question: "What course of action should be taken to utilize the Federalized National Guard during the summer months prior to the re-opening of school in September 1958?" This paper was to be based on the assumption that "The Army will not be relieved, by the appropriate authority, of its present mission in Little Rock prior to the re-opening of school in September 1958."[335] Such a

---

335. (S) M/R, 28 Apr 58, sub: Federalized Ark NG, w/Tabs, item 1465 DCSOPS Journal.

---

paper was developed in some detail and used by Col. Kelsie B. Reaves,

Deputy Director of Operations, in briefing the Chief of Staff and the Secretary of the Army on 24 April. Three alternate solutions were presented: (1) Organize a task force composed of five officers and 50 enlisted men from the present National Guard Force on duty choosing men primarily from the Little Rock area. These men would be attached to Headquarters, U.S. Army Military District, Arkansas, but could be furloughed to their homes on call. (2) Reduce the present force to 175, inclusive of the necessary administrative support personnel, and retain this force in the present area at Camp Robinson. (3) Defederalize the present force immediately upon the close of school. DCSOPS recommended Course two on the grounds that Course One had not been fully explored and that Course three was of doubtful feasibility if the Army were not relieved of its mission prior to the opening of the Fall school term.[336] The Secretary narrowed the choice by ruling out

---

336. (S) Tab C to above.

Course one and a new paper was drawn up for him to use in a meeting with Mr. Adams presenting the alternatives of release at the end of school and the maintenance of a 175-man force through the summer. In the meantime, there had apparently been a change in the thinking at higher levels; in the meeting with Mr. Brucker, Mr. Adams chose the alternative of releasing the Guard, the one that in the talking paper prepared for the Secretary read as follows:

> Release from active military service the present force (407) immediately upon the close of school. This action would be

coupled to an announcement by the President. The President would, in a statement, announce that in the event it was necessary, at any time, to again use troops to ensure that the Court Order would be carried out, he would recall the Arkansas National Guard for that purpose. Such a statement by the President could be considered as a warning and a deterrent to all people concerned.[337]

---

337. (S) Ibid.

Mr. Adams directed that a memorandum recommending this course be drawn up and submitted by the Secretary of the Army to the President. The memorandum drawn up in DCSOPS in cooperation with The Judge Advocate General, after reviewing the existing situation, concluded that

> . . . there will be no requirement during the summer for presence of troops to ensure the orderly execution of the pertinent orders of the Federal Court. Inasmuch as there will be no use for the troops, it is believed that their retention, even though reduced in number, could not be justified in view of the costs involved and the probable adverse effect on morale and discipline of the troops retained. Furthermore, it is doubtful that a legal basis exists for retaining National Guard troops in the active military service when there is no apparent necessity for so doing. The continued presence of troops in the area would tend to generate local as well as national criticism. . . . To insure that the general public recognizes that the President of the United States maintains a continuing determination to protect the rights of all citizens under our constitutional form of government, a public statement should accompany the decision to release from active military service the federalized Arkansas National Guard.

The proposed statement read:

Last September, the wilful obstruction of the enforcement of orders of the United States District Court for the Eastern District of Arkansas regarding the integration of Central High School, Little Rock, compelled the Federal Government to station soldiers in and around this school.

During the ensuing eight months, circumstances have justified the gradual reduction of numbers involved. I have determined now that it will be feasible soon to withdraw the remaining troops.

Accordingly, I have directed that the remaining National Guardsmen be released from Federal service, at the conclusion of the school term on 29 May. Effective on that date, community officials and citizens will have the entire responsibility for the maintenance of law and order.

The law of this land and the lawful orders of its courts must be honored or our nation will lose its vital heritage of freedom under law. I trust that all citizens of our country will recognize my unswerving determination that all of our citizens be insured the equal protection of the laws secured by the Constitution of the United States as interpreted by our courts. I reaffirm this determination and fervently trust that I will not again be compelled to mobilize the National Guard to prevent obstruction to a lawful court order.[338]

---

338. (S) Tab D to above.

Submission of the memorandum was delayed for several days while it was considered by the Department of Justice. Several changes were evidently made in it but the overall solution recommended remained the same. And on 8 May the President formally announced his decision that the Arkansas National Guard should be released from federal service and set the date as 29 May 1958. The President's announcement was somewhat less positive on the point of possible recall of the Guard than had been the initial Army draft. It read:

> Since last September the federal government has stationed soldiers at the Little Rock high school to prevent obstruction of the orders of the U.S. District Court.
>
> Since the summer recess starts at the Central High School on May 28 and since there will be no further present need for the guardsmen, I have directed they be released May 29.
>
> Following that date I trust that state and local officials and citizens will assume full responsibility and duty for seeing that the orders of the federal court are not obstructed.
>
> The faithful execution of the responsibility will make it unnecessary for the federal government to preserve the integrity of our judicial processes.[339]

339. As quoted in Arkansas *Gazette*, 8 May 1958.

In any case, the President's announcement settled the issue and the prescribed timing of the release of the remaining Guardsmen, on 29 May 1958, also cleared the way for the Boys' and Girls' State Encampment. On 13 May, the necessary orders were issued by the Secretary of Defense for the release of all remaining units of the Arkansas National Guard on 29 May, and these were followed by orders from the Department of the Army to Fourth Army to arrange the releases in accordance with what were now well established procedures.[340]

---

340. (1) Msg DA 338409, to CGUSARFOUR, 13 May 58. (2) Msg DA 338597 to CGUSARFOUR, 13 May 58.

While this decision was in the making, the School Board petition came up on 28 April for a preliminary hearing in the U.S. District Court for the Eastern District of Arkansas. The bench for this court being still vacant, the Chief Judge of the Eighth Circuit designated Judge Harry J. Lemley of Hope, Arkansas, to hear the case. After the hearing on 28 April, Judge Lemley issued a statement indicating he intended to give the case a full-scale review. He pointed out that the integration plan was a School Board plan and that the burden of proof that it should be reconsidered rested on the School Board. He required the Board to file a new brief setting forth specifically what new plan it now had, how long a postponement it desired and containing more specific proof of its allegations. Judge Lemley gave the School Board ten days in which to present its new brief and to the original plaintiffs in the case ten additional days to respond. The date for the final hearing was set for 3 June.

The issue was thus joined again in the courts, with both sides presenting the required briefs and engaging in other legal maneuvers during the month of May. But the postponement of the decision until after the end of school meant it would have little effect on the Army's mission, which remained that of enforcing the existing court order until the end of the school year. Any modification of the court order could only affect the question of whether the Army would have a new mission, or resume the old one, when the school year 1958-59 began. The whole question of whether the Army was completely relieved of its mission as of 29 May 1958 remained somewhat questionable even after the President's announcement on 8 May for there was no specific reference to it. However, the Judge Advocate General expressed the opinion that the mission would in fact be terminated by the relief of the last elements of the Arkansas National Guard and that any new action by troops in the integration situation at Little Rock would require a new Presidential Executive Order.[341]

---

341. (1) Text of Judge Lemley's statement in msg, AKMAR 4-104, CHUSARMD, ARK, to DEPTAR, 28 Apr 58, DA-IN-675433. (2) Text of amended School Board petition in msg AKMAR 5-28, CHUSARMD to TJAG DEPTAR,

8 May 58, DA-IN-681289. (3) Further developments in the case covered in AKMAR 5-65, 16 May 58; DA-IN-686107, AKMAR 5-78, 20 May 58, DA-IN-687684; AKMAR 5-97, 26 May 58, DA-IN-690827; AKMAR 5-129, 29 May 58, DA-IN-693271. (4) Memo, TJAG for Sec Army, 19 May 58, sub: Federal Intervention in the Little Rock Ark Dispute, in WHD Defederalization file.

The remaining problem for the Department of the Army, therefore, was to insure that no troubles arose during the last few weeks of school and during the graduation ceremonies that would in effect represent obstruction of the court order. In approaching this problem the old question of the respective responsibilities of the military and the local civil authorities had to be settled anew and this time, indeed, it was a new and more satisfactory solution. On 8 May, Little Rock Chief of Police Eugene Smith indicated to General Walker that he thought it would be a wiser course of action if the baccalaureate (25 May) and graduation (27 May) ceremonies were handled by the city police and suggested a meeting between city authorities and the military for the purpose of formulating a workable plan for division of responsibilities.[342] However, later the same day, after hearing the

342. (FOUO) DCSOPS Journal, item 1493.

President's announcement and consulting other city authorities, the Chief of Police reconsidered and requested that the troops make a show of force at both ceremonies. This point of view was reiterated by city officials in a meeting held on 13 May. The reasoning behind it was quite clearly a fear that segregationists would feel it incumbent on them, in order to save face, to see that some disturbances occurred. General Walker, however, was reluctant for the troops to play any major role, feeling that any considerable show of force would provide ammunition for the segregationists who could claim that the troops were necessary to enforce integration at Central High School from beginning to end of the school year.[343]

---

343. (FOUO) DCSOPS Journal, items 1489-91, 1495, 1499.

There could be no denying however, that there was a potentially explosive situation. As Chief Smith stated it:

> . . . Green would be the first colored graduate from a southern school as prominent nationally as Central High School . . . the stadium would be filled to the brim with curiosity seekers, reporters, photographers, and . . . known troublemakers. . . . He felt that the explosion of a firecracker, a flashlight bulb, or the firing of a pistol containing blanks would be all that was necessary to throw the entire assemblage in a state of panic.[344]

---

344. Ibid., item 1515.

Considering all the factors, General Pachler on 12 May requested that General Walker "submit a written plan for appropriate action in any possible contingency which may affect your mission at Central High School during the period 19-28 May, to include all graduation activities."[345]

345. (C) Msg DA 941641, to CHUSARMD, ARK, 12 May 58.

In response, General Walker on 15 May presented Operation Plan GRADUATION. It contained in fact three plans for three different contingencies. Plan A envisaged a situation in which "local civil authorities have the capacity and indicate full intent to assume complete responsibility," Plan B a situation in which the local authorities had the will but not the capacity "to handle an organized and planned major outbreak of violence," Plan C the case where these authorities exhibited reluctance to assume their normal responsibilities. In the first case, General Walker proposed simply to maintain his troops at Camp Robinson on alert to move to the high school stadium to aid local authorities if necessary; in the second he would move a troop reserve into the basement of Central High School and to the Little Rock Reserve Center and use motor patrols and mobile reserves as necessary; in the third, troops would man all key positions, to include street corners, entrances and exits inside and outside the stadium, both foot and motor patrols would be employed in the Central High School area, and a reserve would be located in the school basement "ready to move to any and all sensitive areas."[346]

346. (C) Msg AKMAR 5-55, CHUSARMD ARK to DEPTAR, 15 May 58 Exclusive Pachler from Walker.

City police now showed determination in their efforts to prevent disturbances at the graduation ceremonies, placing the Army in the last act of the Little Rock drama in the supporting rather than in the main role. They undertook primary responsibility for policing the stadium and the surrounding area at both the baccalaureate and graduation ceremonies, asking only that the Army provide a contingent reserve for any possible major disturbances that might break out despite the careful precautions. Since the Secretary stated his desire that "no hair on the head of one Ernest Green be harmed,"[347] General Walker had to make careful

---

347. (FOUO) DCSOPS Journal, item 1531.

---

provisions for the reserve and be sure that the city police were in fact prepared to handle the situation. The military role nevertheless became secondary.

General Walker's Headquarters aided the police in the preparation of their plans and provided for a close tie-in with the police communications net. The school authorities carefully limited the invitations to seven per student both for the baccalaureate and the graduation. Provision was made for Ernest Green to be escorted to and from the ceremonies in a taxi with a detective escort. More than 90 men were detailed to cover the stadium and operate motor patrols in the surrounding area. It was decided that photographic and press coverage should be limited.[348]

---

348. (FOUO) (1) DCSOPS Journal, items 1516, 1523, 1526, 1531,

1536-38, 1540, 1548, 1549, 1552, 1553. On incidents in period see items 1517, 1529, 1533, 1535, 1541.

The military effort during the last week of school, though it was supplementary, was stepped up to a considerable degree. What was essentially General Walker's Plan B was placed into effect. On 23 May, six additional guards were placed in Central High School making a total of eight and they remained there through the 28th. The two-man reseve at Headquarters, U.S. Army Military District, Arkansas, was also increased to six men. During the baccalaureate services on Sunday night, 25 May, three platoons (40 men each) were placed in the basement of Central High School and two at the reserve center. The two military motor patrols moved about the area lending assistance to more numerous police prowl cars. There was no need for the use of any of this reserve. Little Rock Central High School's first integrated baccalaureate service went off in solemn dignity. The only incidents occurred before and after the ceremony. About one hour before, five Negro boys in a car were apprehended by the police chasing two white boys in another car. The incident seemed to have no relation to what was going on at Central High School. After the ceremony, as the crowd was leaving the stadium, a white boy spat in the face of a Negro girl and was arrested and charged with disturbing the peace.[349]

---

349. (1) Ibid. (2) DCSOPS Journal, item 1537. (3) Msg AKMAR 5-102, CHUSARMD, Ark, to DEPTAR, Sit Rep No 228, 26 May 58, DA-IN-691030.

(4) Operation order No. 6, Hqs USARMD, Ark., 22 May 58, gives military plan for participation in graduation ceremonies. (5) Msg AKMAR 5-99, CHUSARMD, ARK, to DCSOPS, 26 May 58, DA-IN-690912. (6) DCSOPS Sit Rep No. 289, 27 May 58.

The final act, the graduation ceremony, passed equally quietly, though there was clearly greater tension up to the time that Ernest Green received his diploma. Police vigilance was so great that even a home-owner in the vicinity who was moving his personal belongings had great difficulty in persuading patrolmen that he was carrying an empty shotgun for an innocent purpose. Troop dispositions were the same as for the baccalaureate except that, at the special request of Mr. Blossom, the two platoons from the reserve center were quietly and unobtrusively moved in under the west side of the stadium where they were hardly visible to the crowd but were available for immediate action should a disturbance break out. None did. The careful preparations paid off. As reported by the Arkansas Gazette:

> Graduation of one Negro and 601 white students was completed last night without incident at Central High School. The audience was well behaved and didn't even murmur when Ernest Green was given his diploma. Police strength was much in evidence. Army troops were quartered under a part of the stadium and inside the lower gymnasium. Ernest Green was shadowed by detectives as he was led to waiting taxis where he and his family were sped away.
>
> Police and federalized National Guardsmen methodically patrolled the streets bordering Central High School. . . . Any crowds that chanced to form were quickly dispersed. The police appeared unconcerned about the possibility of trouble at the ceremony itself.[350]

350. (1) AKMAR 15-115, CHUSARMD ARK to DCSOPS, 28 May 58,
DA-IN-692282. (2) DCSOPS Journal, items 1550, 1557. (3) Info from
Col. J. F. Ryneska, Chf. WHD, who was an eyewitness.

The following day, 28 May, was the last day of school at Central. It was largely devoted to the clearing up of administrative details such as mailing of report cards and preparations for summer school. The troops spent the day at Camp Robinson breaking encampment and processing for release from the military service. By 1310, CST, 29 May, the last of the National Guard personnel had been discharged except for five men remaining in the detachment of patients at Fort Chaffee. Discharges totalled 383, 35 officers, 4 warrant officers, and 344 enlisted men.

Instructions from the Department of the Army ending Operation ARKANSAS were simple and brief. Messages were dispatched on 28 May to both the Chief of Arkansas Military District and USCONARC stipulating that the provisions of messages dispatched on 24 September 1957 outlining the mission and the special command arrangements for it were terminated as of 2400 CST, 29 May 1958.[351] On this anticlimactic note,

351. (1) DA 341584 to CGUSARFOUR, 23 May 58, sets effective date of discharge at 2400 CST 29 May 58. (2) (FOUO) USARMD Ark Sit Reps 230-231, 28-29 May 58. (3) (FOUO) DCSOPS Journal, items 1556-57, 1560-64. (4) DCSOPS Sit Reps 291-92, 29-30 May 58. (5) Msg DA 343091 to CHUSARMD Ark and DA 343090 to USCONARC, 28 May 58, terminate mission and command

arrangements effective 2400 CST, 29 May 58.

Operation ARKANSAS came to an end.

www.ingramcontent.com/pod-product-compliance
Lightning Source LLC
Chambersburg PA
CBHW081847170426
43199CB00018B/2832